Praise for
The Voodoo Hoodoo Spellbook

"Presented in a down-to-earth, easy to understand style—and jam-packed with a wealth of practical information—*The Voodoo Hoodoo Spellbook* is, without a doubt, a practitioner's fondest dream come true. No magical workspace is complete without it!"
  —Dorothy Morrison, author of *Utterly Wicked* and *Everyday Magic*

"Denise Alvarado's *The Voodoo Hoodoo Spellbook* is a work of considerable value to anyone interested in the workings of magic as performed New Orleans. It is not a tourist-tempting hodgepodge of phony recipes but a serious compilation of authentic rituals, spells, and instructions gathered by a root worker who grew up in the area. As background to the meat of this work, Ms. Alvarado includes a history of this particular folk magic and its practitioners. Whatever the spell or charm you need, you are certain to find it here...and it will be effective! Along with her words, enjoy Denise's beautiful artwork."
  —Raymond Buckland, *Buckland's Book of Gypsy Magic*

"*The Voodoo Hoodoo Spellbook* is overflowing with valuable information pertaining to the theory and practice of authentic Voodoo hoodoo. In addition to a brief historical overview of these practices in New Orleans, here you will find spells, rituals, formulas, and prayers for virtually any conceivable purpose along with correspondence charts arranged by use or purpose for easy reference that will assist you in crafting your own spells and formulas. In short, this book contains everything you need to know in order to practice successful magick in the Voodoo hoodoo tradition. This is a book that you will return to again and again."
  —Carolina Dean, author, associate editor and contributor to
  Hoodoo and Conjure Quarterly Conjure

"A triumph of painstaking and meticulous research. Esteemed author Denise Alvarado, herself raised in New Orleans, has studied mysticism and practiced Voodoo hoodoo and indigenous healing traditions for over three decades. She is an academic anthropologist, cultural psychologist, writer, artist, spiritual adviser and consultant. *The Voodoo Hoodoo Spellbook* is the culmination of the author's decades of practical experience in authentic Voodoo rituals. Wonderfully readable, *The Voodoo Hoodoo Spellbook* will prove a necessary companion to both beginner and experienced practitioner alike. A brilliant and all-encompassing work and an invaluabl￼   ￼tion."
  —Dr. A￼   ￼f *Complete Books of Enoch*

THE VOODOO HOODOO SPELLBOOK

DENISE ALVARADO

WEISER BOOKS
San Francisco, CA / Newburyport, MA

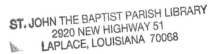

First published in 2011 by Red Wheel/Weiser, LLC
With offices at:
665 Third Street, Suite 400
San Francisco, CA 94107
www.redwheelweiser.com

ISBN: 978-1-57863-513-9

Library of Congress Cataloging-in-Publication Data available upon request

Cover design by Jim Warner
Cover photograph © Karri Cormican
Interior by Kathryn Sky-Peck

Printed in the United States of America
QG
10 9 8 7 6 5 4 3 2 1

The paper used in this publication meets the minimum requirements of the
American National Standard for Information Sciences—Permanence of Paper
for Printed Library Materials Z39.48-1992 (R1997).

Contents

Foreword vii

Disclaimer and Legal Notice viii

Introduction ix

Chapter 1:	The Basics	1
Chapter 2:	The Voodoo Pantheon	25
Chapter 3:	The Saints	55
Chapter 4:	Prayers, Novenas, and Psalms	77
Chapter 5:	Prepare to Mesmerize: Tools, Materia Medica, and Curios	89
Chapter 6:	Candle Magick	101
Chapter 7:	Conjure, Spiritual, and Anointing Oils	111
Chapter 8:	Magickal Voodoo Inks	167
Chapter 9:	Floor Washes	171
Chapter 10:	Spiritual Waters and Colognes	177
Chapter 11:	Spiritual Baths	191
Chapter 12:	New Orleans Gris Gris	201
Chapter 13:	Sachet Powders	217
Chapter 14:	Talismans	225
Chapter 15:	The Spells	233

Final Note from the Author 298

References and Bibliography 300

Resources and Suppliers 303

Index 304

Dedication

*To my children Brandon and Sarah,
and my grandchildren Dylan and Dominic.
You are my inspiration and the true magick in my life.*

Foreword

Here's the dope. Denise Alvarado is a true hoodoo mamba home girl who burned hi-octane conjure in New Orleans where she grew up, and on visits to relatives on the Mississippi bayous, where she was formally introduced to the Voodoo/hoodoo path. Called by the spirits and taught conjuration by family members, she was working the goofer from five years old. That's some serious heat. Denise is no pretender. She's for real. She fixes the formulas, raises the spirits, calculates the mathematics, and works wonders at the old dirt track crossroads.

Crucially, she's also an academic—a formally trained anthropologist and psychologist with fifteen years of clinical experience. What this means is that she personifies the Law of Balance. She combines left-brain, logical thinking with right-brain, creative thinking (unsurprisingly, she's also a great artist). In other words, Denise tempers her magic with good sense and critical thinking—not something you see often in the world of spirituality and the occult.

This healthy duality shines through in *The Voodoo Hoodoo Spellbook*. The book is not only written in a lively compelling style, but its reliability—in terms of exacting research—is simply not found elsewhere. Denise cites all her sources and covers just about everything you could ever want to know about Voodoo, Santería, hoodoo, the saints and psalms, the cult of Black Hawk, and more.

Plus, Denise spills the beans on the mechanics of working conjuration. She shows you how to create your own magical oils, formulas, floor washes, and powders. You'll learn everything from how to make African Juju Oil and Boss Fix Oil (a very handy formulation!) to fixing up Amor Oil and Four Thieve Vinegar. She lists all the spells you are ever likely to need in life—from love and money spells to courtwork and protection spells.

Anyone who has read my writings will know that I'm Voodoo's wild card—a mix of the Joker (trickster) and the Ace of Spades. I ride the hoodoo highway down to the crossroads to pump out the groove with the Graveyard Snake and Ole Satan.

But you can guarantee that wherever it is I'm heading—whatever it is I'm doing—I've got a copy of Denise's *The Voodoo Hoodoo Spellbook* on hand. On every level, this book is worth its weight in gold—and some!

—Doktor Snake
http://doktorsnake.com

Disclaimer and Legal Notice

Efforts were made to ensure that the information contained herein was accurate at the time of this writing. The author and publisher make no representation or warranties with respect to the accuracy, applicability, fitness, or completeness of the contents of this book. The information contained in this book is strictly for educational and entertainment purposes. Therefore, if you wish to apply ideas contained in this book, you are taking full responsibility for your actions. There is no guarantee that your life will improve in any way using the techniques, ideas, and information presented in this book. Self-help and improvement potential is entirely dependent upon the person using the ideas and techniques. Your level of improvement in attaining results depends on the time you devote to developing your skill, commitment to learning the ideas, techniques, principles, and skills mentioned, and your personal belief system. Magic, Voodoo, hoodoo, and energy work are faith-based systems, meaning if you do not believe in your own power to effect change, change is unlikely to occur. Since these factors differ according to each individual, there is no guarantee of your success or improvement level. The author and publisher assume no responsibility for any of your actions, whether you use the information for positive or negative purposes.

Much of the information contained in this book is drawn from folklore collections, recipes given to the author from family, friends, customers, medicine men and women, and healers over the span of a lifetime, recipes from 19th and 20th century formularies, historical accounts of African-based folk magic from slaves in the southern United States, objective evaluation of anthropological literature, and from the personal grimoires of the author. The information contained herein is subject to the interpretation of the author, and may or may not be entirely accurate.

The information contained in these pages is not meant as a substitute for the advice of health or mental health professionals.

Readers should use discretion before performing any rituals or spells. The author is not liable, or in any way responsible, for any actions that readers may take as a result of the information contained in this book. The reader is encouraged to cast spells responsibly.

Introduction

Oral tradition is the cornerstone of indigenous knowledge. It is the means by which our ancestors pass on their wisdom and ways of life so that we may benefit and carry them to generations to come. Today, much oral tradition is finding its way into print. This work represents one effort to preserve the wisdom of our ancestors by writing it down so that it can be enjoyed by all who care to read about it.

While I have written down much of what has been taught to me, I have not recorded those teachings that I was asked to hold in confidence out of respect for tradition. Some things are meant only to be committed to memory, and so in the heart mind they will stay.

Voodoo is a highly complex religion, and hoodoo is a highly complex magico-spiritual practice. I have written this book according to my personal experience and understanding of the New Orleans Voodoo religious, spiritual, and magickal tradition, and it may or may not reflect the opinions of other practitioners of New Orleans Voodoo or hoodoo. The knowledge that I have acquired over the years is the culmination of growing up in New Orleans and absorbing the culture; lifelong learning from family, teachers, and other practitioners; consulting sacred texts; folklore literature; and what speaks to me through divine channels.

This book was written for the individual practitioner, and is not meant as an instructional guide for initiation into any of the religions with their roots in the African Diaspora. It is meant to provide a basic understanding of the nature and properties of the ingredients and practices of New Orleans Voodoo and hoodoo as I understand and interpret them.

Sometimes people seek to "become" priestesses and priests, mambos, houngans, and religious leaders; other times, the spirits seek us out. I was given "the gift" as a small child; the spirits called on me. I was introduced to the Mysteries at the age of five or six by my auntie on the Mississippi bayous. My father taught me about the creatures and minerals of Mother Earth, while my mother taught me about the herbs and plants. As a young girl, I was raised in the Catholic Church, went through catechism, and was confirmed as "Angelique." At sixteen, I was initiated into transcendental meditation at the Hare Krishna temple in New Orleans and given my secret mantra by my guru. I am an ordained reverend from the Universal Life Church Monastery, and have had the privilege of going through a number of rites of passage in the Native American tradition that qualify me to perform various ceremonial activities and function in the role of medicine woman. I am also a formally trained anthropologist and psychologist with fifteen years of clinical experience. I have a broad and deep understanding of many spiritual paths, and consider myself to be a lifelong student of the universe, with much yet to learn. The many paths I have travelled reflect my journey to connect with the ancestors of my Creole ethnicity. I want to make clear, however, that I have not undergone formal initiation into any of the African-derived religions. You will find after reading this book that such initiations are not necessary to practice the brand of Creole Voodoo and hoodoo that is unique to New Orleans.

This book is the revised edition of the original *Voodoo Hoodoo Spellbook* that I had previously self-published. Like most authors, after a time I wished I had written some things differently, added things I initially omitted, and organized things differently. With the support of my new publisher Red Wheel/Weiser and Conari Press, I now have both the opportunity and the excuse to tweak this book to include those changes and make it even better than ever.

I hope that you find this book informational, educational, and most of all, inspirational. It is dedicated to all of those who suffered to keep the tradition alive, to those who carry on the tradition so that it may continue to live, and to those who have yet to come who will find their lives enriched by it.

CHAPTER ONE

THE BASICS

In New Orleans, anyone can practice Voodoo. There is no formal religious initiation rite, no rigid orthodoxy, and there are no standard ways to worship—though there are guidelines. Voodoo is a fluid, adaptable, syncretic, and inclusive spiritual and religious practice that embraces the hearts of all people, no matter their race, creed, or origin. The loas, spirits, orishas, and mysteries—all terms used to describe the divine archetypal forces of Voodoo—are ever-changing, manifesting in infinite ways according to the filter of a given culture and geographic location.

The word *Voodoo* means "spirit of God." Contrary to popular belief, Voodoo is first and foremost about healing. It is a religious system based on three levels of spirit: God, the loa, and ancestors. Voodoo believers accept the existence of one ultimate god referred to as Bon Dieu (Good God), below which are the powerful spirits often referred to as loas. These powerful spirits act as intermediaries between Bon Dieu and practitioners and are responsible for the daily matters of life in the areas of family, love, money, happiness, wealth, and revenge. Finally, ancestor reverence is considered the foundation of New Orleans Voodoo. The loas and ancestors are not worshipped; rather, they are served and revered, respectively.

New Orleans was a major port where multiple cultures converged, and as a result, the influences on New Orleans Voodoo are very diverse. While New Orleans Voodoo as a unique system has no formal initiation rites, many people who practice it are, in fact, initiated into one of its closely related "sister" religions. There are also family lineages in New Orleans that pass down specific traditions that are held in confidence. These are the mambos and houngans who reside in New Orleans, more commonly referred to as priests, priestesses,

1

or kings and queens of New Orleans Voodoo. There are Cuban-inspired Santeros, Haitian-initiated mambos and houngans, Obean rootworkers from the West Indian islands (i.e. Belize, the Bahamas, Dominican Republic), followers of the Spiritualist Churches, hoodoos and rootworkers who incorporate candle magic, spells, and the veneration of Catholic saints, and followers of the Yoruba tradition of Africa. New Orleans Voodoo is highly influenced by Native American spirituality and herbalism, as well. For example, the famous Indian War Chief Black Hawk is a Voodoo saint and is often included in the ritual work of hoodoos and Spiritualists. However, many Spiritualists who venerate Black Hawk deny engaging in hoodoo activities, despite the similarities found between traditions.

This edition of *The Voodoo Hoodoo Spellbook* provides more in-depth information about the history of New Orleans Voodoo as well as a beefed-up formulary that is based on authentic New Orleans *materia medica* as I have learned it. The formulas found in this book may or may not be consistent with rootworker formulas found in other areas of the South. For one thing, there are influences at play in New Orleans that are not present in other areas. For example, the inclusion of Spiritualist oils and Indian spirit products were inspired by the Spiritualist churches and exploited by the hoodoo marketeers. There is the infamous Algiers district of New Orleans where some of the most popular formulas such as Fast Luck derive. And there are the Cleo May and Dixie Love products that cater to ladies of the night and to all women desirous of their effects. Furthermore, French perfumery had a huge impact on the Creoles of high society, and some of these perfume names and ingredients made their way into the hoodoo formulary. The use of Voodoo dolls and doll babies in magick spells has become iconic of New Orleans Voodoo, although their use by genuine practitioners is much more complex than is commonly perceived by the public at large. And gris gris is a completely unique magickal system in New Orleans that involves far more than filling a red flannel mojo bag with a few symbolic items of conjure.

New Orleans Voodoo lacks the rigid orthodoxy found in Haitian Vodou. According to Louis Martiné, drummer, priest, and spiritual doctor with New Orleans Voodoo Spiritual Temple:

> New Orleans Voodoo is the wild child of Voodoo's feral religions, the trick played upon the trickster. In New Orleans Voodoo, where the ultimate authority rests within the individual and his or her living relationship with the loa, there can be no orthodoxy to sit in grand judgment. If judgment were to be meted out, its throne would well bear the word "success." And who is best suited to decide

what is "success" than the involved mind stream as it is now (The Individual), as it was in the past (The Ancestors), and as it will be in all of its future incarnations (The Offspring)?[1]

Because of the proliferation of misinformation on the Internet and in many books about the beginnings of Voodoo in New Orleans and, indeed, in America, I have provided a brief contextual background of its history in the following section. Many aspects of New Orleans Voodoo and hoodoo are direct holdovers from the original African religion and are not just arbitrary additions by contemporary pagans and wiccans. Though there are those obvious recent neopagan influences, I have omitted them and focused this edition of *The Voodoo Hoodoo Spellbook* on the practice of Voodoo and hoodoo in Louisiana and Mississippi, with a special emphasis on New Orleans traditions.

While Voodoo in New Orleans is again becoming more communal, I am from the era of oppression and intolerance that made it necessary for practitioners to go underground and practice in secret by themselves or among their families and trusted friends. Segregation was still alive and well when I was born, and I was among the first children who were "bussed" to schools in black neighborhoods and vice versa. My "in-between" color saved me from being beaten up in school, but I will never forget what it was like to watch my best friend be taunted and beaten because she was white. When I attempted to intervene, I was told by the black kids, "You okay 'cause you brown." I share this story to illustrate the climate of New Orleans from the perspective of a Creole child who received many mixed messages from members of my family and community about my ethnic identity (only claim your French heritage if you must because of your skin color; identify your Hispanic Catholic heritage, but never your indigenous roots . . . all the while holding secret séances, working with the spirits, doing candle magick, learning fortune telling, my mother braiding my hair and telling me stories about being Cherokee, and being taught how to work a Voodoo doll behind closed doors). I am one rootworker who has lived long enough to witness a social climate that, while not completely tolerant by any stretch of the imagination, is more accepting of indigenous beliefs, and contains a segment of the population that not only tolerates but embraces books about Voodoo and hoodoo. The times they are still a-changin', folks. I was born a New Orleans Creole into the Mysteries and this is what I have learned by living it and breathing it.

---

1   Martiné, 1995.

What Is New Orleans Voodoo Hoodoo?

New Orleans is now and has ever been the hoodoo capital of America. Great names in rites that vie with those of Hayti in deeds that keep alive the powers of Africa. Hoodoo, or Voodoo, as pronounced by the whites, is burning with flame in America, with all the intensity of a suppressed religion.

—Zora Neale-Hurston[2]

New Orleans Voodoo originated from the ancestral religions of the African Diaspora. It is one of many incarnations of African-based religions rooted in the West African Dahomean and Central African Voodoo traditions. It became syncretized with the Catholic religion as a result of the massive forced migrations, displacements of the slave trade, and the Code Noir. Slave owners forbade the Africans from practicing Voodoo under penalty of death and, in areas controlled by Catholics, forced many of them to convert to Catholicism. The result was a creolization of the names and aspects of the Voodoo spirits to those of the Christian saints that most closely resembled their particular areas of expertise or power. Under the guise of Catholicism, the religion of Voodoo survived.

Louisiana was founded in 1682 after the King of France, King Louis XIV, embarked upon active exploration of the Mississippi River in order to enlarge his own empire and stop the progress and expansion of Britain and Spain. René-Robert Cavelier, Sieur de La Salle, reached the mouth of the Mississippi River and claimed possession of the river and all the land around it for France. He called the new territory "Louisiane," or "Louis' land." Louisiana's colonial period lasted from 1699, when the French established a permanent settlement in the area, to 1803, when the United States purchased it. New Orleans was designated the capital of colonial Louisiana in 1718. According to the New Orleans Voodoo Museum, New Orleans Voodoo had three distinct phases: African, Creole, and American.[3] Upon examining the historical records, I tend to agree with this categorization. The African phase began in 1719, with the arrival of the first 450 Africans who set foot in New Orleans from the Bight of Benin. According to records of the French slave trade voyages[4] from Africa to Louisiana during the French regime, two-thirds of the slaves brought to Louisiana were from Senegambia.[5] In 1720, 127 more slaves arrived from Senegam-

---

2   From *Mules and Men*, by Zora Neale-Hurston, 1935.

3   The New Orleans Voodoo Museum (n.d.). Voodoo. Retrieved from *www.voodoomuseum.com/index.php?option=com_co ntent&view=article&id=14&Itemid=17*

4   The slave trade is sometimes called the *Maafa* by African and African-American scholars, meaning "holocaust" or "great disaster" in Swahili.

5   Hall, 1992.

bia. In 1721, 196 were from Senegambia, 834 were from Bight of Benin, and 294 were from Congo/Angola. From 1723 to 1747, all of the people stolen from Africa were from Senegambia, with the exception of 464 from Bight of Benin in 1728.[6] Some of the specific African cultural groups that arrived in Louisiana include the Bambara, Mandinga, Wolof, Fulbe, Nard, Mina, Fon (Dahomean), Yoruba (Nago), Chamba, Congo, Ibo, Ado, Hausa, and Sango.[7]

Most references to the African origins of New Orleans Voodoo emphasize the Congo region; however, the historical documents reflect a significant population of people from Senegambia, including some practicing Muslims (which makes sense, given Senegambia was under the rule of the Islamic Almoravides Empire; though, many resisted the conversion to Islam and maintained their traditional African religions and beliefs). The reason that so many Sengambians were sold into slavery in Louisiana was because the slave trade was organized by the Company of the Indes, a privately owned company licensed by the King of France, who held an exclusive trade monopoly in Senegal and Louisiana during the years of the African holocaust.[8]

From a geographic perspective, Senegambia refers to a large region between Senegal and the Gambia rivers. One might assume that since the region is so large, the culture would be heterogeneous. On the contrary, there were many commonalities among the differing cultural groups, as evidenced by the similarity of language groups. It might be likened to Scandinavian culture; while Scandinavia is comprised of three different countries (Denmark, Sweden, and Norway), they are related linguistically and culturally. If you can speak one Scandinavian language, you can typically understand (i.e. speak and read) the other two.[9] Examination of the traditional practices of the people from the Senegambia region reveals a far greater influence on New Orleans Voodoo than has been previously recognized. For example, gris gris, a religiomagical tradition from Senegambia, is one of the hallmarks of New Orleans Voodoo.

The first slaves in Louisiana were not African, however. They were Native Americans, most of whom were warriors. Some of the Native American tribes in the area at the time were the Natchez, Choctaw, Cherokee, Tunica, Tamira, Chaouchas, Chickasaw, Illinois, Houma, Arkansas, and Miami. The indigenous

---

6   Jean Mettas, *Autres Ports* (Paris, 1984), Vol. II of Mettas, *Répertoire des expéditions négrières francaiwses au XVIIIième siècle.*, ed. Serge and Michelle Daget, as cited in Hall, G. M. (1992). *Africans in Colonial Louisiana*, Louisiana State University Press: Baton Rouge.
7   Hall.
8   Hall, 1992, *Africans in Colonial Louisiana*, Louisiana State University Press: Baton Rouge.
9   The Scandinavian languages are classified as Northern Germanic languages or Scandinavian languages. Having lived in Norway when I was 12 and 13 and being fluent in Norwegian, I found it relatively easy to communicate with others in other Scandinavian countries.

peoples from various tribes were captured and sold into slavery by both the British and the French. In fact, indigenous people were bought, sold, and exported from Louisiana to the West Indies at a ratio of two Indian slaves for one African slave. Even though the export of slaves was outlawed by 1726, the slave trade continued, albeit on a smaller scale.[10]

Enslaved Africans joined enslaved Native American Indians when they arrived in Louisiana. Many times they lived under the same masters. Like the Native American Indians, the enslaved Africans were not the passive, submissive people so often depicted in print and media. Among the Mande, for example, there was the principle of *fadenya,* meaning "father-childness." Fadenya is the cultural principle of the innovator, the one who rebels against social order, and the one who travels "to foreign lands to gain special powers and rewards that are eventually brought back for the benefit of the village."[11] The rebels are the ones who are considered heroes.

By the time the African slaves arrived, the Indians already had experience as escapees. The Indians who escaped retreated to the nearby swamps, and some even remained in the city, literally hiding in plain sight. They were well organized and heavily armed. It comes as no surprise that the Africans and Native Americans banded together to escape, and steal food, supplies, and weapons. They organized to raid settlers for more supplies and wreaked all kinds of havoc for their masters and the colony. The colonizers feared a great uprising by the joining together of these two populations, and with good reason. By 1729, the Natchez, in cooperation with recently arrived Africans, wiped out the entire tobacco settlement of the Company of the Indes, which had been in control of the colony along with approximately one-tenth of the French population. By 1731, the Company of the Indes officially turned its Louisiana concession over to France.

Undoubtedly, the French and the British allied with the various Indian nations and used these alliances to their benefit. They used slaves in battles that would turn African against Indian, Indian against African, and Indian nation against Indian nation. They dangled the carrot of freedom as incentive for alliance with both groups. They played upon the preexisting intertribal conflicts among Indian tribes. Arming slaves in any great number made the colonizers even more nervous, but they needed their assistance to achieve the goal of maintaining control over the colony.[12]

---

10 Charles Edward O'Neill, *Church and State in French Colonial Louisiana: Policy and Politics to 1732* (New Haven, 1966); Nancy M. Miller Surrey, *The Commerce of Louisiana During the French Regime, 1699-1763* (1916, rpr. New York, 1968); Hall, G. M. (1992) *Africans in Colonial Louisiana*, Louisiana State University Press: Baton Rouge.

11 Ibid, 55.

12 For more details about the development of Afro-Creole culture in colonial Louisiana in the eighteenth century, the reader is referred to *Africans in Colonial Louisiana* (Hall, 1992).

The gumbo of cultures that comprised colonial Louisiana included people of French, Canadian, Spanish, Latin American, Anglo, German, Irish, English, Scottish, Jewish, Native American, and African descent. In addition to joining the Native Americans, the first African slaves also encountered the social rejects from France who were exiled to New Orleans, many of whom were made into indentured servants. France and Spain were fighting over Mobile and Pensacola, leading to mass desertions among French and Swiss soldiers. Consequently, New Orleans was comprised largely of rejects, deserters, and African and Indian slaves. The shared desperation among the diverse groups of people led to a degree of cooperation that seemingly transcended status and race.

Eventually, France was defeated in the French and Indian War and abandoned North America. New Orleans and the west bank of the Mississippi were ceded to Spain. During the years of Spanish rule (1763 to 1803), the white population almost doubled and the slave population grew 250 percent.[13]

In 1803, the United States purchased the Louisiana territory. Shortly after this time, there were several influxes of immigrants from St. Domingue (Haiti); the first consisting of an estimated one thousand refugees. According to Debien and le Gaedeur, another nine thousand refugees arrived indirectly from St. Domingue via Cuba in 1809. While some of these refugees settled in New Orleans, most of them made their homes west of the Atchafalaya Basin in St. Martinville and the surrounding area.[14] Because of the large number of Haitians settling in this area, it became known as *le Petit Paris,* as residents attempted to recreate their lives as they had been in St. Domingue.[15] Undoubtedly, the spirits followed the refugees, and thus we can see how some of them became part of the New Orleans Voodoo pantheon.

From 1719 to about 1830, Voodoo in New Orleans was much like it was in Africa. The main difference was a merging of the different African cultures and region-specific religious practices. But the languages, dances, and traditions were decidedly African. The direct influence of African tradition, however, was eventually cut off when the importation of slaves from outside of the United States became illegal in 1808.

The Creole phase is marked by the convergence of distinctly different cultures, the loss of African languages, and the development of the Creole language. This phase was in high gear during the years between 1830 to 1930, when Voodoo peaked in cultural influence. The Creole language became the primary language, the African rhythms of Voodoo dances gave birth to jazz, and Voodoo Queens

---

13 Hanger, 1997.
14 Speedy, 1994; Spitzer, 1997.
15 Spitzer, 1997.

emerged. Gris gris continued as a system of coping with the daily problems of life. Voodoo rituals merged with Mardi Gras and other celebrations to the point that many activities that were Voodoo in origin went unnoticed by the ordinary person.[16] New Orleans Voodoo had integrated elements of European folk magick, Native American spirituality and herbalism, African Voodoo, and Catholicism. Catholic saints took a prominent place in New Orleans Voodoo at this time, masking, but not replacing, the loas of the traditional African Voodoo religion.

The American phase occurred after 1930, when New Orleans Voodoo became a business referred to as hoodoo. Voodoo was exploited by popular media and commercialized by people looking to make a quick buck. Voodooists became uncomfortable with the distorted imagery that was emerging and went underground. Community events and rituals that had once characterized it during the Creole phase disappeared. Practitioners became increasingly isolated, giving way to a growing number of individual practitioners called rootworkers. The term *hoodoo* began to replace *Voodoo*, and neighborhood drugstores began to be a major source of hoodoo and conjure materia medica. The popularity of gris gris remained, but the original meaning and purpose behind it seemed to fade into the shadows.

Characteristics of New Orleans Voodoo Hoodoo

Once the outward and public expression of the religion went underground, many people believed Voodoo all but disappeared in the twentieth century. There is a common presumption that any "authentic" Voodoo in New Orleans disintegrated into gris gris as if gris gris were a less important system (see Jacobs and Kaslow, 1991, for a discussion on the influence of Voodoo in New Orleans Spiritualist Churches). This perception is undoubtedly due to a lack of understanding of the religious context of gris gris and its association with Voodoo and Islam in Africa. Instead, gris gris is likened to a mojo bag and not recognized as a religious tradition. The misinformation is further perpetuated by contemporary and popular authors, hoodoo marketeers, and other ill-informed individuals who continue to publish and republish the same misinformation.

The term *Voodoo hoodoo* is commonly used by Louisiana locals to describe our unique brand of New Orleans Creole Voodoo. It refers to a blending of religious and magickal elements. Voodoo is widely believed by those outside of the New Orleans Voodoo tradition to be separate from hoodoo magick. However, the

---

16 The New Orleans Voodoo Museum (n.d.). Voodoo. Retrieved from *www.voodoomuseum.com/index.php?option=com_co ntent&view=article&id=14&Itemid=17*

separation of religion from magick did not occur in New Orleans as it did in other areas of the country. The magick is part of the religion; the charms are medicine and spiritual tools that hold the inherent healing mechanisms of the traditional religion and culture. Voodoo in New Orleans is a way of life for those who believe.

Still, there are those who separate Voodoo and hoodoo. Some hoodoo practitioners integrate elements of Voodoo, and some do not. Some incorporate elements of Catholicism or other Christian religious thought into their practice, while others do not. How much of the original religion a person decides to believe in and practice is left up to the individual. Some people don't consider what they do religion at all, preferring to call it a spiritual tradition or African American folk magic. Throughout this book, I use the term *Voodoo hoodoo* in reference to the blend of the two aspects of the original religion as found in New Orleans Voodoo and as a way of life. A fellow New Orleans native and contemporary gris gris man Dr. John explains it this way:

> In New Orleans, in religion, as in food or race or music, you can't separate nothing from nothing. Everything mingles each into the other—Catholic saint worship with gris gris spirits, evangelical tent meetings with spiritual church ceremonies—until nothing is purely itself but becomes part of one fonky gumbo. That is why it is important to understand that in New Orleans the idea of Voodoo—or as we call it gris gris—is less a distinct religion than a way of life.[17]

New Orleans Voodoo evolved to embrace aspects of the "fonky gumbo" of cultures in the nineteenth century and as a result, it is distinguishable from other forms of Voodoo and hoodoo found in other areas of the country. For example, there is a blend of Spiritualism, African Voodoo, Native American traditions, Santería, Catholicism, and Pentecostalism. An additional hallmark of New Orleans Voodoo hoodoo is the borrowing of material from European and African folk magic, Kabbalistic influences, ancestor worship, and strong elements of Christian and Jewish mysticism, such as the use of various seals and sigils. In fact, for many practitioners, the Bible is considered a talisman in and of itself, as well as a primary source for magical lore. The psalms and the saints are aspects key to hoodoo practice for many practitioners, though not all.

New Orleans Voodoo is unique in its use of Spirit Guides in worship services and in the forms of ritual possession that its adherents practice. There is candle magick, and there used to be Voodoo séances (I don't know how prevalent these are among practitioners today). The Voodoo-influenced Spiritual Churches that

---

17 Rebennack & Rummel, 1994, p. 159.

survive in New Orleans are the result of a mingling of these and other spiritual practices. I should point out that Spiritualists will typically say that they have nothing to do with Voodoo or hoodoo. Still, some of the spiritual practices are extremely similar, whatever you call it.

A most important difference, however, is the retention of elements of the various religious practices from the different African cultural groups that arrived on the Louisiana Coast. For example, there is gris gris from Senegambia; the "serpent cult" of Nzambi from Whydah, or Li Grande Zombi as it is known in New Orleans; the obvious influence of fetishism, the nkisis or "sacred medicine," from the Congo basin of Central Africa; and the Bocio figurines from the Gulf of Guinea and the Congo Kingdom.

Catholicism

Among the enduring influences in New Orleans Voodoo today are elements of Catholicism. This is the direct result of Louisiana's Code Noir or Black Code. It was written specifically to control the behavior and religious practices of slaves and free Africans and ordered the Jews out of the colony. It served to reinforce the notion that the status of those with darker skin was always lower than people of lighter complexions and contact between "racial" groups was intentionally disrupted.[18] The Code Noir imposed only one religion—Catholicism.

According to the Community College of Denver, the Code Noir initially took shape in Louis XIV's decree of 1685, and while the code was modified on several occasions, it is the original document that established the main lines for the policing of slavery right up to 1789. The very first article expels all Jews from the colonies and insists that all slaves be instructed as Catholics and not as Protestants. For the most part, the Code concentrated on defining the condition of slavery (passing the condition through the mother, not the father) and establishing harsh controls over the conduct of those enslaved. Slaves had virtually no rights, though the code did enjoin masters to take care of the sick and old.[19]

The influence of Catholicism in New Orleans Voodoo and hoodoo is evident in the presence of the various saints and the use of the psalms in magickal and healing works. Those who incorporate Catholic elements may or may not be practicing Catholics. There are significant populations of practitioners who utilize these elements for their poetic and inspirational nature value as opposed to a strictly religious one.

---

18 Brown & Hill, 2006.
19 Community College of Denver (CCD), (n.d.) Retrieved from *www.roebuckclasses.com/201/conquest/codenoir.htm*

Gris Gris

A distinguishing characteristic of New Orleans Voodoo is its emphasis on gris gris as a magickal system. Gris gris is both a noun and a verb, referring to a powder or poison, a ritually prepared object such as a doll, or a small cloth bag filled with magickal ingredients. Gris gris also refers to the act of working the gris gris (spell or charm). Gris gris is an integral aspect of life that can be traced back to the African Muslims and to Senegambians. Gris gris is discussed in detail in chapter 12.

Serpent Worship and Li Grande Zombi

Li Grande Zombi (also called Damballah Wedo) is the major serpent spirit of worship among New Orleans Voodooists. In New Orleans Voodoo, snakes are not seen as symbols of evil as in the story of Adam and Eve. Snakes are considered to be the holders of intuitive knowledge—knowing that which cannot be spoken. Women often dance with serpents to represent the spiritual balance between the genders. Voodoo rituals in New Orleans almost always include a snake dance to celebrate the link to the ancient knowledge. The origin of Li Grande Zombi can be traced to the serpent deity Nzambi from Whydah in Africa. According to the Bantu Creation story, Nzambi is the Creator God:

> Nzambi exists in everything and controls the universe through his appointed Spirits. In the beginning only Nzambi existed. When he was ready to create, millions and millions of pieces of matter swirled around him counterclockwise until Ngombe was born. Ngombe is the universe, the planets, the stars and all physical matter. Nzambi then created movement, and the matter that he had created began to change and drift apart. So, he decided to create a being that could traverse the universe and mediate between matter and space. Nzambi focused on a fixed point and gave life to a being who was simultaneously man and woman, a manifestation of the nature of Nzambi, called *Exú-Aluvaiá*.[20]

Another description of Li Grande Zombi is provided by Louis Martiné, priest, spiritual doctor, and elder of the New Orleans Voodoo Spiritual Temple:

> The Grande Zombie is the Temple Snake, a defining element of New Orleans Voodoo and a loa of great stature. The Grande Zombie of New Orleans Voodoo is best not confused with the Zombie of Haitian Voodoo which has been described as a ritually animated corpse. The Temple Snake bears little physical or spiritual resemblance to such a being. The Grande Zombie can fill many roles and

---

20 Alvarado, 2010, p. 19.

perform many ritual functions. In the context of this Order of Service the Temple Snake is the umbilical cord, the connection between the Mother and the child.[21]

Some people prefer to honor Li Grande Zombi by purchasing a live boa constrictor or python, but this is not recommended unless you know how to take care of one and have the appropriate enclosure and willingness to feed it the live food it requires. Even though these creatures can become accustomed to eating frozen mice, rats, or rabbits, it is not the optimal choice. Remember, these serpents grow to be very large, and they can be dangerous.

So how does one use a large snake in Voodoo ceremony without being bitten? Well, one way is to be sure that the snake has been fed prior to the ceremony. The other issue is how familiar the snake is with people and activity. Snakes should be conditioned through exposure to tolerate such stimuli; a well-trained eye for snake behavior is required to maintain safety for the serpent and the people present. Still, there are always the risks of startling the animal or overstimulating it, not feeding it enough, or allowing an inexperienced person handle it. With so many things to consider, it is best to use a snake fetish or doll instead of a live animal, and to rely upon the experience of the Voodoo Queen to bring out her snake when called for in a ritual. Individual practitioners have no real need to acquire one of these creatures.

The use of the powers of Li Grande Zombi and snakes in general is commonly found in hoodoo, especially the use of snake sheds in the preparation of gris gris, conjure powders, and oils. Strength, power, retribution, and renewal are among the qualities associated with snake sheds in conjure. Snake imagery is also seen in the phenomenon called "live things in you." This is a condition in which a person believes they have been hoodooed and as a result there are live things, oftentimes snakes, living inside the body. The afflicted person will report being able to feel the snakes crawling around under their skin or in their bellies.

Snake conjure can also involve drawing a person to you. One way this is done is by taking hairs from your head and naming them for the one you desire. The hairs are then placed in a bottle during a gentle rain and the bottle is allowed to fill up with rain water. The bottle is then sealed and kept near the front door of the home. Within a few days, the hairs are said to swell up and turn to into snakes. The power of the snake is believed to be so strong that the one desired will be unable to withstand the urge to come to your home.

---

21 The Order of Service that Martiné refers to is a departure from the usual litany of Catholic prayers that open a typical Voodoo service. Catholicism was not a part of the original African religion, and so it is not always done this way by practitioners, particularly those for whom Catholicism doesn't "fit." The order of service provided by Martiné in the New Orleans Voodoo Spiritual Temple reflects an evolving and adaptable religion, one that reflects the universal tradition that embraces faiths outside of the Catholic paradigm as part of the ceremonial process.

The old-timers will say that in order to become skilled at conjuring, you have to get the gift and/or permission from the snake. One way this was done in the past was by eating the brains of a snake so that the wisdom of the serpent would be transferred to the eater. Conjurers were also expected to lie down in the woods and call upon the snakes to come and crawl all over their bodies. If they were able to calmly look at the serpents in the eyes without flinching, they were believed to be fit to be a conjurer.

Zombies

The belief in zombies is an exceptional aspect of New Orleans Voodoo that stems from Haitian Vodou. A zombie is a living person who has not died; rather, it is a person who is under the influence of powerful drugs administered by a bokor (a priest skilled in the art of sorcery). Believed to be dead, the affected person is buried in a grave. The bokor later digs up the person and gives them an antidote. At this time, the bokor also captures the victim's Ti Bon Ange (a part of their soul referred to as the zombie astral) and puts it into a clay jar and keeps it. The victim awakens from near death but loses his or her free will. The victim is then forced into a life of slavery, serving only the bokor.

Although many people believe in zombies, there are only a few documented cases. The most famous of these cases concerns Felicia Felix-Mentor, a Haitian woman believed to have been made into a zombie in the early part of the twentieth century. While gathering information for the book *Tell My Horse,* author Zora Neale Hurston encountered the supposed zombie and photographed her.[22] In 1982, Wade Davis, a Harvard ethnobotanist, discovered that a person could be turned into a zombie by means of folk pharmacology. He presented his theory for zombies in two books, *The Serpent and the Rainbow* (1985) and *Passage of Darkness: The Ethnobiology of the Haitian Zombie* (1988). As a result of his travels to Haiti and subsequent investigations of Haitian Vodou practices, Davis claimed that a living person can be turned into a zombie by introducing two special powders into the bloodstream: one, coup de poudre (meaning "powder strike" in French), which includes the powerful neurotoxin found in the pufferfish called tetrodotoxin (TTX), and two, dissociative drugs such as datura. When

---

22 Felicia Felix-mentor. (n.d.). Retrieved from *wn.com/Felicia_Felix-Mentor*

combined, these powders reportedly bring on a death-like state. Davis also popularized the story of Clairvius Narcisse, a Haitian man said to have been turned into a living zombie in this fashion. This case was the subject of his book, *The Serpent and the Rainbow.*

In New Orleans, there arose the tradition of the zombie bottle. Zombie bottles are created in a secret mystical tradition that requires a great deal of skill and knowledge. Only a few Voodoo conjure artists still create these special and unique magickal fetishes. They are each completely unique, individual creations made for a specific person or family as a guardian of the home.

Over the centuries, people across cultures have had their own versions of the genie in the bottle. Africans have been known for their colorful blue bottles hung on the outside of their huts for the purpose of capturing evil spirits. This practice was brought by slaves to the southern United States, where you can find bottle trees in the countryside.

Often zombie bottles will contain more than one spirit. It is believed that whoever owns the bottle also owns the spirit or spirits residing inside the bottle. The spirit is there to do your bidding and will not respond to anyone other than its owner.

Stories abound about strange things happening once a zombie bottle is brought into the home. If you are tuned in, the spirits inside have been known to sing or speak. They are said to be great protectors of the home and are sometimes placed beside the front door to ward off evil and negativity. Others choose to create a special place on an altar for them and feed them special foods that keep them happy. In Louisiana, they sometimes function as the house protector and take orders from the home owner as they sit on a shelf or mantle, fiercely protecting whomever they are told to defend.

Voodoo Dolls

Voodoo dolls are derived from the fetishism brought to New Orleans by the African slaves.[23] This practice of image magic with dolls was also commonly used by some of the Native American cultures, as well as in European folk magic and witchcraft.[24] The use of Voodoo dolls reportedly peaked during the reign of the infamous Voodoo Queen, Marie Laveau.[25] Voodoo dolls are made as gris gris—as sacred vessels to represent or house a spirit. Although they are most commonly depicted as objects of revenge in popular culture, approximately 90 percent of the use of Voodoo dolls

---

23 Herskovitz, 1964; Teish, 1985.
24 Alvarado, 2009, Blier, 1995; Herskovitz, 1964; Lang, 1900.
25 Teish.

in New Orleans is centered on healing, finding true love, or spiritual guidance. In New Orleans, Voodoo dolls are largely sold as souvenirs, curios, and novelty items. Refer to my book, *Voodoo Dolls in Magick and Ritual,* for an in-depth discussion of the history and evolution of Voodoo dolls in New Orleans.

The Mardi Gras Indians

There's a great secret in New Orleans with regards to Voodoo hoodoo that is often overlooked. It is perhaps one of the most unique aspects of New Orleans culture, particularly during Mardi Gras and St. Joseph's Day celebrations. With their elaborate costumes and fabulous performances, the Mardi Gras Indians' flamboyant displays sometimes cause the average onlooker to miss the important role they played in the history and shaping of New Orleans Voodoo hoodoo. Their contributions to the enduring Voodoo hoodoo tradition lie in the transmission of cultural knowledge via chants, dance, and music. Their authentic African rhythms are used in the rituals and celebrations of major Voodoo holidays and rituals.

Indeed, little is understood about the specific Mardi Gras Indian tribes and their activities outside of local legend. Only those who grew up in their neighborhoods would be aware of their presence and influence. New Orleans Mardi Gras is full of secret societies, and the Mardi Gras Indians are among them. They are tribal in every sense of the word; like in any tribe, or any gang for that matter, there are secrets to uphold and measures to be taken to ensure outsiders remain just that—outsiders.

The phrase "Mardi Gras Indians" is used for the benefit of outsiders, as the Indians do not refer to themselves as such, preferring to use "Black Indian" or to identify as a member of a tribe. I remember hearing lies about the Black Indians of New Orleans when I was growing up . . . they aren't really Indians, they're just *masking up* for Mardi Gras . . . they aren't really fighting, they're just putting on a show. Again, these are popular misconceptions put forth by the uninformed. According to Big Chief Bo Dollis of the Wild Magnolias in a 2000 interview,[26]

> At that time my mama wouldn't let me mask—not with Brother Tillman, anyway. He was kind of rough. He'd come home at the end of Mardi Gras Day and his suit would be bloody, you know, he'd get into humbugs . . . Oh yeah, they were still fighting. But most of the time it would happen when they'd meet a gang from downtown, and I didn't go that far. [27]

---

26 Sinclair, J. and Taylor, B. (2000). *Wild Indians Down in New Orleans: an interview with Big Chief Bo Dollis of the Wild Magnolias,* Blues Access 43. Retrieved January 10, 2011: *www.bluesaccess.com/No_43/magnolias.html*
27 Sinclair, J. and Taylor, B. (2000).

The masks worn by the Mardi Gras Indians honor the Native Americans that helped enslaved Africans to escape. Masking is also a means of acknowledging the mixed blood of Africans and Indians, an important part of African heritage overlooked when judging only by the color of one's skin. They have their own Creole street language that is believed to be part Choctaw, part Yoruba, part French, part Spanish, and mostly unknown.

On Mardi Gras and on St. Joseph's night, one member of a Mardi Gras Indian tribe, the spy boy, runs reconnaissance missions around his gang's path, looking for feathers and listening for chants of rival gangs.

It is no coincidence that the Mardi Gras Indian tribes meet up at the street corner crossroads and proceed to walk through them while pounding out foot-stomping beats on the points of specific spirits, singing songs that call on various Voodoo spirits, and referencing military preparedness. Upon careful observation, one can see similarities between the Black Indians of New Orleans and the Rara celebrations in Haiti, which begin on the eve of Lent just as carnival ends.[28]

There are more than fifty Mardi Gras Indian tribe names from in and around the New Orleans area. The oldest is Creole Wild West, founded in the eighteen hundreds. Some, like the Wild Squatoulas and Medallion Hunters, are no longer active. Others, such as Fi-Yi-Yi and Congo Nation, haven't yet reached their peak. One thing is for sure: when it's Mardi Gras time in the Crescent City, the streets are graced with colorful Indian costumes, confrontations, and call-and-response style chants and Indian second line rhythms. If you are ever in New Orleans during the Jazz & Heritage Festival or Mardi Gras, join the second line of the spectacular walk-around parades. You won't be sorry.

During the rest of the year, there is warfare among Mardis Gras tribes and rival gangs. The main focus is turf—who is the strongest and the best—and all year long they prepare for the "show" by creating their elaborate costumes, which are second to none (the trannies of New Orleans run a close second, admittedly, but in my opinion no one will ever out-costume the Black Indians).

If you really want to get inside the psychology of the Black Indians, listen to their music. You will hear rhythms straight from Africa and learn about a culture that has changed little for 250 years. Listen to the songs listed below, as they provide a snapshot of an aspect of New Orleans culture that is intimately tied to the experiences of the original slave inhabitants of Louisiana.

---

28 The reader is referred to *Rara! Vodou, Power, and Performance in Haiti* by Elizabeth McAlister (2002).

- "Jockamo," Sugar Boy Crawford & the Cane Cutters
- "Handa Wanda Pt. 1," Wild Magnolias
- "Big Chief Got a Golden Crown," Wild Tchoupitoulas
- "My Gang Don't Bow Down," Flaming Arrows
- "Yella Pocahontas," Champion Jack Dupree
- "New Suit," Wild Magnolias
- "My Indian Red," Dr. John
- "Second Line Pt.1," Bill Sinigal & the Skyliners
- "Big Chief," Professor Longhair
- "Iko Iko," the Dixie Cups

One of the most popular songs of the Mardi Gras Indians is "Iko Iko," a song originally penned by Sugar Boy Crawford in November 1953 on Checker records and called "Jock-A-Mo." The song tells of a "spy boy" or "spy dog" (a lookout) for one band of Indians encountering the "flag boy" for another band. He threatens to set the flag on fire. Many artists have covered the song and have sung the words phonetically and thus incorrectly, without understanding their meaning. In reality, no one really knows what they mean or what language it is, but there are many theories. According to Dr. John on the liner notes to his 1972 album, *Dr. John's Gumbo*:

> Jockamo means "jester" in the old myth. It is Mardi Gras music, and the Shaweez was one of many Mardi Gras groups who dressed up in far out Indian costumes and came on as Indian tribes. The tribes used to hang out on Claiborne Avenue and used to get juiced up there getting ready to perform and "second line" in their own special style during Mardi Gras. That's dead and gone because there's a freeway where those grounds used to be. The tribes were like social clubs who lived all year for Mardi Gras, getting their costumes together. Many of them were musicians, gamblers, hustlers and pimps.

Another theory is that Jockamo is actually an old African festival called *Jonkonnu*. It is believed that this festival began during the sixteenth and seventeenth centuries. The slaves were allowed to leave the plantations during Christmas to be with their families and celebrate the holidays with African dance, music, and costumes. The tradition continued after emancipation and Junkanoo has evolved into an organized parade with sophisticated, elaborate costumes and unique music among people living in the Bahamas. It is also celebrated in Miami and Key West, Florida, where the local African American populations have their roots in the Bahamas.

Yet another theory is that *Jockamo* is a corruption of the word *Jonkonnu,* which is further adulterated when it is translated as "John Canoe." John Canoe is said to be either the name of a slave trader or the name of an African tribal chief who demanded the right to celebrate with his people.

Okay, now let's think about that one. If *Jockamo* is indeed an adulteration of John Canoe (or the other way around), is it logical to think that on the one day of the year that the slaves were allowed to celebrate, they were going to celebrate their enslavement? Were they really singing and dancing and partying with the name of a slave master? Do I need to point out the flaw in this theory?

I am more inclined to accept the theory that it is a derivative of the African festival Jonkonnu, or one pissed off tribal chief. Of course, my rejection of the slave master theory wouldn't hold water from a scientific standpoint, because words cannot always be translated in isolation. We would have to look at the whole of the song to determine what it really means, and that's just way beyond the scope of this book. Suffice it to say that what we have is a continuation of African and Indian traditions that hold much mystery to us all.

> The world in which you were born is just one model of reality. Other cultures are not failed attempts at being you; they are unique manifestations of the human spirit.
>
> —*Wade Davis*

Characteristics of New Orleans Voodoo Hoodoo Folk Magick

Fortunately, there are a lot of the old traditions that we do know and understand. At the core of New Orleans Voodoo hoodoo are African folkloric practices such as crossing and uncrossing, using spiritual baths and washes, laying tricks, creating gris gris, crossroads magic, and foot track magic.

Crossing and Uncrossing

Simply put, *crossing* refers to spiritual works that cause harm or bad luck, while *uncrossing* refers to works that reverse it. A number of products are used to aid in putting an end to crossed conditions, particularly when used in conjunction with one or more of the psalms. For example, products such as uncrossing crystals, oils, sachet powders, incenses, and even chalk are believed to be particularly effective when used in conjunction with the 37th psalm. The word *cross* is virtually synonymous with the words *hex, jinx,* and *curse.*

Foot Track Magic

Foot track magic involves throwing powders and gris gris in the path of a targeted person. That individual will suffer from unusual problems and a streak of bad luck after they have walked on it. The belief is that the toxic properties of the powder or gris gris will be absorbed through the foot and "poison" the individual. Ailments such as back problems, difficulty walking, edema, and difficulty concentrating are some of the complaints of those who have been victimized in this fashion. Foot tracks can also be used for other purposes, such as keeping a lover from wandering off.

There are two methods of foot track magic: the direct method and the sympathetic method. The direct method is when the powder or other substance is thrown on the ground or a bottle is buried and the person's foot actually touches or walks over it. Some folks take care and throw down the mess in an "X" pattern. I was always told you just throw it where you know the person is going to walk. The second method involves capturing the person's footprint by gathering the dirt from an actual footprint of the target, or by taking an old sock or shoe and doctoring it with some other powder.

You can put a hoodoo on a person by filling an old shoe with red pepper and placing under their house.

Floor Washes

Floor washes are used to remove negativity from the home or business or to bring good fortune, increase the number of customers, or attract love. Florida Water is commonly used as a floor wash. A ritual floor washing typically starts at the back of the premises and ends at the front doorstep. The top floor is washed from the ceiling to the floor, and this is repeated on each floor. Extra time is spent scrubbing the doorway. For best results, the floors, corners of the rooms, closets, doorsteps, walls, fabrics, and furniture are washed. The left over water is thrown out of the front door in the direction of the east, if possible. In the old days in New Orleans, urine, and especially the urine of a child, was frequently used as an ingredient in a floor wash, as was red brick dust.

Laying Tricks

Laying tricks is another reference to the throwing of special herbs, powders, and gris gris in a place where the intended target will touch it, usually by walking on it. It also refers to the concealing or disposing of magickal objects by strategically placing the ingredients in certain places in order to *fix the trick*, or seal the deal.

For example, if you want to keep your partner faithful, you could take a pair of your lover's dirty underwear, tie them in a knot, and bury them in their backyard. If it is an enemy work, then bury the work in the person's yard, or under their doorstep or porch or somewhere else they are inclined to walk. If it's a money spell, you could bury the spell in the yard of a bank, or, if you can get away with it, in the yard of a treasury mint. If you are a gambler, bury it in a potted plant or in the garden or yard of the casino. Following this train of thought, the same can be done for court case spells (in the courtyard), blessings (in the churchyard), school success (schoolyard) . . . you get the picture.

The following are some frequently employed places for laying tricks.

Buried in a building structure. A common place for laying tricks is in construction sites, because the tricks will last forever—or at least for as long as the building stands. Bank construction sites are good for attracting money; courthouse sites are good for keeping the law away; hospitals and doctor's offices are good for healing; and church sites are good for protection.

Placed in a chimney. To bless the home, a trick can be laid inside a chimney.

Buried in a garden or potted plant. When you want to attract love, luck, fertility, or success, bury a trick in a garden in spring and summertime or in a potted plant anytime. A trick to work against someone else can also be planted in the person's garden or in a potted plant at their place of residence.

Buried in the earth in the home yard. To ground a trick and keep it working, bury it in someone's yard. Plant good luck works in your own yard, under your porch, or beneath the front steps for fixing blessings, love drawing, money drawing, and protection. Plant a bad luck trick in someone else's yard to hex them.

Placed under carpets or rugs. This is reflective of adapting hoodoo to modern times. When you don't have a yard to work with, the same principle can be employed by placing a trick under someone's rug or carpet.

Buried under the enemy's doorstep or porch. To hex or jinx and enemy, place a trick under their doorstep or front porch.

Placed in food or drink. This method is typically employed in domination spells, to keep a mate faithful, or in enemy works. Scrape some skin from the bottom of your foot and bake it in some food that will be eaten by someone you wish to dominate or jinx. Add semen or menstrual blood in your lover's food or drink to keep them bound to you.

Thrown into a fire. To neutralize a jinx, burn it in a fire and spread the ashes around a tree. For example, to cause harm to your enemy, burn a bad wish written on paper in a fire and spread the ashes around their doorstep or front porch. Prayers and well wishes can also be accomplished in the same manner. Burn a special prayer in a fire and scatter the ashes near the home for special blessings.

Placed in clothing or on objects. For love spells, money spells, protection spells, and court cases, mojos are often sewn into clothes, curtains, pillowcases, and mattresses.

Disposed at a crossroads. To dispose of ritual remains such as candle wax, ashes from incense, and the like, leave them at a crossroads. Bad luck tricks can also be disposed of in the middle of a crossroads where cars will run over them and destroy them. Tossing coins in the middle of a crossroads is considered good luck.

Buried in a cross mark indoors. As an alternative to a crossroads, an artificial crossroads can be created by making a cross mark indoors. The basic method of creating an indoor crossroads is by drawing an "X" with cornmeal, chalk, or cascarilla on the floor. The cross mark is used for fixing spells, harming an enemy, or as part of protection spells and likely has its origin in the Kongo cosmogram.

Buried in a graveyard. Ritual objects used in extreme magic—like causing serious illness or death—can be buried in a graveyard.

Thrown in running water. Throwing a spell into running water is best used for wishes and banishing.

Placed in a tree. Trees are believed to absorb negativity and evil, so bad works are often buried at the base of trees to neutralize them.

Placed in a bottle. An old practice with origins in the African Congo involves making wishes and placing cobalt blue bottles onto branches of a tree to make a bottle tree that functions as a talisman. My mama always had a bottle tree in the yard. This practice used to be common in the South, but over time the practice seemed to fade away. In recent years, however, it seems as if bottle trees are beginning to make a comeback all over the country.

Spiritual Baths

Spiritual bathing is an ancient practice. In hoodoo, spiritual baths are taken to cleanse oneself of negativity or to bring good luck. Almost always, when someone goes to a rootworker for treatment, a spiritual bath will be part of that treatment. A person is directed by the conjuror to put special herbs, oils, or other ingredients in the bath water to bring about the desired change. This is often done in conjunction with the recitation of special psalms. Removing negativity requires washing oneself with a downward stroke, while bringing luck or fortune requires washing oneself in an upward motion. The left over water can be used in other spellwork, added to floor wash, or disposed of at a crossroads.

Magickal Oils, Incenses, and Sachet Powders

For thousands of years and across cultures, the belief that plant and animal aromatics (or "odours," as they are referred to in the old texts) have psychological, natural, and supernatural effects on human beings. Ancient magicians regularly made use of anointing oils, incenses, and powders as a means of consecrating themselves, their altars, or other ritual items, or to alter their state of consciousness. Instructions for preparing sacred oils and anointing formulas are provided in biblical texts as well as in Egyptian papyri, European grimoires, and other ancient and sacred books. As the art of perfumery developed alongside the science of pharmacology, the formulas of the various hoodoo oils, ointments, and powders coincided with this evolution. In New Orleans, the influence of Egyptian and French perfumery on the magickal formulary is quite pronounced, though often unrecognized. The ancient use of oils, powders, and incenses for psychological stimulation, as aphrodisiacs, in religious and spiritual contexts, for psychic development, for healing, and for magickal influence persists to this day in their application in hoodoo.

The Hoodoo Altar

Before you begin any hoodoo work, you will need a place to do your rituals. This means you will need a quiet place where you won't be disturbed, and a surface such as a table, box, chest, or even a large flat stone. Some people set aside a portion of the floor to use as an altar, or they use a dresser top, with ritual supplies stored underneath. You will need basic items and some extra items to personalize your altar. Note that not all works require the use of an altar. For those that do, the instructions I am providing here are just the basics.

Cover your altar with a white cloth, and place two white candles at the back on either end. Figures or pictures of saints or other religious images should be placed at the back, between the two white candles. Place your incense burner in front of the image and in the middle of the altar, and to the right of that keep some holy water or a bowl of water that you have blessed. These are the basics of the hoodoo altar.

You can add fresh-cut flowers, special stones, a dish of salt, and a small dish of graveyard dirt, if you wish. The important thing is to not place anything on your altar that doesn't belong there. Altars can range from the very basic to the extremely elaborate.

Your altar and everything on it should be blessed or consecrated. Your candles should be blessed and dressed. All of the bowls and other containers should be washed with salt water, conjure water, Florida water, or Holy water. Directions for dressing your candles are provided in the chapter on candles, and instructions for how to consecrate your ritual objects are provided in a later chapter as well.

As you become familiar with working with the various spirits, you will learn how to set up altars for each spirit or family of spirits. For individual magickal works, however, the altar will be as individual as the work is itself.

The Ancestral Altar

Anyone who wishes to develop a Voodoo spiritual practice should create an ancestral altar first. This altar can honor your biological ancestors, the universal archetypal ancestors, or both. Any and all connection to the spirit world is dependent upon the strength of your ancestral connection.

The following are some guidelines for creating your own ancestral altar. Follow your intuition when creating your altar, and feel free to add to or subtract from the suggestions below.

How to Create an Ancestral Altar

To create an altar you will need:

- A table, flat stone, or shelf
- White cloth
- Photos and mementos of your ancestors
- White candle
- Glass or crystal bowl of water
- Fresh-cut flowers
- Incense
- A portion of each meal of the day
- A dish with nine different types of earth, including graveyard dirt

Drape the white cloth over the table or shelf. If using a stone, leave it bare. Place the glass bowl of water in the center of the table and the white candle behind the bowl. Arrange the photos and mementos, flowers, and bowl of earth on the altar in a manner that pleases you. The bowl of food should go in front of the bowl of water. You can add a small white candle in the bowl of food as well.

How to Address the Ancestors

First, light the incense to purify your surroundings. Sprinkle a little fresh water on the items on your altar, including the earth, to give respect to your ancestors. Light your candle and offer it to the four sacred directions—east, west, north, and south—then place it behind the bowl of water. Begin speaking to your ancestors by introducing yourself. Say something like,

> "Greetings, ancestors, my name is _____, son/daughter of _____ and _____, and I come with a pure heart to honor you with these offerings.

> "I honor [Say all of your ancestors names out loud]. I honor all of those remembered and forgotten, who were associated with my ancestors as friends, companions, and loved ones. I love, honor, and respect all who have gone before me.

> "To all my relations, all grandmothers and grandfathers, all elders and ancient ones, to all the creatures, plants, and living things of our Mother Earth, I offer my reverence and gratitude. I thank you for your guidance and protection, seen and unseen.

> "For all those who suffered so that we may carry on the traditions, for those who died prematurely, in a violent manner, or to anyone in particular need, I offer this special prayer so that you may rest in peace through the intercession of the four archangels and the Seven African Powers."

Say the prayer to the Seven African Powers here, followed by a sincere prayer of your own. You can now talk to your ancestors about your problems and ask them for guidance. When you are finished, offer them the food and drink and thank them for listening. Take a moment and meditate on your life, focusing on your blessings and abundance. Visualize passing on all that is good to your ancestors who have gone before you and to those yet to come. To conclude, pour water on the ground and say "Aché!" Let the candles burn out if possible.

At any time, you can focus on the positive aspects of your loved ones and pour water for them. Do this daily or weekly, while saying their names out loud. You can remember them by offering them some of the food you eat every day. A point of clarification: we do not worship our ancestors. We honor and respect them, and ask for their guidance.[29]

---

29 From *A Guide to Serving the Seven African Powers* by Denise Alvarado.

CHAPTER TWO

THE VOODOO PANTHEON

The spirits that comprise the Voodoo pantheon are the result of the forced mingling of various tribal groups because of slavery. In an incredible feat of psychological and spiritual survival, the tribal groups were able to combine their very different religious practices into one Voodoo practice that is no longer "pure" according to African standards. However, in the throes of slavery, the stolen people created new practices that incorporated not only their own rites and deities, but the rites and deities of other cultural groups. The original African rites spread to Haiti, Cuba, Brazil, the West Indies, the Dominican Republic, and other parts of the United States, where they began to take on characteristics of the local cultures. There are literally hundreds of spirits, and the list is always growing.

The spirit forces in New Orleans Voodoo and Haiti are referred to as *loas* (lwas), *mystères,* and *invisibles.* In Santería and Yoruba they are known as *orishas.* They are not deities; rather, they are comparable to saints or angels in Western religions in that they act as mediators between a distant Creator (Bon Dieu, or Good God) and humanity. It is not uncommon for New Orleans practitioners to acknowledge the loas found in Haiti, the orishas of the Yoruban tradition and Santería, the Catholic saints, the spirits of ancestors, zombie spirits, Native American spirits, archangels, and spirits that are uniquely New Orleanian in origin. In fact, it is not unusual to refer to spirits, saints, angels, and archangels as loas. The voodooists' relationship with the loas differs from saints and angels in that the loas are not merely petitioned with prayer—they are served. They are distinct entities with their own personal preferences and individual sacred rhythms, songs, dances, ritual symbols, and special forms of servitude.

In the Yoruban tradition, the *orishas* are God's ambassadors, ruling the fortunes of humankind, as well as the forces of nature. Their aspects are determined by their elemental natures. Thus, the orisha of lightning is also the orisha of sudden inspiration, vengeance, and dance; the orisha of the ocean is the orisha of motherhood, femininity, and creativity. In this way, the orishas represent ancient archetypal forces, a notion reflected in the phrase, "Las Sietes Potencias," or the Seven African Powers.[30]

For a more in-depth discussion of the Seven African Powers, including instructions for how to construct altars for each one and how to petition them, refer to my book, *A Guide to Serving the Seven African Powers*.

The Nations

The pantheon of Voodoo spirits is organized according to nations and more formally in Haitian Vodou according to rites. Two of the major nations are Rada and Petro. Some mistakenly refer to the Rada loa as "good" and the Petro loa as "evil." This is misleading; the Rada loa can be used to make malevolent magic, while the Petro loa can heal and do beneficial workings. They are more accurately referred to as "cool" and "hot," respectively.

You will find that contemporary hoodoo has little if anything to do with the Voodoo nations. It is for the sake of being thorough with regards to the religious aspects of New Orleans Voodoo that I have provided this information. A New Orleans Voodooist will not serve all of the spirits listed, but will recognize and acknowledge the existence of these and many, many more.

Rada Loas

A major family of loas, the Rada loas consist of older, beneficent spirits who can be directly traced to Dahomean Voodoo. Rada loas are guardians of morals and principles and related to Africa, whereas Petro loas are connected to the New World. According to Milo Rigaud (1953), the Rada loas include (this is a partial list):

- Agwé
- Ati Bon Legba (meaning "tree of justice" in Fon)
- Loko
- Ayizan
- Damballah Wedo

---

30 New Orleans Voodoo Loas, HauntedAmericaTours.com. (n.d.). Retrieved from *www.hauntedamericatours.com/voodoo/voodooloasneworleans*

- Ayida Wedo
- Maitresse and Grande Erzulie
- Erzulie Freda
- La Sirène
- La Baleine
- Marassa
- Maitre Kalfou (Master of the Crossroads)
- Baron La Croix
- Baron Samedi
- Manman Brigit

Some loas (such as Erzulie) have both Rada and Petro manifestations. Their traditional color is white (as opposed to the specific colors of individual loas) and they are associated with the element air. There are also loas classified in various combinations with other nations, such as Rada-Dahomey (i.e. Legba Ati Bon, Sobo, Ayizan, Erzulie Freda, etc.) and Rada-Nago-Congo (La Sirène, La Baleine).

Petro Loas

The Petro loas are generally the more fiery, occasionally aggressive, and warlike loas assumed to have originated in Haiti under the unforgiving conditions of slavery. Their rites feature whip cracking, whistles, and ignited gunpowder. In addition, Petro drumbeats are swifter and more syncopated than the Rada rhythms. The Petro rites are an integral part of the Haitian Vodou initiation ceremony (Kanzo), the rite by which serviteurs are initiated as priests and priestesses (houngans and mambos). Erzulie Dantor is considered the "mother" of the Petro nation and is one of the most important Petro loas. Other Petro loas include (this is a partial list):

- Ogun Changó (Petro, Nago)
- Lemba File Sabre (Nago, Petro)
- Manman Pemba
- Damballah la Flambeau
- Trois Carrefours (Three Crossroads)
- Grande Brigitte (Petro, Rada)
- Captain Zombi
- Jean Zombi
- Erzulie Toro (the Bull)
- Erzulie Gé Rouge (Red-Eye)

Their traditional color is red and they are associated with the element fire. In New Orleans, Petro spirits often designated as *la flambeau.*

Congo Loas

The Congo loas are thought to descend from the *Lemba,* an ethnic group in southern Africa who claim a common descent belonging to the Jewish people. The entire northern area of Haiti is especially influenced by Congo practice. Congo spirits are associated with the element water and include, but are not limited to, the following spirits:

- Simb'bi d'leau
- Grande Alouba
- Canga
- Lemba Zapou (Congo, Petro)
- Sinigal (Congo, Senegal)
- Man Inan
- Laoca (Congo Legba)
- Manman Pen'ba (Congo, Petro)

Nago Loas

Originating from Nigeria (specifically the Yoruba speaking tribes), this nation includes many of the Ogun spirits:

- Ogou Fer
- Ogou Changó
- Ogou Bha Tha Lah (Mixed Nago)
- Ogou Baba
- Ogou-Tonnerre (nago, Petro)
- Lemba File Sabre (Nago, Petro)
- Ti Jean

Guede Loas

Although the guede are included in the section about Voodoo nations, they are not considered a nation; rather, they are a family of loas. The *guede* (ghede) are the spirits of the dead. They are traditionally led by the Barons (La Croix, Samedi, Cimitière, Kriminel), and Manman Brigit, though these classic guede spirits are included among the Rada loas. The guede are loud, rude, crass, sexual, and a lot of fun. Their traditional colors are black, purple, and white.

The Seven African Powers

The Seven African powers are the most memorable divinities of the Yoruban pantheon. They are common to all Yoruban faiths, but they are not always considered to be the same deities. Though it may be confusing to some, the orishas appear alongside the loas in New Orleans Voodoo as well as on hoodoo altars. Following is a list of the Seven African Powers, their associated saints, and their attributes as I have learned them.

Papa Legba (Ellegua, Elegba, Liba, Laba, Labas)

In Haitian Vodou as well as New Orleans Voodoo, Papa Legba is the intermediary between the spirits and humanity. He is the most important loa because he stands at a spiritual crossroads and grants or denies permission to speak with the spirits of Guinee. In New Orleans, the gates of Guinee are considered to be the portal to the afterworld.

If you have lost or misplaced something, ask Legba to help you find it. Like St. Anthony, he can help you find lost objects.

Legba is believed to speak all human languages. He is always the first and last spirit invoked in any ceremony, because his permission is needed for any communication between humans and the loas—he opens and closes the gates to the spirit world. Legba is petitioned to remove obstacles and open the doors to opportunities.

In Yoruba, Ellegua is mostly associated with Papa Legba because both deities share the role of the god of the crossroads. Legba also shares similarities to Orunmila, the orisha of prophesy who taught mankind how to use the mighty oracle Ifá. Legba, Ellegua, and Exú are similar, but they are not the same spirits.

Papa Legba usually appears as an old man on a crutch or with a cane, wearing a broad-brimmed straw hat and smoking a pipe, or sprinkling water. The dog and rooster are sacred to him. Because of his position as "gatekeeper" between the worlds of the living and the mysteries, he is often identified with St. Peter, who holds a comparable position in the Catholic tradition. He is also depicted in Haiti as St. Lazarus, or St. Anthony. Legba's wife's name is Adjessi.

In Yoruban mythology, Ellegua is an orisha associated with "opening the ways," or crossroads, as well. Often depicted as a child or a small man, he is a playful trickster god. Worshippers often place a cement head with a metal spike in the top and cowrie shells for eyes and mouth as a representation of Ellegua behind their front door. He is believed to protect the entryway and prevent harm from entering the home. Receiving a consecrated Ellegua head is part of the Santería initiation known as Los Guerreros (the Warriors). Ellegua is the messenger of the orishas and guardian of the doors; without him nothing can be accomplished. His child aspect is likened to the Catholic saint El Niño de Atoche.

Legba and Ellegua are said to like candy, toys, and coconut as offerings, or anything children would enjoy. In return, they help people overcome various problems.

- Identification: Holy Infant of Atocha, St. Peter, St. Anthony, St. Lazarus
- Feast day: January 1st
- Numbers: 3 and 21
- Colors: Red and black

Ogun (Ogoun)

Ogun is the chief of the Warriors and the Spirit of war, blood, and iron, similar to the spirit of Ares in Greek mythology. He is the patron of civilization and technology. Ogun is responsible for tools of progress, like farming equipment and surgeon's knives, and commands the leaders of society, such as policeman, doctors, and the military. As such, he is mighty, powerful, and triumphant; however, he can also be dangerous and destructive. He is often called upon to bring work to the unemployed and to give us the tools we need to realize our goals, whatever they may be.

Ogun gives strength through prophecy and magic. He is associated with locomotives, and offerings are often made to him at railroad tracks. A favorite offering to Ogun is three railroad ties. In Candomble, he is associated with St. George, the dragon slayer; in Lukumi, Santería, and Palo Mayombe, he is syncretized with St. Peter; in Voodoo, St. Joseph. In New Orleans he is referred to as Joe Feray. Ogun is one of the husbands of Erzulie Freda and is a husband of Oshun and Oyá in Yoruba mythology. According to legend, Ogun is a son of Yemayá and Orungan. In all his incarnations, Ogun is a fiery and martial spirit. He can be very aggressively masculine, but can rule the heads of female or effeminate male initiates to whom he takes a liking. He is also linked with blood, and is for this reason often called upon to heal diseases of the blood. However, because Ogun enjoys blood offerings, it is considered inadvisable to petition Ogun with a bleeding wound or while menstruating.

- Identification: St. George, St. Peter, St. Joseph
- Feast day: June 29th
- Numbers: 3 and 7
- Day of the week: Tuesday, Wednesday & the 4th of each month
- Colors: Green and black

Changó (Xango, Shango)

Changó is a warrior, the orisha of lightning, dance, passion, fire, thunder, and power. He is the epitome of all things masculine, and the dispenser of justice and vengeance on behalf of victims. He has the power to help win wars, defeat enemies, and gain power over others. He brings victory over enemies and all difficulties. Petition Changó for domination and strength in all matters, to cleanse and renew a community, or to ensure victory over difficulties.

Changó was a royal ancestor of the Yoruba, the third king of the Oyo and deified after his death. His most popular symbol is the double-bladed axe (oshe). He is represented under the colonial guise as St. Barbara, and is sometimes associated with Vodou's Petro loa, Erzulie Dantor.

According to Yoruba and Vodou belief systems, Changó hurls bolts of lightning at his followers, leaving behind imprints of stone axe blade on the earth's crust. Worship of Changó provides a great deal of power and self-control. Changó altars often contain a carved figure of a woman holding a gift to the god with a double-bladed axe sticking up from her head. The axe symbolizes that this devotee is possessed by Changó.

Changó has three wives: Oshun, Oba, and Oyá. Because of her excellent cooking, Oshun is his favorite. Oyá was Changó's third wife, known for stealing the secrets of his powerful magic.

As the legend is told, Changó lived in a home next to his three wives, who also had their own homes. He spent time eating and sleeping with each of his wives. Oba noticed that when Changó went to Oshun's home he would eat all of the food that she prepared for him; yet, when he came home to her he would just pick. Desiring a closer relationship with her husband, Oba asked Oshun how she kept Changó so happy. Oshun was offended by the inquiry and became filled with resentment. For one, Oba's children would inherit Changó's kingdom because they were his first children. Oshun's children would not have nearly the same status, being born from his concubine. Out of jealousy, Oshun decided to play a trick on Oba by telling her a lie. Oshun told Oba that she had cut off a small piece of her ear and dried it many years ago. She pulverized her dried ear into a powder and sprinkled it on Changó's food. According to Oshun, the more Changó ate, the more he desired her. Excited by this information, Oba ran home to prepare Changó's favorite meal. She thought that if a little piece of Oshun's ear produced such a great effect, her whole ear should drive Changó crazy with desire for her and he would forget Oshun forever. Oba sliced off her ear and stirred it into Changó's food. When Changó came home, he sat down and began to eat without looking at his bowl. When he finally looked down, he saw Oba's ear floating in the stew. Thinking Oba was trying to poison him, Changó drove her from his house. Oba ran away, sobbing. She fell to earth to become a river, where she is still worshipped today. As an orisha, Oba is the goddess of marriage and is said to destroy marriages in which abuse occurs.

- Identification: St. Barbara
- Feast day: December 4th
- Numbers: 4 and 6
- Colors: Red and white

Obatalá

Obatalá is the creator God, the androgynous sky king of the white cloth. He is the supreme deity of the Yoruba pantheon. Obatalá is the eldest of all orishas. His color is white, containing all the colors of the rainbow. He rules the mind and intellect, cosmic equilibrium, male and female. Obatalá is considered to be beyond the sphere of direct communication. In New Orleans, the serpent spirit Damballah Wedo shares many of the same attributes.

According to mythical stories, Obatalá created the human body through the power of the supreme deity Olorún, while Olorún (God) breathed life into them. Obatalá descended from the sky to Ilé Ifé, Nigeria. He brought with him a cockerel, a pigeon, and a calabash full of dirt. After throwing the soil upon the waters, he set the cockerel and pigeon upon the pile of dirt. They scratched and scattered it around to create the rest of the dry land that became the earth's surface. Somewhere along the line of creation, Obatalá got drunk on palm wine and screwed up by creating defective people. That is how he became the patron deity of handicapped individuals. Hence, Obatalá must never be worshipped with palm wine, palm oil, alcohol, or salt. His worshippers may eat palm oil and salt, but never drink palm wine.

- Identification: Our Lady of Mercy
- Feast day: September 24th
- Numbers: 8 and all its multiples
- Color: White

Oyá (Yansa)

Oyá is the orisha of winds and hurricanes, lightning, fertility, fire, and magic. She is the guardian of cemeteries and the underworld. She is also the orisha of change and cuts through stagnation with her machete and sword of truth. In this way, she clears the way for new growth.

In Yoruba mythology, Oyá is the Goddess of the Niger River. Her purpose is ancestral connection and success in the marketplace, and she is called upon when a great change is needed. Oyá is a powerful warrior, and the wife of Changó. She epitomizes female power and righteous anger. Her full name is Oyá-Yansan, which means "mother of nine." Oyá has been syncretized in Santería with the Catholic images of Our Lady of Candelaria (Our Lady of the Presentation) and St. Theresa. In Brazilian Umbanda she is represented by Saint Barbara.

- Identification: Our Lady of Candelaria (Our Lady of the Presentation), St. Teresa, St. Barbara
- Feast day: February 2, 9
- Day of the week: Friday
- Colors: All colors except black. Her main color is wine.

Yemayá (Yemoja, Iemanja)

Yemayá is the Mother of the Seven Seas, the Creation Goddess, and Yoruban orisha of fertility and motherhood. She offers protection to women. She is likened to the patron saints Lady of Regla, and Mary, Star of the Sea. Often depicted as a mermaid, she is associated with the moon, ocean, and female mysteries. She rules the subconscious and creative endeavors. She is the governess of the household and of matters pertaining to women, including childbirth, conception, childhood safety, love, and healing. Extremely compassionate and merciful, Yemayá rules the dreamtime, oversees the moon, deep secrets, ancient wisdom, salt water, sea shells, and the collective unconscious.

According to legend, Yemayá originated in Egypt as the goddess Isis. It is thought by some that the Nubian slaves who returned to different parts of Africa may have brought Isis with them under the new name of Yemayá. It is said that Yemayá gave birth to the fourteen Yoruban goddesses and gods. When her uterine water broke, it caused a great flood and created the oceans. The first human man and woman were borne from her womb.

Yemayá goes by a number of different names, including Queen of Witches, Mother of Fishes, The Constantly Changing Woman, The Ocean Mother, Mother of Dreams and Secrets, Mother of Pearl, and Yemayá-Olokun (a powerful dream aspect). Yemayá's counterpart in Vodou is called La Sirène, the mermaid. She is related to Mami Wata (Mamma Water), the African water spirit.

According to a popular legend, Yemayá chooses her students. Sometimes a person will disappear for seven years and return with tales of having learned the ways of magick and healing in Yemayá's undersea home. Her offerings are often doves, but *never* fish, as these are considered her children.

- Identification: Our Lady of Regla and Mary, Star of the Sea
- Feast day: September 7th
- Day of the week: Saturday
- Colors: Crystal and blue

Oshun (Ochun, Oxum)

In Yoruban mythology, Oshun is the orisha of love, intimacy, beauty, wealth, and mediation. She rules the "sweet waters"—rivers, brooks, streams, and water in the body. She is a sweet, loving, and generous spirit who is the force of harmony. However, she is known to have a terrible temper and is capable of absolute destruction. According to the Yoruba elders, Oshun is the "unseen mother present at every gathering," because she represents the cosmological forces of water, moisture, and attraction.

Oshun is the consummate business woman. She is known as Iyalode ("female chief of the marketplace") and is the mother of things outside the home.[31] She answers prayers quickly and effectively, so she is also known as Laketi ("she who has ears"). When Oshun possesses her followers, she dances, flirts, and then weeps because of the deep sense of empathy she has for the suffering of the world. No one can ever love her enough, and she holds the pain of knowing that the world is not as beautiful as she knows it could be. [32]

In New Orleans Voodoo, Oshun is celebrated as the orisha of love, beauty, witchcraft, and creativity, especially dance. She watches over pregnant women and ensures safe deliveries. She is believed to own all of the wealth in the world, and is most generous. She carries a pumpkin as her purse that overflows with an abundance of creativity and joy, as well as all that is needed to keep her servitors free of want. While she is the epitome of beauty, she also has other manifestations who live in stagnant waters that will eliminate uncleanliness. She is mostly petitioned for issues of love, prosperity, magic, fertility, and family. In 1996, the Mardi Gras Krewe of Oshun was founded in honor of this great Yoruban goddess.

According to legend, Oshun gave birth to Elegba, the divine messenger of aché in the universe and also the timeless trickster. She is one of three spirits married to Changó, the orisha of fire, thunder, and power.

In one story, it is said that Oshun was forced into prostitution in order to feed her children. The other orishas did not approve of her behavior and took her

---

31   Matory, J. L. (2005). *Sex and the Empire that is No More*. New York: Berghahn Books. p xxvi.

32   For more information, refer to Miguel A. De La Torre, "Dancing with Ochún: Imagining How a Black Goddess Became White," in *Aesthetics within Black Religion: Religious Thought and Life in Africa and the African Diaspora*, Anthony Pinn, ed., Cambridge University Press, pages: 113-134.

children, which left her in utter despair. She wore the same white dress every day until it eventually turned yellow because of all the tears she cried. She went to a river and began washing her dress. Another river orisha called Aje'-Shaluga fell in love with her as he watched her washing her dress. He gave her some money and jewelry that he collected from the bottom of the river where he lived. Oshun used these items to free her children, and ultimately married Aje'-Shaluga.

- Identification: Our Lady of Charity (la Virgen de la Caridad)
- Feast day: September 8th
- Numbers: 5 and all multiples of 5
- Colors: Yellow and amber

Other Important Loas

While the Seven African Powers are of obvious importance in the New Orleans pantheon, there are a number of other spirits of equal importance. Not all Voodooists serve all of these spirits, though. As there are literally hundreds of loas, the following is but a partial list.

Adjassou-Linguetor

Adjassou Linguetor is the loa of spring water. She has eyes that bulge out and a terrible temper.

Agassou (Monsieur Agassou, Yon Sue, Vert Agassou)

Agassou, or Monsieur Agassou as he is sometimes called in New Orleans, is a spirit of African origin, said to be the offspring of a divine mating between a spotted panther and Princess Aligbonoun of Togo. In the most simplistic descriptions of this loa, he is defined as the guardian of the traditions of Dahomey and the Royal Leopard King of Africa. Further discussion about this loa with practitioners of related African-derived traditions and research into his background reveals a much more complex story.

Agassou is characterized differently among traditions and African regions. According to some Haitians, Agassou is sometimes represented by a crab and considered a companion of Met Agwe. According to African informants, the crab represents Mami Wata, the spirit that came from the Mina/Ewe people of Togo.

In New Orleans, Tallant (1946), Pitkin (1904), and Ellis (1965) all report that Saint Anthony of Padua is petitioned as Yon Sue or Monsieur Agassou and that he manifests as a great guardian who protects Voodooists from those who would  interfere with their freedom to worship the spirits of Africa. The confusion here is about who is actually being petitioned and how syncretization works. A particular Catholic saint being syncretized with an African spirit does not make the two one and the same. The descendents of Agassou who choose to seek help from Yon Sue are not confused about who they are working with. Agassou is petitioned for protection and for money. I would suggest using his vévé along with a statue of St. Anthony of Padua and a figure of a spotted panther or leopard when working with him.

Agwé (Met Agwe, Agoué)

Agwé is the New Orleans loa who rules over the sea, fish, and aquatic plants. He is the patron loa of fishermen and sailors. He is alternately married to Erzulie Freda or La Sirène, and he may have had an affair with Ayida Wedo, the rainbow serpent and wife of Damballah Wedo.

Offerings to Agwé are left on constructed rafts that are floated out to sea. His color is usually blue, and he is syncretized with the Catholic St. Expedite as well as Saint Ulrich, who is depicted holding a fish. His vévé is a boat with sails. He is associated with Bayou St. John, Lake Ponchartrain, and the Mississippi River in New Orleans.

Annie Christmas

Annie Christmas is unique to New Orleans and known to be the epitome of woman-strength. She is the female incarnation of Ogun and is said to be a railroad worker in old New Orleans. Annie Christmas can be served with a machete, rum, undercooked meat, iron, railroad objects, and clanging metal. Her altar and offerings can be placed on the floor next to Ogun's altar.

Ayida Wedo

Ayida Wedo is a loa of fertility, rainbows, and snakes, and is a companion or wife to Damballah. She represents the sky powers, and the rainbow is her symbol. She functions as protector of the cosmos and giver of blessings.

Long ago, the serpent spirit Damballah created the world. He used his seven thousand coils to form the stars and the planets in the heavens and to shape the hills and valleys on earth. He used lightning bolts to forge metals and make the sacred rocks and stones. When he shed his skin he created all the waters on the earth. And when the sun showed through mist settling on the plants and trees, a rainbow was born. Her name was Ayida Wedo. Damballah loved her and made her his wife. They are still together today, the serpent and the rainbow.

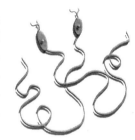

Ayizan

Ayizan is the loa of the French marketplace, commerce, and herbal healing. She represents love and is associated with Vodou rites of initiation. Ayizan is regarded as the first or archetypal mambo (priestess), and associated with priestly knowledge and mysteries, particularly those of initiation. She is the protector of religious ceremonies. She is syncretized with Saint Clare and said to be married to Papa Loco. Her symbol is the palm frond, and she doesn't drink alcohol. On Palm Sunday, people gather the leaves and use them as an offering to her. Her colors are gold, yellow, white, and silver. In New Orleans she is often represented with the color pink and is given sugar cane syrup, yams, and plantains, along with palm fronds, as offerings.

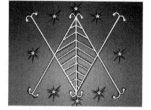

Azaca-Medeh

Azaca Medeh is the loa of farmers, agriculture, and healing. After the Haitian Revolution, Azaca Medeh appeared in the Haitian Vodou pantheon when slaves were able to own property. He is typically depicted as a peasant carrying a straw bag, and he loves to eat. He is a kind and gentle loa. Azaca Medeh is identified with Saint Isadore. His feast day is May first, which is Labor Day in Haiti. His colors are denim blue, green, and white. His sacrifical animal is the red rooster and offerings include cornmeal, corn cakes, sugar cane, coffee, and cane syrup.

Azaca-Tonnerre (see Diable Tonnere)

Azaca Tonnere is in the same family of loas as Azaca Medeh. Azaca Tonnere is the loa of thunder. He is referred to as Diable Tonnere in New Orleans.

Babalú-Ayé

Babalú-Ayé is the spirit of epidemics, illness, and disease, but is also the deity who cures. Though originally associated with smallpox, many of today's worshippers appeal to Babalú-Ayé for healing from HIV/AIDS. In Santería, he is syncretized with St Lazarus.

Babalú-Ayé is said to be the rightful owner of the earth and a special advocate for the poor. Babalú-Ayé is traditionally pictured in blue, brown, red, white, and purple, and is offered rice, wheat, corn, beans, chickpeas, garlic, onions, smoked fish, and possum in divination rituals. His sacred implements include a rattle and two crutches, which are decorated in purple and gold. A power object associated with him is a broom made from palm fronds and decorated with cowry shells and beads.

Baron Samedi

Baron Samedi is a loa of the dead, along with his numerous other incarnations Baron Cimetière, Baron La Croix, and Baron Criminel. He is the ultimate suave and sophisticated spirit of death, usually depicted with a black top hat, black tuxedo, dark glasses, and cotton plugs in the nostrils, as if to resemble a corpse dressed and prepared for burial in Haitian style.[33] He has a white, skull-like face, talks through his nose, and tells crude but funny jokes. He is known for disruption, obscenity, debauchery, and for having a particular fondness for tobacco and rum. As well as being the all-knowing loa of death, he is a sexual loa, frequently represented by phallic symbols. He is the head of the Guédé family of loas, and married to the loa Manman Brigit.

Baron Samedi stands at the crossroads, where the souls of humans pass on their way to Guinee. Baron is a protector of children and is petitioned for sick children. He has authority over zombies and decides whether or not people can be changed into animals.[34] Since Baron Samedi is the lord of death, he is the last resort for healing because he is able to decide whether to allow the dying to cross over or to allow them to recover. In Haiti, he is associated with St. Gerard Mejella.

Black Hawk

Black Hawk was a famous leader and warrior of the Sauk American Indian Nation. Contrary to popular belief, he was not a hereditary civil chief of the Sauk, though he did inherit a sacred medicine bundle. Rather, he was an appointed war chief. During the War of 1812, Black Hawk fought on the side of the British. Later he led a band of Sauk and Fox warriors against settlers in Illinois and present-day Wisconsin in the 1832 Black Hawk War. After the war, he was captured and taken to the eastern United States, where he and other Brit-

---

33 Hurbon, L., 1995. *Voodoo: Search for the Spirit.*
34 Haiti: List of Central Loa. (n.d.). Retrieved from *www.webster.edu/~corbetre/haiti/voodoo/listlwa.htm*

ish band leaders toured several cities. Black Hawk died in 1838 in what is now southeastern Iowa.

The Spiritualist churches of New Orleans honor the Native American spirit of Black Hawk. Black Hawk is also considered a Voodoo saint, and is often included in ritual work wherein worshipers become possessed and gain the power to heal and prophesy. He is served by many hoodoo practitioners as well.

Because of exploitation by hoodoo marketeers, the image of the Indian spirit guide has had a big influence on commercial hoodoo products. The image can be seen on many hoodoo products such as Indian Spirit incense and room spray by the E. Davis Company. The Indian motif is significant in the art and organization of the Mardi Gras Indians, as well.

In the Native way, Black Hawk is an elder. Elders are revered and given the utmost respect. This is translated in hoodoo and Spiritualism into Father Black Hawk, though his given name in Mesquakie is Ka-Tai-Me-She-Kia-Kiak. Few can pronounce his given name, so it is hoodooized as Father Black Hawk. Black Hawk was born into the Thunder clan, and sometimes he wows his servitors by announcing his arrival with a loud clap of thunder.

Father Black Hawk is invoked routinely by the bishops in the Spiritualist churches in New Orleans. His altar in the Spiritualist church is that of a teepee with a plate of incense on the floor in the front. He is frequently found alongside images of St. Michael, guardian of Israel, and Dr. Martin Luther King. This trinity represents three oppressed races and functions as a symbol of strength and victory. Rootworkers who serve him keep him in a metal bucket with sand or dirt, along with a hatchet, tomahawk, and a spear. Father Black Hawk is petitioned by individuals from their homes. He is typically evoked for help with money and protection, justice, release from prison, to win court cases, and to overcome tragedy. He is the consummate warrior, and wants to fight your battles for you. They say he will come to those who have enough patience to sit still. Black Hawk likes spaghetti and meatballs, red beans and rice, bread, and fruit, and is served these dishes on Wednesdays and Sundays. He is approached at his altar. To set up a home altar to Black Hawk, you need a bucket of sand and a statue of an Indian warrior. Some people will use a combination of seven different dirts taken from seven different places of power. I have dirt from the Rock River in Illinois where he was born and where he fought in the Black Hawk War. I added dirt from a crossroads, along with graveyard dirt, mud dauber nest, and sand from the Gulf Coast where I grew up. These dirts, along with several others, make for a powerful representation of Mother Earth. The number seven in Native American cosmology represents the seventh sacred direction of the medicine wheel, which is the place where the people, self, and all living things reside. Of course you can have a variation on this theme, as I did for my first altar. I had a small statuette of him that stood in a Native American bowl full of sand from the Gulf Coast.

Surrounding the statue in my Black Hawk bucket are a number of rocks that have personal and cultural significance. In the Native way, rocks are considered the elders of Mother Earth and the keepers of ancient wisdom. I also have a bear fetish that was carved from stone by my son's father (a full-blooded Navajo), a small clay pot made by a Native American, and my quilled medicine wheel that I wore at Sundance. The bucket sits on a small Indian blanket. A beaded golden eagle feather that I use in Native American church ceremonies lies on the back of the bucket. His spear, which is thrown to reach a distant goal, and a tomahawk, used to cut a right of way, are also in his bucket. As can be seen, everything placed in, on, or around his bucket holds special significance.

It is usually a good idea to burn sage, cedar, or sweet grass while petitioning Black Hawk. Some people insist on giving him whiskey to "fire him up," but I find this to be an amplification of the stereotype that depicts the drunken Indian juiced up on fire water. This is an image that is offensive to Native peoples. He can be equally fired up by offering him lightning-struck wood (remember, he is of the Thunder clan) or respectfully offering him Indian tobacco, which is the tradition of his people. To petition him, put on some traditional Indian music or play a drum or flute. Offer him some Indian tobacco and food. Then recite one of the prayers to Black Hawk in chapter 4, followed by a heartfelt prayer of your own. Then you can talk to him and tell him what you need.

Blanc Dan-I (Dani Blanc, Damballah Wedo)

This loa is similar in many ways to Obatalá. He is a "cool" loa concerned with compassion, fairness, and love. In New Orleans, Blanc Dani or Dani Blanc is often another reference for Danballah Wedo, which makes sense, given the association of Obatalá with Damballah Wedo. Blanc Dani has been syncretized with the Catholic St. Michael.

Damballah Wedo

Damballah Wedo is depicted as a serpent god, and is closely associated with snakes. Damballah is the wise and loving father of all the loas and, along with his wife Ayida Wedo, is the loa of creation. One of the most important and popular of all the loas, he is both a member of the Rada family and a root loa. Dam-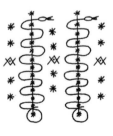

ballah's color is white and his offerings are an egg on a mound of flour. When he manifests in ritual, he does not speak but only hisses like a snake. He is syncretized with the Catholic figures of Moses or St. Patrick. When referenced as Blanc Dani or Dani Blanc, he is syncretized with St. Michael. He is sometimes referred to as Li Grande Zombi.

Dan Petro

Dan Petro is the New Orleans loa of farmers. He originated from the African loa Danh.

Diable Tonnere (see Azaca Tonnere)

Diable Tonnere is the loa of thunder in New Orleans.

Dr. John

Dr. John is one of the loas unique to New Orleans. According to Doktor Snake, Dr. John was "the famed and flamboyant Voodooist who operated in New Orleans during the nineteenth century . . . specializing in healing, selling gris-gris and telling fortunes."[35] Apparently, he claimed to be a Senegalese prince and had the ceremonial scars on his face to prove it. Dr. John was known for his money charms, which served him well as evidenced by the large amount of wealth he accumulated while he was a Voodoo doctor. Because of the power of his gris gris, he has been elevated to the status of loa in New Orleans Voodoo, and often referred to as Father John in Spiritualist circles.

Dr John is petitioned largely for healing purposes, given his knowledge of the healing herbs and plants and his reputation as a great doctor. Among Spiritualists, he is considered a great guiding spirit who controls other spirits. He is also a great defender against evil.[36]

Louis Martiné of the New Orleans Voodoo Spiritual Temple has played an intergral role in facilitating the elevation of Dr. John to loa status. One way he has done this is by writing the Litany of the Good Doctor. The Litany, or Priye Ginen (African Prayer) plays an important role in many Voodoo ceremonies. It is a long prayer that calls out the names of the saints and the loas in the the opening ritual. Martiné wrote the following litany in honor of Dr. John, to be said when petitioning him. The reader is referred to Martinés book *A Priest's Head, A Drummer's Hands: New Orleans Voodoo: Order of Service* for a wonderful description of

---

35 2000, p. 34-36.
36 Jacobs & Kaslow, 2001.

New Orleans Voodoo drum rhythms and the unique order of service for Dr. John. Martinié's service for Dr. John includes the following litany:

Doctor John.
Honor and respect to you.
I remember your name.
I say your name.
Before my eyes sits the issue of your hands;
    in both document and signature.
Within me my mind and heart remember you.
Doctor John.
John Montanée.
Born of Africa.
Live in New Orleans.
Husband to Mathilde and Armantine.
Father of John Montennet, born the third of November, 1856.
And of many others.
Owner of a coffeehouse in New Orleans.
Worked as physician and Indian doctor.
Passed on August 18, 1885 at seventy years.
Doctor John.
Loa of New Orleans.
Loa of Drummers.
Loa of doctors in the spiritual path.
Guide my hands on this drum.
Guide my hands in this work.
Doctor John.
Speak in wisdom to my mind.
Speak in understanding to my heart.
Help me to play the rhythms of awakening to my spirit.
Touch and be touched. (Martinié, 2005)

Ellegua

The great trickster who owns the crossroads is called Ellegua. He enables mankind to communicate with the other orishas and is always honored first. He is often referred to as Papa Legba, but they are not the same spirits. Ellegua is petitioned to clear the path so we may realize the attainment of our goals. In his child form, he often represents our desires, wishes, and impulses.

Erzulie Dantor

Erzulie Dantor is the Voodoo goddess of love, romance, art, jealousy, passion, and sex. Dantor supports independent businesswomen and is the patron of women's finances. She is also the patron loa of lesbian women and a fierce protector of women and children experiencing domestic violence. She is a patron loa of New Orleans. Erzulie Dantor offers protection and possibilities beyond the imagination.

Erzulie Dantor is a mulatto woman who is often portrayed as the Black Madonna, or the Roman Catholic "St. Barbara Africana." In New Orleans, she is often called Our Lady of Perpetual Help. She has tribal scars on her cheek. She is considered heterosexual because she has children, but she loves women fiercely, and will defend them to the death. Dantor loves knives and is considered the protector of newly consecrated Voodoo priests and priestesses, as well as of women who have been betrayed by a lover. She is highly respected and much feared due to her woman power. Most Haitian women serve Dantor, as do Voodooists in New Orleans. Enlightened men also serve Dantor—especially men who honor, love, and respect women. Many women invoke Erzulie Dantor against their partners (male or female) should they become violent.

Erzulie's personal story is a tragedy. She was a warrioress who fought with her people during the Haitian Revolution. However, her own people cut out her tongue so that she would not tell their secrets should she be captured. Thus, she is mute and can only produce a clicking sound with her tongue She is often pictured with her daughter Anais, who serves as her translator and interpreter.

Erzulie Freda

Erzulie Freda is the loa of romantic love and is the epitome of femininity and compassion. She is invoked to help find a lover, or to renew a love relationship. She is also a powerful magician who can counter the blackest of magick and evil. Beauty, love, and sensuality are her creations. To those who serve her, she can offer wealth, prosperity, and luxury. She possesses great beauty, grace, and sensuality, and demands cleanliness of her children. Erzulie's domain is water and she lives on the river banks. In the Rada aspect, Erzulie is the spirit of beauty, jewelry, dancing, luxury, and flowers. Her colors are light blue and pink. Sometimes her clothing will be shown in rose and white. She wears three wedding bands for her three husbands: Damballah, the serpent god; Agwé, the god of the fishermen; and Ogun, the god of iron. Erzulie is not promiscuous; rather, she is a goddess with a large heart.

Erzulie's symbols are a heart, a mirror, and a fan. She often weeps tears of sadness, joy, or frustration. Her animal is a white dove. She is associated with the Lukumi Orisha Oshun.

Exú (Eshu)

Exú (Ey-shu) is one of the most well-known spirits of the Yoruban religion and related African-derived traditions. Exú is a powerful spirit who functions as divine messenger and gatekeeper to the spirit world. He sits at the crossroads, offering choices and possibilities to humankind. Exú represents balance: day and night, old age and youth, black and white, construction and destruction. He encompasses male sexuality, strength, and fertility, and is privy to the mysteries of life and death. Exú is the lord of chaos and trickery, and the keeper of the life force/energy (ashé). Nothing can be accomplished in the human world or the spirit world without his permission. He is translator and bridge between humans and the natural world—the sacred and the profane. Every living thing has a personal Exú.

Exú goes by many different names among the African-derived religions. For example, he is known as Eshu in the Orisha-Ifá system of the Yoruba, as well as in the Candomble, Santería, and Lukumi religions. He is often likened to Legba in Haitian Vodou and New Orleans Voodoo. In Cuba he is likened to Eleggua, and in West Africa he is known as Esu. In Palo Mayombe, he is known as Lucero. However, these spirits are not the same entity. Exú is sometimes associated with the Catholic Saint Anthony and Saint Michael.

In the Afro-Brazilian tradition commonly referred to as Umbanda, Exús are considered a family of spirit-deities. It is believed that Exús are the spirits of people who were considered to be either frightening, very well educated, or experts in a given field when they were alive. Exú Meia-Noite, for example, is said to be the spirit of a great doctor who knows all the secrets to healing.

Exú functions as door opener. He can remove obstacles and open doorways to new opportunities. As divine messenger, Exú sees all and is all-knowing. He knows good and evil, and can be equally cruel and generous. However, his actions are always justified and logical—never random. He has a very close relationship to the orisha of divination, Orunmila (Orunla). He is the master of the buzios, a form of divination that uses cowry shells. At the same time, Exú does not need an oracle to be able to foretell the future. As master magician, Exú is knowledgable and capable of doing black or white magick. He knows all the formulas and spells. In fact, his spells and talismans are so powerful that it is said that they are impossible to destroy. He can be invoked to do manipulative magick, but only by those foolhardy enough to try.[37]

Gran Bwa

The Gran Bwa (Big Wood) is the master of the Sacred Forest of the Island below the Waters, which is the place that the loas call home, and to which the newly dead travel. He is the protector of all wild animals, and knows the secrets of herbal medicine and of magic hidden in herbs. He is likened to St. Sebastian and St. Christopher in the Catholic tradition. He represents the forces of nature in New Orleans religion.

Gran Bwa is a very loving loa with a great sense of humor and is full of advice. He is apparently proud of the fact that he has a big, stiff penis. Gran Bwa can be petitioned for healing, prosperity, and general advice. He is the loa who must be called upon before one is ordained into Voodoo priesthood.

Some of Gran Bwa's favorite things include sweet potatoes, yams, green bananas, black pigs, goats, distilled rum, wild berries, acorns, and any type of food from the woods.

Gran Ibo

Gran Ibo has experience of the ancient, the oldest of old, beyond memory, in the roots of the beginning of time. She is most commonly known as the Swamp Witch, so called because the bayou swamp is the place she calls home. Gran Ibo is a loa of wisdom and patience. She sits and waits, watching and embracing the heart of the swamp. She holds the secrets of the mysteries that lie therein. She knows the magic and the medicine found within her little sisters, who are the healing plants and herbs of the forest. She knows the power of the water. Through her, the roots, plants, herbs, and flowers of the swamp communicate to the Voodooist.

This goddess is a wise hermit, her home in the solitude of nature away from prying eyes. Her sacred animal is the yellow canary who whispers secrets of the mysteries into her ears. Canaries lead the soul to the ancestral realm. Give Gran Ibo and her canary food, blue-gray candles, swamp plants, plants with healing properties, seeds, and love and respect.

Gran Ibo is excellent with oils and incenses. She has inner peace, bliss, and foresight. She is not rash or impulsive. She understands and hears all the languages of life forms around her. If you lie, she will see right through you. She is the loa of the Vodou tradition called Congo.

---

37 Excerpted from Alvarado, D., 2010. *Exu, the Divine Trickster*, Create Space.

Grand Maître

The original supreme being of Haitian religion is Grand Maître. He is considered by some New Orleans practitioners to be too remote for personal worship.

Guede

The guede are a family of spirits associated with death. They live in cemeteries and visit Catholic churches at night. On November 2, the faithful visit cemeteries and light candles in honor of the dead. There are countless guede spirits, with Baron Samedi and Papa Guede being the most popular. Guede are generally good and generous spirits; both Papa Baron and Gran Brigitte have great healing power. It is believed the Guede can decide the fate of a person near death by allowing him or her to recover or make the transition to the afterlife. They are particularly fond of young children and protect them from harm. Unless it is the will of the Ultimate Creator, guede spirits do not allow children to die before they have lived their lives.

The guede control the crossroads at which every human must pass on the way to the afterlife. In the Haitian culture and New Orleans Voodoo, it is believed that permission must be obtained from Papa Baron (Lord of the Dead) in order to communicate and connect with ancestral spirits. In every major cemetery in Haiti, Papa Baron is represented by a black cross mounted on a small tomb.

Kalfu (Carrefour, Kalfou)

Kalfou is Legba's Petro manifestation. Kalfu also has dominion over the crossroads, but he controls the shadow forces of the spirit world as well. Kalfu oversees the in-between points of the crossroads and allows the crossing of bad luck, deliberate destruction, misfortune, and injustice.[38]

While Legba controls the positive spirits of the day, Kalfu controls the malevolent spirits of the night.[39] Kalfu is described as being strong, tall, and muscular. When he appears at a ceremony, everyone present will stop speaking because he allows evil loas in. He claims that most of the chief loas know him and that he works with them. He is sometimes depicted as demonic, but Kalfu denies this. He is a respected loa, but he is also feared and not well-liked. He is an expert sorcerer and closely associated with black magic. Ceremonies for him are often held at the crossroads. In New Orleans he is known as Mait' Carrefour.

---

38 Deren, M., 1953. *Divine Horsemen: The living Gods of Haiti.* New York: Vanguard Press .
39 Ibid.

La Sirène

La Sirène is the enchanting loa of the sea and the treaures that lie therein. She is often depicted as a mermaid, sitting on a rock, gazing at her reflection in the water while combing her long black hair. She is sometimes considered an aspect of Erzulie Freda or an aspect of the loa La Baleine, the spirit of the whale. La Sirène is the loa of wealth, musical arts, love, beauty, and dreams. She is the queen of the sea and has the ability to hypnotize people with her beautiful songs. She is known to grant gifts of extreme wealth and luck. La Sirène is especially honored in New Orleans Voodoo; when petitioned, she is offered shrimp, seaweed, and seawater. In return, she blesses her followers with gifts of music, wealth, and beauty. La Sirène's ritual colors are blue and green, and her offerings include sea glass, pink champagne, combs, sacred songs and chants, and sweet white wine—but never fish, as these are her children.

La Sirène epitomizes seductive power. She is the wife of Agwé and the mistress of Ogun. Petition La Sirène when you need luck and money, or when you need to enhance your seductive power, sensuality, and sex appeal. Make her happy and she will give you quick results.

Lemba

A deity of the Congo religion, Lemba is worshipped in the African-derived religions of Haiti, Brazil, and New Orleans.

Les Mort

Les Mort in Haitian Creole is the collective term for the dead. Ancestor reverence forms the foundation of the Voodoo religion. This refers to our personal and collective ancestors and the loas who were once human.

Li Grande Zombi

Li Grande Zombi is the most important loa in the New Orleans Voodoo pantheon. His name is most commonly linked to the name of Marie Laveau's pet snake, a huge boa constrictor or royal python (ball python) who was worshipped at her New Orleans Voodoo rituals on Bayou St. John. St. John's Eve, which falls on June 23, is the day when the biggest Voodoo gatherings were held, and even members of "polite society" were invited—including reporters, prominent citizens, and the police. It is also the day that some believers claim the ghost of Marie Laveau rises from the dead. To this day, it is still the most important Voodoo holiday in New Orleans. But, as has already been discussed in a previous chapter, Li Grande Zombi did not begin or end with Marie Laveau.

Limba

Limba is one of the New Orleans loas, believed to live among the rocks. He has an insatiable appetite and persecutes, kills, and eats people. Even his own devotees are not safe from his hunger.

L'inglesou

A Haitian loa who lives among rocks and ravines, L'inglesou is said to kill those who offend him.

Loco

In the Voodoo religion, Loco (Papa Loko) is a loa of vegetation and a patron of healers and healing plants, especially herbs and trees. Loco is the husband of loa Ayizan, and is considered the first houngan. As the spiritual parents of the priesthood, Loco and Ayizan are two of the loas associated in the kanzo (priesthood) initiation rites. They are both powerful guardians of "reglemen," and the correct and appropriate form of (Haitian) Vodou service. He comes from the royal lineage of Dahomey and his sacred number is 41. His feast days are January 6 and May 1, his colors are green, yellow, and white, and he is served on Wednesdays.

Mait' Carrefour (see Kalfu)

The New Orleans Voodoo lord of crossroads and loa of magicians. He is the loa who stands in balance to Legba. Mait' Carrefour controls the malevolent spirits of the night and the in-between points on the crossroads. His symbol is the crossroads and his color is black.

Manman Brigit (Brigit, Brijit)

In Voodoo, Maman Brigitte (Grann Brigitte, Manman, Manman Brigit, Manman Brijit) is the mother of cemeteries, the loa of money and death, and the wife of Baron Samedi. She may be related to the "triple" Celtic goddess of poetry, smithcraft, and healing, Saint Brigit, as her name is Irish in origin. She is usually depicted as a white woman. The first woman's grave in a cemetery in Haiti is dedicated to her. Her colors are black, purple, and white; her number is nine; and her particular days of service include Monday and Saturday. Her sacrificial animal is a black chicken. She drinks rum laced with hot peppers—"gaz lakrimojen Ayisyen" (Haitian tear gas), and like her husband and the rest of the guede spirits, she is a "potty mouth" and uses profanity. Maman Brigitte is known to rub her private parts with hot peppers, and those who appear to be faking possession by her in a Vodou ceremony may be subjected to this test, which they obviously would not pass if their possession is not genuine. She is a very sexual dancer, and her skill in the banda dance is legendary.[40]

Maman Brigitte is invoked to cure those who are near death as a result of magick. She will protect gravestones if they are marked properly with a cross.

Mami Wata

Mami Wata is an African water spirit who makes an appearance in the New Orleans pantheon. She is depicted as a mermaid and a snake charmer. Mami Wata provides kind and nurturing guidance, and good fortune in the form of money.

Marrassa

The Marassa are the divine twins. They are children, but are more ancient than other loas. As spirits, they can exhibit the behaviors of children, both positive and negative. They love toys, but will sometimes throw tantrums. They are considered very sacred, and have the ability to heal and clairvoyant powers. According to Milo Rigaud, the Marassa are "Love, truth and justice. Directed by reason. Mysteries of liaison between earth and heaven and they personify astronomic-astrological learning. They synthesize the Voodoo loa as personification of divine power and the human impotence. Double life, they have considerable power which allow them manage people through the stomach. They are children mysteries."[41]

The Marassa are somewhat different from standard loas. While they are twins, there are three of them. While they are male and female, they are both male *and* female—an example of the Haitian worldview's capacity to retain two seemingly contradictory concepts. The Marassa are commonly syncretized with the Catholic twin brothers Saints Cosmas and Damien.

In Vodou, Marassa Jumeaux are the ghosts of deceased twin children. They symbolize of the elemental forces of the universe.

Marie Laveau (Laveaux)

The Voodoo Queen of New Orleans. More than anyone else, Marie Laveau put New Orleans Voodoo on the map with her powerful magic and infamous ceremonies held in what are now Congo Square, Bayou St. John, and Lake Ponchartrain. Oral

---

40   Mambo Racine Sans Bout (1996). *Noninitiates service for Baron*. Retrieved from *www.rootswithoutend.org/emporium/baronserv.html*

41   Rigaud, M. (1992). *Voodoo Diagrams & Rituals*, Trilingual edition.

tradition suggests that the occult part of her magic mixed Roman Catholic beliefs and saints with African spirits and religious concepts. She is believed to have been born in 1794 in a French and Spanish city, where the Catholic Church dominated the lives of its citizens. She is celebrated every year on Saint John's Eve, the foremost Voodoo holiday in New Orleans. Saint John's day corresponds with the summer solstice. This same celebration has taken place for almost three hundred years; many of those years in Congo Square, though today the celebrations are much more discreet.

There are many legends about Marie Laveau that stem from the folklorists and newspaper reports of her day; they are mostly sensationalized accounts of her orgiastic Voodoo parties on Bayou St. John or Lake Ponchartrain. Most of these accounts tend to dismiss any real spiritual powers she possessed, and instead attribute her skills to conning as opposed to cunning. One such example is from Anna Riva's *Modern Herbal Spellbook*. In it, she refers to Marie Laveau in the usual regurgitated manner:

> To conjure business, it is alleged that Marie Laveau made "hoodoo" charms to frighten people into coming to her to counteract a spell which she herself had put on the person secretly. Her gris gris is made of an image of a person sprinkled with saffron, salt and gunpowder and wrapped into a piece of black paper. After planting the charm in the victim's home or place of business, she simply waited for them to discover it to come to her for help since her reputation in these matters was well known all over New Orleans.[42]

First, is there any truth to the assertion that Marie Laveau would cross someone just to get them to come to her for the uncrossing, and thus make money off of them? This is similar to the "lore" that minimizes her legitimacy and authenticity as a practitioner. She is said to have listened to town gossip while working as a hairdresser and used that information to "know" what she knew. She is also said to have paid off poor black household servants to get inside information about their wealthy white slave masters to use to her advantage. Is any of it true?

The writings that report the "lore" of Laveau's conning were written through the eyes of racist white people (anthropologists, folklorists, and newspaper reporters, for example) and hoodoo marketeers. This is the stuff that people focus on, and it has become almost gospel because it has been cited and rewritten so many times. Africans and indigenous people have historically been regarded as inferior intellectually, and as superstitious, savage, and ignorant. Just look at the writings of Puckett, Ellis, Hyatt, and Tallant for examples.

---

42 Riva, A. (1974) *The Modern Herbal Spellbook*. International Imports.

Then consider what they are saying, ignoring the racist and superior overtones: that Laveau gathered information about her demographic, she built business alliances, she marketed her talents, she built her clientele, she was a shameless self promoter (perhaps), and most importantly, she had satisfied customers and got results. She was good at what she did. Not only was she good; she was so good that she is often considered to be the one single person who made a business out of New Orleans Voodoo. All of the things she reportedly engaged in during her time were necessary for success in business. If her activities were written in these terms instead of the way they were portrayed in the literature, her authenticity as a Voodoo Queen would not be questioned and her business acumen would be celebrated.

That is the problem I have with these types of writings. She may have engaged in some magickal manipulations—the folklore certainly supports it. But that doesn't mean she wasn't effective or powerful—in my opinion, she was. Otherwise, she would never have risen to the status of loa in her own right in the New Orleans Voodoo pantheon.

Marie Laveau's mother was Indian, and she believed in Damballah Wedo, and the religion straight from Africa. I often wonder if Laveau's Catholicism wasn't in part another of her brilliant business strategies for getting and keeping clients that found her devotion to Catholic saints palatable.

Marinette

Marinette is a powerful and violent loa of the Petro family. She was the mambo who first summoned the djab Ezili Danto to kickstart the Haitian Revolution. She is very skilled in herbal healing. The owl is one of her symbols, and she is served outside. Offerings are given to her in a special straw woven bag that is hung from a tree far away from the temple. She drinks gasoline as opposed to water or rum, and is served with pine bundles called bwa pin.

Mary Magdalene

Mary Magdalene is revered by sex workers in New Orleans for her sacred sexuality. She is petitioned by women for help with troubles.

Mombu Mombu

This New Orleans loa stammers and causes storms of torrential rain.

Ochosi

Ochosi is known as the hunter, the divine tracker and the master of the woods. He is the patron orisha of justice and assists in court cases and legal disputes. His colors can be black and green (like Ogun), although he has also been associated with yellow, blue, and sometimes lavender.[43] He is depicted wearing a leopard or deerskin tunic. His sacred tools are the bow and arrow, and deer antlers are placed on his altar. The deer, goat, hen, and parrot are sacred to him. Since he is one of the warriors, his feast day falls on the same day as Ogun, on January 17th. Ochosi is syncretized as Saint Norbert.

Papa Guede

Papa Guede is the lord of cemeteries in New Orleans and is considered the counterpart to Baron Samedi. He waits at the crossroads to escort souls into the after-

life. Like all the barons, he has a very crass sense of humor. Papa Guede is considered to be the corpse of the first man who ever died. He appears as a short, dark man with a high hat on his head, a cigar in his mouth, and an apple in his left hand. It is said that he has a divine ability to read minds and to know everything that happens in both worlds. If a child is dying, Papa Guede is prayed to. It is believed that he will not take a life before its time, and that he will protect the little children.[44]

Papa Lebat

One of the things that I find to be brilliant about Voodooists is their incredible resiliency. How they were able to take the oppressive tactics of the Catholic Church and find a way to embrace the "new" God and saints into something that made sense to them is nothing short of a miracle. They were smart enough to learn about the religion and find commonalities, and then cloak their own spiritual beliefs behind the mask of Catholicism. While many times you will read that the saints "became" the loas, this is not the case. When the slaves prayed to Legba through St. Anthony of Padua (in New Orleans), they were not in the least bit confused about who they were praying to. St. Anthony is not Legba, and Legba is not St. Anthony. Of course the Church did not know this, and bought the act of saintly devotion hook, line, and sinker.

43 Rev. Severina (2011). Predictions. Retrieved from *www.neworleansvoodoocrossroads.com/prophecies.html*
44 Guédé. (n.d.). Retrieved from *en.wikipedia.org/wiki/Gu%C3%A9d%C3%A9*

When people are traumatized, they seek to make sense of their experience in any number of ways. Sometimes they cope through self abuse, substance abuse, or even taking on the role of the abuser and hurting others. Other times, they do what Sitting Bull called "redefining the battle." When people are able to find meaning in the worst of experiences, they find the path to healing. A good example of how this was done by the Voodooists of old New Orleans is in the story of Papa Lebat. In the late 1700s and early 1800s, a Catholic priest named Father Jean Baptiste Lebat attempted to eradicate Voodooism in New Orleans. Voodooism was the work of the devil, he believed, and it had to be stopped. Many years of oppression and suffering resulted from his efforts; yet, Voodooists were able to take this evil man and turn him into a Voodoo loa. What Father Lebat did had significant social and spiritual consequences on devotees of Voodoo, so how and why was he elevated to the status of loa? Well, they simply gave him the opposite function in the spiritual realm than he had played in the physical realm. Instead of oppressor and squelcher of spirit, he became the road opener and protector. As Papa Lebat, he serves the same function as Papa Legba. He is invoked before each ceremony, and is asked to clear the way, provide protection, and remove obstacles so that we may serve freely.

Pie

Pie is a loa who is held responsible for making floods. Pie, a grave soldier, lies at the bottom of ponds and rivers.[45]

Shilibo No-Vavou

New Orleans spirit of pure joy. According to Reverend Severina at the Voodoo Crossroads Temple in New Orleans,

> Shilobo is the aspect of the four elements who animate intellectual activity, abundance of ideas, clarity of thought, completion of understanding. I see Shilibo also reflecting the four as one who wishes to be assisted by this Spirit must be well balanced between air, water, fire and earth. Shilibo has been associated for me with both solstice and epiphany. Indeed the understanding and clarity given by Shilibo often comes as "an epiphany."[46]

---

45 Pustanio, A. New Orleans Voodoo Loas. HauntedAmericaTours.com. (n.d.). Retrieved from *www.hauntedamericatours.com/voodoo/voodooloasneworleans/*
46 2011 Predictions. (n.d.). Retrieved from *www.neworleansvoodoocrossroads.com/prophecies.html*

Simbi

Simbi are a family of serpent deities associated with the element water. They are the loas of magic and psychic power, the bearer of souls to all places, and the creative principle. As the water snake loa, Simbi is the master of the rains, river currents, and marshes, and is most closely associated with Moses and the Magi. Simbi oversees the making of charms, and is very helpful with all magical work, including divinations and granting second sight. He has a very gentle nature and usually lives near marshes and ponds. As the master of all magicians, he can bring an incredible amount of power to any ritual or spiritual work. His color is green and his symbol is the water snake. Speckled roosters are sacrificed to him.

Sobo

A New Orleans Voodoo spirit, particularly of thunder and lightning, Sobo is one of the Rada loas. Sobo looks like a handsome soldier. He is believed to forge sacred thunderstones by hurling a thunderbolt to the earth and striking an outcrop of stones, which forces a piece of stone resembling an axe head to the valley floor. The stone must lie there for a year and a day before it can be touched by a houngan. Sobo's sacred animal is the ram.

Sousson Pannan

In New Orleans Voodoo, Sousson Pannan is an evil and very ugly loa whose body is all covered with sores. He is known to drink liquor and blood.[47]

Ti Jean Quinto

Ti Jean Quinto is a rude spirit who lives under bridges. He usually assumes the form of a policeman.[48]

Ti Jean Petro

A New Orleans Voodoo snake deity, the son of Dan Petro.

47 Pustanio, A. New Orleans Voodoo Loas. HauntedAmericaTours.com. (n.d.). Retrieved from *www.hauntedamericatours. com/voodoo/voodooloasneworleans/*
48 Ibid.

CHAPTER THREE

THE SAINTS

There are more than ten thousand Roman Catholic saints. "Veneration" describes a particular popular devotion to the saints. Although the term "worship" is often used, it is intended to mean "to honor or give respect." This is similar to the manner in which the loas are perceived in Voodoo. Divine worship is properly reserved only for the Creator (Bon Dieu) and never to the saints. As intermediaries, they can be asked to intervene on behalf of those still on earth.

When a saint is assigned to a particular cause or profession, they are considered patron saints to those specific causes. Patron saints may be invoked against specific illnesses or disasters. They are not believed to possess their own power, but only that granted by the Creator. The bodies of saints are considered holy and their remains and personal belongings are considered holy relics.

One of the hallmarks of New Orleans Voodoo hoodoo is the incorporation of elements of Catholicism, especially the saints. In the Voodoo tradition, many of the loas are associated with a Catholic saint (sometimes more than one), and in fact, the saints often play a more integral role than the loas in magick. Although religious structures no longer force believers to conceal their faith, this syncretism is still popular. In South America and the Caribbean, representations of santos (saints) are more often representations of orishas/loas than objects of Catholic devotion—although they are often both!

In New Orleans Spiritualist circles, several Native American and folk saints are included in the pantheon. Black Hawk, Sitting Bull, and Running Water are some that make appearances in the Spiritualist churches. Other spirits can include ancestors, Old and New Testament biblical figures, saints, noncanonical saints . . . the list is endless. As with all of the saints, whether they are Catholic or Native American, not every practitioner works with every saint. Everyone is said to have their own spirit guide or guides. On the other hand, some practitioners may not include any saints in their work at all. This is reflective of the unique and individualized nature of New Orleans spiritual and religious traditions.

While the saintly associations are popular, let there be no mistake: Voodooists past and present know exactly who they are praying to. Although the loas and orishas have corresponding saints, they are not one and the same. They serve similar functions, but there are important differences. One of these is that the saints are not considered deities or spirits; however, they are believed to reside with deities in the upper world. Prayers are directed to a particular saint or deity along with an offering in accordance with the need. This is called religious magic and saintly devotion.

For many people, buying a statue of a saint is not a financial option. Thus, a practice developed whereby an image of the saint could be used in place of a statue. In order to prepare the image to be a suitable substitute for a statue, it is fed with guinea peppers or grains of paradise seeds (*Aframomum méléqueta*) by placing the seeds in a small red flannel bag attached to the back of the image. This practice is referred to as "feeding the saint."[49]

Knowing the saints, their associated purposes, and corresponding loas is essential to New Orleans Voodoo and hoodoo. Take your time and become familiar with them. A very good book about the saints and their use in hoodoo that I highly recommend is *The Magical Power of the Saints: Evocation and Candle Rituals* by Ray Malbrough. In the meantime, following is a list of saints who are experts in specific areas of need. It is a partial list at best, but it's enough to get you started. The names of the saints, their corresponding Voodoo loas or orishas, purposes, and feast days are provided for your reference.

---

49 Malbrough, R. (2003). *hoodoo Mysteries*. St. Paul, MN: Llewellyn Publications.

Table 1: Catholic Saints, Folk Saints, Spiritualist Saints, and Angels

Saint/Angels	Loa/Orisha	Purpose	Feast Day
Archangel Chamuel	N/A	Angel of comfort, divine love, a powerful healer. Chamuel heals family dysfunction, grief, and assists with relationships and creativity. Chief of the Order of Powers and one of the Sefiroth, he leads those who protect the world from fearful and lower energies. Said to be one of the two angels who comforted Jesus in the Garden of Gethsemane.	September 29th
Archangel Gabriel, St. Gabriel the Archangel	Papa Loko	Angel of communications workers, postal workers, clergy, artists, prophecy, adoption, and those seeking to conceive a child. Gabriel's name means "God is my strength." He is the angel of resurrection, mercy, and peace and benefactor of "Messengers." Defender of the element of water and the west.	September 29th
Archangel Michael, St. Michael the Archangel	Blanc Dani, Ogun, Damballah Wedo, Lenglesou	Leader of the archangels and Prince of the Seraphim. Patron of grocers, mariners, paratroopers, police, soldiers, law enforcement, and the military. The angel of protection, courage, justice, and strength. Defender of fire and of the south. In hoodoo, he is used to overcome obstacles, defeat enemies, remove evil, and fight sickness. Also associated with divination in Louisiana Voodoo.	September 29, November 8th
Archangel Raphael	N/A	Patron of travelers, sciences, medicine, the blind, happy meetings, nurses, physicians, dominations, and powers. Drives out evil, brings joy, love, and laughter, is custodian of the Tree of Life and of healing powers. Considered the head of the guardian angels and a member of the cherubim. Defender of the element of air and the east. Like Obàtálá, those suffering from addictions can petition Archangel Raphael for assistance.	October 24, September 29th

Saint/Angels	Loa/Orisha	Purpose	Feast Day
Archangel Uriel	N/A	Uriel's name means "God is light," "God's light," or "Fire of God" because he illuminates situations and has the gift of prophecy, especially with regards to natural disasters. Call upon Archangel Uriel to help in these events, or to heal and recover in their aftermath. Angel of nature, spiritual understanding, and students. He can be called upon to help with school and educational pursuits. He is considered the angel of wisdom and ideas, literature, and music. Ruler of magick, devotion, alchemy, sudden changes, ("the winds of change"), astrology, universal cosmic consciousness, divine order, distribution of power and universal flow, emergencies, judgment, enlightenment, and insights.	September 29th
Black Hawk	N/A	Revered in Spiritualist circles and among hoodoo practitioners. He is known as "Father Black Hawk," and is petitioned for justice and to fight your battles for you.	December 17th
Holy Death (Santisima Muerta, La Santa Muerte)	N/A	While not indigenous to New Orleans, this folk saint of Mexico has found her way onto the altars and in the works of some hoodoos as an all-purpose saint. She is especially revered by the downtrodden, outcasts, the poor, and criminals, though her use is certainly not limited to these folks. La Santa Muerte will grant your prayers—but only in exchange for payment, and that payment must be proportional to the size of the miracle requested. The punishment for not meeting one's debt to her is believed by many to be terrible. Hence, she is not a spirit to be toyed with. This saint is NOT recognized by the Catholic Church.	N/A
Holy Guardian Angel	N/A	Personal guardian, guide, and protector. Benzoin is a good incense for the Holy Guardian Angel.	October 2nd
Infant Jesus of Atocha (El Niño de Atoche, Santo Niño)	Legba, Ellegua	Patron of the abandoned (desamparados). Miracle worker, prayed to for healing from illness, freedom from punishment, guilt and sin, those caught in an unfair legal system, miners, immigrants, victims of poor labor, economic conditions, and crime, and the seriously ill.	The first Sunday in May

Saint/Angels	Loa/Orisha	Purpose	Feast Day
Jesús Malverde	N/A	Folk saint of drug traffickers and for those in need of protection from crime. Some say he is a mythical saint with no evidence of a real person upon whom he is based.	May 3rd
Miraculous Mother	N/A	Brings good things in life. Petitioned when a miracle is needed.	November 27th
Our Lady of Charity (Caridad del Cobre)	Oshun	Protection of home, finding love, bringing prosperity. Patroness of Cuba.	August 1st
Our Lady of Guadalupe	N/A	Patron of the Americas, patroness of Mexico, protectress of the unborn. Invoked to overcome fear, for protection from jinxes, for help with financial issues, and to receive special blessings and miracles.	December 12th
Our Lady of Mercy	Obàtálá	Invoked for compassion and mercy, studies, mental clarity.	September 24th
Our Lady of Perpetual Help	N/A	Invoke when in need of assistance, an act of mercy, or an act of uninterrupted piety. Her help will not cease anywhere, any time, or for any reason. Even if a person is in the worst possible situation, Our Lady always will help the one who prays to her.	June 27th
Our Lady of Prompt Succor (see St. Mary)	Erzulie Dantor	Our Lady of Prompt Succor is a religious title given to the Blessed Virgin Mary, the mother of Jesus, by the Roman Catholic Church. It refers to a statue of the Madonna kept in a shrine in New Orleans. She is also known as Notre-Dame de Bon Secours. She is known for protecting, by her intercession, the city of New Orleans during the Great Fire of 1812. She is the principal patroness of the state of Louisiana, the Archdiocese of New Orleans and the city of New Orleans. She is called upon to intervene on New Orleans' behalf when a hurricane has threatened.	Jan 8th, August 21st
Our Lady of Sorrows	Erzulie Freda	Her feast commemorates either five dolours (sorrows), from the imprisonment to the burial of Christ, or seven dolours, extending over the entire life of Mary.	June 19th, Sept 15th

Saint/Angels	Loa/Orisha	Purpose	Feast Day
Queen Esther	N/A	Revered among Spiritualists, spirit guide of Spiritualist Church founder Leafy Anderson, represents empowerment for women.	May 24th
St. Abo the Perfumer of Georgia	N/A	Patron saint of perfumers. Abo's profession in Baghdad was that of a perfumer, and he excelled as maker of fine perfumes and ointments.	Jan 8th
St. Agatha	N/A	Invoked by sufferers of diseases of the breast and considered to be protectress against fire. She is considered a martyr because she was sentenced to have her breasts torn by two slaves with iron shears. Her body was exposed to the flames but to increase the torture, she was not permitted to be burned to death, but taken back to her dungeon to die in agony.	February 5th
St. Agnes	N/A	Patroness of maidenhood and the children of Mary.	January 21st
St. Alex (San Alejo)	N/A	Traditionally, a pink candle is burned for those imprisoned and a purple candle is used against occult enemies. Light his candle on Sunday and pray to him for protection.	July 17th
St. Anne	Anaisa Pye (Dominican Vodou), Gran Manbo Batala (Haitian Vodou)	"St. Anne, St. Anne, I need a man." This little prayer is said by people in search of a male partner. She is considered to be the patroness of mothers and grandmothers.	July 26th
St. Anthony Of Padua	Legba, Ellegua	Patron of sailors, pregnant women, amputees, fishermen, and the poor. He is invoked against shipwrecks and in order to find lost objects, by women to find a husband, to conceive a child, and to ensure safe childbirth. He is also invoked to see that mail and packages are safely delivered. Finder of lost objects, works wonders and is petitioned for luck.	June 13th

Saint/Angels	Loa/Orisha	Purpose	Feast Day
St. Barbara (Santa Barbara)	Changó	Patron of the United States Army and soldiers. Invoked against tempest and lightning, and all explosions of firearms and gunpowder, because, according to the legend, after her father had followed her into the mountains and cut off her head for embracing Christianity, a fearful tempest with thunder and lightning arose, and God caused a fire to descend upon him, in which he was utterly consumed. For love and friendship, to conquer enemies, delivery from sudden death, to strengthen faith and protect from evil, light a red candle dedicated to St. Barbara.	December 4th
St. Benedict	N/A	Patron to many, including agricultural workers, cavers, civil engineers, coppersmiths, dying people, erysipelas, Europe, farmers, fever, gallstones, Heerdt (Germany), inflammatory diseases, Italian architects, kidney disease, monks, nettle rash, Norcia (Italy), people in religious orders, schoolchildren, servants who have broken their master's belongings, speleologists, spelunkers. Petition for protection against poison, witchcraft, sorcery, and temptations.	July 11 (Roman Catholic calendar of saints), March 14 (Byzantine Rite), March 21 (on local calendars and in the General Roman Calendar of 1962)
St. Bernadette	N/A	Visionary and messenger of the Immaculate Conception petitioned for healing.	April 16th
St. Brigit	Manman Brigit	Regarded as the patroness of fallen women, not because she was at any time of her life unchaste, but because Henry VIII.'s palace of Bridewell, (i.e., beside the well of St. Bride or Bridget), was converted into a house of correction for refractory females. She is represented in Christian art with a lamp in one hand, typical of heavenly light and wisdom, and a cross in the other.	October 8th
St. Cecilia	Oshun	Patroness of music and musicians, she invented the organ, and consecrated it to the service of God.	November 22nd

Saint/Angels	Loa/Orisha	Purpose	Feast Day
St. Christopher (San Cristobal)	Gran Bwa	Protection during travel. Invoked to be exempt from the perils of earthquake, tempest, and fire.	July 25th
St. Clare of Assisi, St. Claire (Santa Clara)	Ayizan, Gran Silibo Vavou	Patron saint of sore eyes. Foundress of an order of nuns now called "Poor Clares." Clairvoyance, the ability to see spirits of the dead. Also associated with divination in Louisiana Voodoo.	August 11th
St. Cyprian	N/A	Patron saint of witches, conjurers, root doctors, and spiritual workers, both good and evil. Against demons and witchcraft.	September 26th
St. Dymphna	N/A	Patron saint of the mentally ill, petitioned for mental disorders, demonic possession. St. Dymphna was an abused woman and so she offers hope to women everywhere. Frequently used to overcome drug abuse and depression.	May 15th
St. Elias (San Elias)	Oshosi	Honored for his mysticism, asceticism, prophesy; denouncing rulers for their injustice, their infidelity, and their oppression of the people; his orthodoxy, his miracle-working, his concern for the poor, and his appearance with the Messiah at the Holy Transfiguration (Matt 17:1-8)	July 20th
St. Expedite (San Expedito)	Baron Lacroix	Patron saint of emergencies, shopkeepers, dealers, examinees, schoolboys, sailors, and navigators, and everyone who needs a quick solution for their problems. St. Expedite is invoked in urgent causes and for quick solutions, especially in the settlement of business and legal proceedings, and for overcoming obstacles that are in the way of financial success.	April 19th
St. Francis d'Assisi	Orunmilla or Orulla (Santería)	Patron of animals and the founder of the Franciscan Order of Preaching Friars. Depicted in Christian art with a lamb and a lily, the emblems of meekness and purity, and the stigmata, or five wounds of the crucified Christ.	October 4th
St. George the Martyr	Ogun	For soldiers, animals, and livestock (cattle and herds), the patron of soldiers.	April 23rd

Saint/Angels	Loa/Orisha	Purpose	Feast Day
St. Gerard Mejella	Baron Samedi, Guede	The patron saint of expectant mothers, especially those experiencing difficulties and in need of a miracle. His gift of reading consciences was well known, and he had the faculties of levitation and bi-location associated with certain mystics. Also associated with divination and communicating with the dead in Louisiana Voodoo.	
St Gregory the Wonder-Worker	N/A	For protection against thieves.	November 17th
St. James the Greater	Ogun	Universally regarded as the patron of pilgrims to the Holy Land, because after establishing the Christian religion in Spain, he returned to Judaea on a pilgrimage and was there beheaded. Great military patron of Spain.	July 25th
St. Joan of Arc	Marinette, Al Anima Sola	Patroness of soldiers and of France. Also associated with divination and the ability to hear and understand spirits in Louisiana Voodoo. She was condemned to death as a heretic, sorceress, and adulteress, after being tricked into making some incriminating, yet honest statements. She was burned at the stake on May 30, 1431 at the age of 19.	May 30th
St. John the Baptist	Ogun, Agonme Tonné	Patron of silence and protector against slander, associated with bridges and running water.	June 24th, May 16th, August 29th
St. Joseph with infant Jesus (San Giuseppe)	Papa Loko	Considered the patron saint of families in New Orleans. Can help find a job, sell or rent house. Sympathetic defender of lovelorn men. New Orleanians who suspect their wives of infidelity will often come to St. Joseph for his help. They reason that since his wife had someone else's baby, he will understand their plight and come to their aid.	March 19th
St. Jude (San Judas Tadeo)	N/A	For impossible situations and desperate causes. Burn a dark green candle to ask him for special favors. Usually petitioned as a novena for nine days.	October 28th
St. Lazarus	Babalú-Ayé, Legba	Patron to the poor, beggars, lepers, and the sick. Invoke for healing.	June 21st

Saint/Angels	Loa/Orisha	Purpose	Feast Day
St. Lucy	N/A	The patroness of writers, the blind, and the poor, on account of her boundless charity. She is invoked by persons afflicted with diseases of the eye.	December 13th
St. Luke	N/A	Patron saint of physicians, surgeons, and painters, in accordance with the tradition that he painted a portrait of the Virgin. Beside him is usually an ox, symbolical of sacrifice.	October 18th
St. Margaret	N/A	Patroness of female innocence and virtue, and the special patroness of women in childbirth. Margaret is one of the Fourteen Holy Helpers, and she spoke to St. Joan of Arc.	July 20th
St. Martha	N/A	Considered to be the patroness of drummers in New Orleans and is called upon by women seeking husbands. Also the patroness of good housewives, servants, and cooks. She answers those who petition her quickly.	June 29th
St. Martin de Porres	Guede, Changó	Patron of barbers, beggars, and drunkards. November 11th, or Martinmas Day, was originally the Vinalia, or Feast of Bacchus, among the Romans. When the Christian Church merged Bacchus into St. Martin, those who were employed in the vineyards came to look upon the saint as their patron; while drunkards were recommended to invoke him to save them from their besetting sin. Fights against racial injustice and is associated with Changó. Petition for comfort, health, friends, good life.	November 3rd, 11th
St. Martin Caballero	Ellegua	Patron saint of those who hope strangers will aid them. Invoked for business, drawing customers. Because the horse he rides is associated with the lucky horseshoe, he is also a favorite saint among gamblers.	November 11
St. Mary (Holy Mary, Virgin Mary, Good Mother, Mother of All, Lady Luck)	N/A	Also known as the "lovely lady dressed in blue," she is believed to be in direct contact with Bon Dieu.	August 15

Saint/Angels	Loa/Orisha	Purpose	Feast Day
St. Mary Magdalene	N/A	Patroness of frail and penitent women, because she threw herself at the feet of our Lord, weeping bitterly for her sins. In New Orleans, she is the patroness of prostitutes and can be petitioned by all women for matters of the heart. She is also the patroness of hairdressers and hairstylists, perfumeries, perfumers, and phamacists.	July 22
St. Moses	Simbi	Also associated with divination and magic in Louisiana Voodoo.	November 25
St. Patrick	Damballah Wedo	Patron of Ireland, whose people he converted to Christianity. Known for driving the snakes out of Ireland, is ironically, yet logically, associated with Damballah Wedo, the sacred serpent of New Orleans Voodoo. He no longer chases away the snakes; this belief is now interpreted as chasing away and subduing one's enemies.	March 17th
St Paul	Papa Loko	Patron saint to writers and journalists.	June 29th
St. Peter (without the key)	Legba, Ellegua	Is used to bring success.	June29
St. Peter (with the key)	Legba, Ellegua	Used same as above but for quicker success. Holds the keys to the gates of heaven and with his keys can unlock tricky situations and closed doors. Patron of bakers, bridge builders, butchers, fishermen, harvesters, locksmiths, cobblers, masons. Petitioned for foot problems, fever, longevity.	January 16, Veneration of the Precious Chains of the Holy and All-Glorious Apostle Peter, June 29
St. Philip(Neri)	N/A	Considered the "cheerful saint."	May 26
St. Raymond (St. Maroon)	N/A	Stop gossip and slander, silence enemies, keep the law away.	January 7
St. Rita	N/A	Gives assistance to women who are victims of domestic violence, providing them with incredible strength when they thought they had none. She is the patroness of impossible cases.	May 22

Saint/Angels	Loa/Orisha	Purpose	Feast Day
St. Roche	Sobo, Zobo	St. Roche was chosen as our patron/benefactor, being sought in New Orleans Voodoo for his healing intercessions. He devoted his whole life to the service of those who fell victim to the plague; consequently his intercession is invoked by the pious in times of pestilence. He is also the patron of dogs and those who love them.	August 16th
St. Rose	Grande Erzulie	The saint with the key to open the doors to paradise. She is also the provider for women of a new husband or a better boyfriend.	August 23
St. Teresa of Avila	Oyá	the patroness of Spain, represented in Christian art kneeling in prayer, with an angel a short distance above, piercing her heart with a flametipped arrow, in token of the Divine love with which she was animated. St. Teresa is the patron saint of headache sufferers. Her symbol is a heart, an arrow, and a book.	October 1, October 15
St. Thomas More	N/A	Patron saint of lawyers.	June 22
St. Vitus	N/A	One of the Fourteen Holy Helpers and the patron of epileptics, those afflicted with St. Vitus' Dance (named after him}, dancers, and actors, and is a protector against storms. He is often invoked by persons who are addicted to oversleeping.	June 15th
San Simón (Maximon)	N/A	folk saint venerated in various forms by Mayan people of Western Guatemala. San Simon is referred to as "Champion of the Hopeless" by some folks because of his ability and willingness to work with just about anyone for just about anything. He is able to grant wishes of any kind, if you offer him the right gifts. San Simón is believed to be a Catholicized form of the pre-Columbian Mayan god Mam (meaning Ancient One).	October 28
Sitting Bull	N/A	Indian Spirit known as the "medicine man," petitioned for wisdom and patience.	N/A

Some Important New Orleans Saints and Spirit Guides

Some New Orleans saints are worth expounding on a bit more than others. Among these are Saint Anthony, Saint Expedite, Saint Jude, Saint Joseph, and Our Lady of Prompt Succor.

Saint Anthony

Saint Anthony of Padua lived from 1195 until 1231 AD. His feast day is June 13th, which is the anniversary of his death. He is widely recognized as a miracle worker. Saint Anthony is also invoked when a person is lost. As a result, many people call upon him to help them reconcile with a lost lover. He is also asked for help in finding a mate. Because Saint Anthony finds lost people, his aid can also be requested when praying for someone who is severely struggling, and who seems to be a lost soul. In some countries, Saint Anthony is prayed to by travelers and vacationers for safe journeys, particularly over the seas. Hence, he is the patron saint of sailors and fishermen in Spain, Italy, France, and Portugal. According to some stories, sailors keep a statue of Saint Anthony on the mast of the ship, and appeal to him for safety while at sea.

If you wish something returned to you, turn an image of St. Anthony upside down by a St. Anthony candle. Carry the amulet and pray to St Anthony until your request is granted.

Call his name, visualize your lost item, explain how important it is to you to find it, and sincerely ask for his aid. You will find your missing object, especially if you recite the following prayer:

> Saint Anthony, Saint Anthony, please come down,
> My _____ is lost, and must be found.

In New Orleans, it is said that Marie Laveau always kept a statue of St. Anthony in her front yard. When she was "doing a work," she would turn the statue upside down. The upside-down position of the statue of St. Anthony let visitors know not to disturb her. When she was done with her work, she would turn the statue right side up again and avail herself to visitors.

Saint Expedite

Saint Expedite is the patron saint of those who need fast solutions to problems, who strive to put an end to procrastination and delays, and who seek financial success. His feast day is April 19th. In New Orleans Voodoo, he often represents Baron LaCroix, one of the guede spirits of death.

According to a legend, Saint Expeditus was a Roman centurion in Armenia who was beheaded during the Diocletian Persecution in 303. On the day he decided to become a Christian, the Devil took the form of a crow or a snake and told him to postpone his conversion until the next day. Instead, Expeditus stomped on the animal and killed it, proclaiming, "I'll be a Christian today!" But how did St. Expedite end up in New Orleans? According to *saintexpedite.org,* one story is as follows:

> There is an old tale about the arrival of Saint Expedite in New Orleans. The story goes that in outfitting the Chapel of Our Lady of Guadeloupe, the priests sent off to Spain for a large and beautiful statue of the Virgin, and many months later, by ship, they received TWO crates instead of one. They opened the first and it contained the statue of Mary, which they had commissioned, and then they turned to the unexpected second crate, which only bore the legend EXPEDITE on the outside. This they opened, to find the statue of a Roman centurion. In their simple ignorance, they mistook the shipping instructions, EXPEDITE, meaning, "expedite this shipment" to be the name of a saint.

While this is an interesting story, I doubt that the people of New Orleans made such an ignorant mistake. Perhaps that is my personal bias, but I just don't buy it.

In hoodoo, it is customary to offer St. Expedite pound cake, flowers, and a glass of water. In New Orleans, we typically offer him Sara Lee pound cake. He is believed to grant any request within his power, provided the petitioner recommends his invocation to others. In this tradition, his image in the form of holy cards and medals is used in gambling charms and crossing rituals.

Some important things to remember when working with St. Expedite are:

- Only petition St. Expedite for positive purposes.
- Set up an altar dedicated to him.
- Only ask for one favor at a time.
- Be respectful.
- Don't forget to pay him for his help.
- Don't forget to honor him publicly after he has helped you.
- Don't forget the Sara Lee pound cake!

Saint Expedite's Altar

Saint Expedite's altar should be set up in a triangle pattern. Use red candles, except when asking for money—in that case you should use green candles. You can also use a glass-encased candle with his image on it. Whichever candle you use, place it at the back of the altar; this is the tip of the triangle formation. In the front to the left, place an ordinary glass of water; in the front to the right of the triangle, place the statue or image of Saint Expedite in the form of a picture or holy card.

Petition St. Expedite on Wednesdays, though he can be petitioned any day of the week. Wednesday is the day dedicated to Mercury, the messenger god of the Romans. It is fitting to have a Roman soldier and a Roman deity honored on the same day.

Here is a popular spell that you can use to petition St. Expedite for just about anything you need fast.

Saint Expedite Spell to Get Things Fast

Perform this spell on a Wednesday. Light a red candle that you have annointed with Red Fast Luck Oil (Algiers formula) or St. Expedite Spiritual Oil. I use a cinnamon candle to heat the spell up even more if the case is of the utmost urgency. Set up the altar as indicated in the prior section. Write your petition on a piece of paper and place it under the candle. Then, say the following prayer:

> *Saint Expedite, you lay in rest.*
> *I come to you and ask that this wish be granted.*
> *_____ (Express exactly what you want, and ask him*
>   *to find a way to get it to you.)*
> *Expedite now what I ask of you.*
> *Expedite now what I want of you, this very second.*
> *Don't waste another day.*
> *Grant me what I ask for.*
> *I know your power, I know you because of your work.*
> *I know you can help me.*
> *Do this for me and I will spread your name with love and honor*
> *so that it will be invoked again and again.*
> *Expedite this wish with speed, love, honor, and goodness.*
> *Glory to you, Saint Expedite!*

Recite the prayer once a day until your prayer is answered. Allow the candle to burn down. When your request is granted, place fresh-cut flowers in the glass of water. Thank St. Expedite by offering him a piece of Sara Lee pound cake (In New Orleans we are rather adamant about this, but I have heard reports from others that using any brand of pound cake will do) and be sure to tell someone how he has helped you. If you do not thank him in this manner, it is said that he will take back your request and then some, so be sure to remember this step.

Saint Joseph (San Giuseppe)

St. Joseph is highly venerated in New Orleans. On St. Joseph's Day (March 19th) he is honored with lavish altars, good food, and celebration. He stands beside Black Hawk and Moses in the Spiritualist churches as a patron saint of social justice.

New Orleans was a major port of entry for Sicilian immigrants during the late nineteenth century, and they brought the tradition of St. Joseph altars with them. Between 1850 and 1870, the U.S. Census Bureau estimates that there were more Italians concentrated in New Orleans than in any other U.S. city, which explains why the tradition of St. Joseph is almost exclusive to New Orleans.

Within the Roman Catholic tradition, St. Joseph is the husband of Mary and earthly father of Jesus Christ, and is honored as the patron saint of families, fathers, expectant mothers, travelers, immigrants, house sellers and buyers, craftsmen, engineers, and working people in general. Joseph is also the unofficial patron against doubt and hesitation. Because Joseph died in the arms of Jesus and Mary, he is considered the model of a devout believer who receives grace at the moment of death. Thus, he is considered the patron saint of a happy death.

The Feast of St. Joseph is a citywide occurrence. Both public and private St. Joseph's altars are traditionally built. The altars are usually open to any visitor who wishes to pay homage. The food is distributed to charity after the altar is dismantled.

There are also parades in honor of St. Joseph and the Italian population of New Orleans that are similar to the many marching clubs and truck parades of Mardi Gras and St. Patrick's Day. Some groups of Mardi Gras Indians stage their last procession of the season on the Sunday prior to St. Joseph's Day, otherwise known as "Super Sunday," after which their costumes are taken apart.

Over the years there developed a tradition of St. Joseph having a special power in real estate transactions and home sales. However, the formal tradition of burying St. Joseph in the earth began hundreds of years ago in Europe. When an order of nuns needed more land for a convent, they buried medals of St. Joseph in the ground and prayed to him for help. They were apparently successful, and so, hoping for a little heavenly intercession, thousands of home sellers and real estate agents nationwide perform a ritual where a statue of St. Joseph is buried upside-down on a property to make it sell very fast.

The first St. Joseph altar was built in New Orleans in 1967 by members of the Greater New Orleans Italian Cultural Society (GNOICS). The tradition expanded to his feast day and continued yearly until it became the citywide event it is today. The origin of this practice can be traced back to the Middle Ages, when starvation was rampant and Joseph was petitioned for relief. The altars were an act of gratitude for his intercession. The families of farmers and fisherman built altars in their homes to share their good fortune with others in need. Tradition dictates that no expense should be incurred to build the altar, and no profit should be made from it.

Altars created for St. Joseph are typically large, three-tiered, and elaborate, and have many food items on them. The different food items have special symbolism and meaning to the Church. Because the Feast of St. Joseph occurs during Lent, there is no meat on the altar. Instead there is fish. The fish represent the twelve Apostles, Jesus, and the miracles of the loaves of bread and fish. The fish also serves as a reminder of the Last Supper. In addition to fish, there are fruits, vegetables, salads, wine, cakes, cookies, blessed breads, fava beans, and symbolic pastries. The blessed bread is created in symbolic shapes and is edible, while the symbolic pastries are not. It is said that during terrible storms, a piece of this blessed bread from the altar of St. Joseph can be tossed outside, a prayer recited, and the storm will subside.

Fava beans are considered lucky, and a bowl of these lucky beans is kept on the main altar. Petitioners are given one to take the luck and blessings of St. Joseph with them. Fava beans are kept in the kitchen to ensure a pantry full of food, or in the pocket to ensure a wallet full of money. These are the perfect curio for a lucky mojo or gris gris bag, or can simply be carried alone in a pocket or kept on a home altar.

Another tradition is the hammer and nails. Hammers and nails are given out to those attending the feast, along with instructions for to hammer the nails into the frames of their front doors to receive the blessings of St. Joseph for their homes.

Saint Jude

St. Jude Thaddeus is the patron saint of impossible causes. St. Jude is turned to in times of despair and seemingly hopeless causes, including depression, grieving, unemployment, and sickness. There is a St. Jude shrine located in the Our Lady of Guadalupe Chapel in New Orleans. It is located to the left of the main altar and includes a relic of St. Jude. In the 1930s, parishioners praying to Jude had their prayers answered, which resulted in a tradition of regular novenas to St. Jude (that continue today) and the erection of a shrine to him (which is still maintained today).

Prayers to St. Jude can be in the form of special novenas or be as simple as "St. Jude, pray for us," or "Thank you, St. Jude." He is often prayed to during hurricane season.

Hurricane Prayer

Our Father in Heaven, through the powerful intercession of Our Lady of Prompt Succor and St. Jude, spare us from all harm during this hurricane season, and protect us and our homes from all disasters of nature. Our

Lady of Prompt Succor and Saint Jude hasten to help us. We ask this through Christ Our Lord. Amen.

Queen Esther

Esther is a queen of the Persian Empire in the Hebrew Bible, the queen of Ahasuerus, and heroine of the biblical Book of Esther. In preparation to see the King, Esther went through a purification ritual using oil of myrrh and sweet odours for six months:

> Now when every maid's turn was come to go in to king Ahasuerus, after that she had been twelve months, according to the manner of the women, (for so were the days of their purifications accomplished, to wit, six months with oil of myrrh, and six months with sweet odours, and with other things for the purifying of the women. [Esther 2:12, KJV]

The founder of the Spiritualist church, Leafy Anderson, identified Queen Esther as one of her spirit guides. Queen Esther is a powerful symbol for women, being both female and Jewish. She provides support for women in positions of spiritual power, and shows women the way out of traditions that typically do not permit women to hold such roles. She encourages women to defy the men who will tell them they can't, they shouldn't, and they won't. She stands and opens the door for women with the support of the Creator, who wants his daughters to stand strong and independent and be true to their spiritual calling. There is nothing a woman can't do, so long as they believe in the divine love and support of Queen Esther. Devotees wear pink and burn pink and white candles when petitioning Queen Esther.

Feast Days

Catholic religious holidays became Voodoo holidays for the corresponding loas. For instance, celebrations for the guede, personifications of dead ancestors, take place on All Saints' Day and All Souls' Day. The saints, archangels, and loas are celebrated on various days of the year. Below is a partial list of the annual Feast Days of Voodoo. [50]

New Orleans Moveable Feasts

Movable feasts are holy days whose dates are not fixed to a particular day of the calendar year. According to Christian doctrine, they move in response to the date of Easter, which is itself a moveable holiday.

---

50   Hoffman, G. (n.d.) retrieved from *www.hauntedamericatours.com/Voodoo/Voodoohollidays/*

- Mardi Gras (Fat Tuesday)—Carnival lasts a week, but only the one day is an official holiday
- Good Friday
- Easter
- Voodoo Hurricane Protection ritual held in July
- Two private rituals at the tomb of Marie Laveau, held second weeks in July and November

January

1—Ellegua, Legba—to remove obstacles and open the doors to opportunities

2, 3, 4—Breaking the Cakes (Case Gateaux). A three-day Haitian Vodou holiday when "feeding of the Loa" occurs. A great feast that can take a week to complete and which involves numerous offerings and services

6, 7, 8—Feast days of Jasper, Balthazar, and Melchior (For obtaining gifts and prosperity)

6—Les Rois (King's Day). Simbi Dlo, Simbi Andezo and Simbi Anpaka are celebrated on this day in Northern Haiti

17—Ogun (For work, opportunities, protection from accidents and firearms)

February

2, 9—Oyá, Mistress of the cemetery (For change, readying for battle, protection from bad weather)

25—Ritual feeding of the springs (manger tetes d'l'eau)

March

16—Loko Davi, eating of the ritual wood and of its guard

19— Loko Attisou and Osanyin, as syncretized with St. Joseph; celebrated in New Orleans for healing and nourishment from nature

20—Legba Zaou (Eating consists mainly of a black goat)

25—Oshun, Our Lady of Charity. For love, abundance, charity, passion, creativity

April

19—St. Expedite. For quick solutions, especially in the settlement of business and legal proceedings, and for overcoming obstacles that are in the way of financial success

22—Earth Day. All loas and orishas (For renewing one's vows to make one's life sacred and in harmony with the whole Creation)

27—Danbala Wedo

29—Breaking the jugs (casse canarie), deliverance of the souls from purgatory

31—Feeding the dead (mange-les-morts)

May

12—Feeding of different loas

15—Ochosi, the Divine Hunter. For justice, court cases, re-establishing balance and universal harmony

18—Feeding of Grande Aloumandia

20, 21—Sim'bi blanc

30—Sung masses (chante-messes) in the Roman Catholic Church

June

23—St. John's Eve, rituals for Marie Laveau

24— St. John the Baptist, also called St. John's Eve, Legba, St. John's Eve, John the Conqueror, holiday coincides with summer solstice, celebrated in New Orleans every year by Mambo Sallie Ann Glassman at St. John's Bayou. To celebrate the summer, the warmth, fire, and nourishment from the sun. For opportunities, good luck and to re-align with cosmic forces

28—M'sieu Guimeh Sauveur, Mystere Grande Delai. Common table served for Maetresse Erzulie, Maetress Tenaise, and Maetresse Mam'bo

July

25—Papa Ogou or St. James the Greater (Sheep and goats are offered)

26—Common table for Grande Saint Anne, also known as Mystere Grande Delai and Grande Aloumandia

29—Ogun, Maetresse Silverine, and Maetresse Lorvana. Offer flowers in lieu of food

August

2—Black Madonna, Virgin of the Angels. For solace, protection, fertility, to give up one's sorrows, and for protection of mothers and children

25—Communion table for Dambalah Wedo, also known as St. Louis, the King of France

29—L'Orient, one of the most important mysteres

30, 31—Agwé. For intuition and wisdom, offerings of goats and peppers are made.

September

7—Yemayá. For appeasement of sorrows, abundance, love and fertility, protection of the home

8—Oshun, Our Lady of Charity. For love, abundance, charity, passion, creativity, and the arts (See also March)

24—Obatalá, Our Lady of Mercy. For universal peace and harmony

25—Roi Wangol and Mousondi

29—Manman Aloumandia

30—Maetresse Delai

October

4—Orunmila. For divination, psychic powers, prophetic knowledge

24—Erinle. For healing all

30, 31—Masses sung in the Roman Catholic Church; communion table of forty scarves of different colors, exposed to the peristyle and "served"

31—Halloween. To make hallowed before the rites of the ancestors and to dispel evil forces through disguise and trickery

November

1—Day of the Dead, Baron Samedi, Manman Brigitte, Ghede. Rites to the ancestors according to your own familial or ethnic tradition

2—Fet Gede (Feast of the Dead). Known in the Catholic tradition as All Soul's Day, the day to celebrate the lives of the ancestors.

3—St. Martin de Porres. For healing and for those who have made healing professions their chosen path

25—Eating the yams (manger-yam)

December

4—Changó. For vitality, health, courage, victory in battles, to repel enemies and negative works and evil spells

10—Ganga-Bois

12—Our Lady of Guadalupe. For miracles, abundance, solace in times of trials and troubles, healing, and strengthening one's faith

12, 13, 14—Feeding the sea (Agoueh r oyo)

17—Babalú-Ayé. For healing, particularly skin ailments, for abundance

21 through 25—Winter Solstice, Christmas, Ellegua, El Nino de Atocha, Infant Jesus of Prague. To celebrate the coming return of the sun, to prepare for the winter months and their unseen transformation that will lead to new birth in springtime, to realign with the cosmic forces. Birth of Jesus celebration

25—Bath of Christmas. Leaf rubbing, medical treatments, and baths to bring good luck for the coming year.

31—Yemayá (La Madre de Agua). For protection of mothers and children, for fertility and abundance, to usher a new year of compassion and well-being and wealth in all things.

CHAPTER FOUR

PRAYERS, NOVENAS, AND PSALMS

I n hoodoo and New Orleans Voodoo, some important Catholic prayers are central to many ceremonial and ritual activities. Though there are some differences among practitioners, there are enough commonalities to warrant including some of them here. For example, the Litany of the Saints will often precede the opening of a Voodoo ceremony, as will the Rosary for the Dead, Our Father, Hail Mary, and Apostle's Creed.

In hoodoo, the Bible is considered by many to be the greatest conjure book and most powerful talisman in the world. Moses is honored as the consummate conjurer. He is said to have acquired his power through the names he used for summoning God and performing miracles, like parting the Red Sea. This is one reason why you will often find the Bible used in consecration ritual and psalms used in hoodoo magick.

Prayers

I have listed a few of the important prayers here, along with some other helpful prayers for specific purposes. Some of the prayers, like the Litany of Saints, are too long to list here. See another of Ray Malbrough's books, *Hoodoo Mysteries: Folk Magic, Mysticism, and Rituals* for this and other prayers.

The Apostle's Creed

I believe in God, the Father Almighty,
the Creator of heaven and earth,
and in Jesus Christ, His only Son, our Lord:
Who was conceived of the Holy Spirit,
born of the Virgin Mary,
suffered under Pontius Pilate,
was crucified, died, and was buried.
He descended into hell.
On the third day He arose again from the dead.
He ascended into heaven
and sits at the right hand of God the Father Almighty,
whence He shall come to judge the living and the dead.
I believe in the Holy Spirit, the holy Catholic Church,
the communion of saints,
the forgiveness of sins,
the resurrection of the body,
and life everlasting.
Amen.

Hail Mary

Hail Mary, full of grace
The Lord is with thee
Blessed art thou among women
and blessed is the fruit of thy womb, Jesus.
Holy Mary, Mother of God, pray for our sinners
Now and in the hour of our death,
Amen.

The Lord's Prayer

Our Father, who art in heaven
Hallowed be thy name.
Thy Kingdom come, thy will be done,
on earth as it is in heaven.
Give us this day our daily bread,
and forgive us our trespasses

as we forgive those who trespass against us
And lead us not into temptation
and deliver us from evil,
For thine is the kingdom, the power, and the glory,
Forever and ever.
Amen.

Prayer to Black Hawk

Oh Great Spirit, hear my voice, I believe in your power and your ability to defend me.
In the name of all that is good, I ask for your help with this battle, my battle, with those who intend to harm me.
Oh Powerful Indian Spirit, you are the Great Chief and you know my problems.
Help me with your warrior medicine and guide me to safety with your Divine protection.
Faithful Indian Spirit, I humbly ask for your protection.
With your warrior shield, shield me from the attacks of my enemies.
With your bow and arrow, protect me from the evil thoughts and actions hurled towards me.
With your hatchet, cut the chains and ropes that bind me.
With your feathers, brush away the negative energy surrounding me.
With your eyes, see that no jealousy and envy penetrates me.
With your peace pipe, create harmony where there is discord.
Black Hawk, have my back and be a watchman on the wall.
See that no evil befalls me.
Fight the battle to destroy those who will harm me.
Take revenge on my behalf and destroy the insurrection of the wicked.
Protect me from all evil, danger, slander, and threat.
In peace and protection walk before me.
In strength and wisdom walk beside me.
In honor and courage walk behind me.
In power and resolve fly above me.
In truth and beauty walk below me.
This prayer I ask not just for myself but for all of my relations past and present, and for those yet to come,
Amen.

Prayer to the Seven African Powers

Oh, Seven African Powers, who are so close to our Divine Savior, with great humility I kneel before thee and implore your intercession before the Great Spirit. Hear my petition and grant me peace and prosperity. Please remove all of the obstacles that cause me to stray from the Beauty Way. Oh Olofi, I trust in the words "ask and you shall receive." Let it be so! Amen.

Prayer to St. Gerard Majella

O Great St. Gerard, beloved servant of Jesus Christ, perfect imitator of your meek and humble Savior, and devoted Child of the Mother of God: enkindle within my heart one spark of that heavenly fire of charity which glowed in your heart and made you an angel of love. O glorious St. Gerard, because when falsely accused of crime, you did bear, like your Divine master, without murmur or complaint, the calumnies of wicked men, you have been raised up by God as the Patron and Protector of expectant mothers. Preserve me from danger and from the excessive pains accompanying childbirth, and shield the child which I now carry, that it may see the light of day and receive the lustral waters of baptism through Jesus Christ our Lord. Amen.

Prayer to St. Joseph for Protection

Gracious St. Joseph, protect me and my
family from all evil as you did the Holy
Family. Kindly keep us ever united in
the love of Christ, ever fervent in
imitation of the virtue of our Blessed
Lady, your sinless spouse, and faithful in devotion to you.
Amen.

Unfailing Petition to St. Joseph

Holy St. Joseph, Spouse of Mary,
be mindful of me, pray for me, watch over me.
Guardian of the paradise of the new Adam,
provide for my temporal wants.

Faithful guardian of the most precious of all treasures,
I beseech thee to bring this matter to a happy end,
if it be for the glory of God,
and the good of my soul.
Amen.

A Prayer to St. Michael

St. Michael, Archangel, defend us in battle.
St. Michael, Archangel, defend us in battle.
Be our protection against the wickedness
Be our protection against the wickedness
and snares of the Devil.
and snares of the Devil.
May God rebuke him, we humbly pray;
May God rebuke him, we humbly pray;
And do thou, O Prince of the Heavenly Host,
And do thou, O Prince of the Heavenly Host,
by the power of God, thrust into hell Satan and all the other evil spirits
who prowl about the world
by the power of God, thrust into hell Satan and all the other evil spirits
who prowl about the world
seeking the ruin of souls.
Amen.

—Pope Leo XIII

Novenas for Special Intents

The novenas are special prayers that are said in conjunction with seven day candles, which are encased in glass and designed to burn for seven consecutive days. When using one of these candles, you should pray to the saint of your intent while kneeling before the novena candle. You can usually find the prayer(s) printed on the candle's glass container. It is best to say the novena prayer(s) at the same time each day.

When praying your novena, make the sign of the cross and say, "In the name of the Father, the Son, and the Holy Spirit. Amen," before and after your novena prayer(s). Make your petition following your prayer. When your petition is granted, be sure to keep any vow that you made.

St. Barbara

Oh, St. Barbara, as your last words to Christ Jesus, before the sword severed your head from your body, were that all those who invoked His Holy Name in memory of you, may find their sins forgotten on the Day of Judgment. Help me in my tribulations, console me in my afflictions, and intercede for me and for my family in our needs. Amen.

St. Benedict

Say once a day for nine days, especially beginning on March 12th and ending on March 20th, the eve of the Feast of St. Benedict:

O glorious St. Benedict, sublime model of all virtues, pure vessel of God's grace! Behold me, humbly kneeling at thy feet. I implore thy loving heart to pray for me before the throne of God. To thee I have recourse in all the dangers which daily surround me. Shield me against my enemies, inspire me to imitate thee in all things. May thy blessing be with me always, so that I may shun whatever God forbids and avoid the occasions of sin.

Graciously obtain for me from God those favors and graces of which I stand so much in need, in the trials, miseries, and afflictions of life. Thy heart was always so full of love, compassion, and mercy toward those who were afflicted or troubled in any way. Thou didst never dismiss without consolation and assisted anyone who had recourse to thee. I therefore invoke thy powerful intercession, in the confident hope that thou wilt hear my prayers and obtain for me the special grace and favor I so earnestly implore (mention your intentions here), if it be for the greater glory of God and the welfare of my soul.

Help me, O great St. Benedict, to live and die as a faithful child of God, to be ever submissive to His holy will, and to attain the eternal happiness of heaven. Amen.

St. Expedite

Oh, Glorious Martyr and Protector, St. Expedite! We humbly ask to have fortune and prosperity for our country, that the sick get well, the guilty get pardoned, the just be preserved, and those who abandon this valley of tears rest in the Light of the Lord and the souls of the dearly departed, rest in peace. (Mention your request). Amen.

St. Jude

Most Holy Apostle, St. Jude, Faithful Servant and Friend of Jesus, pray for me who am so despaired in this hour of great need. Bring visible and speedy help for I promise you, O Blessed St. Jude, to be ever mindful of this great favor. I will never cease to honor you as my most special, most powerful patron. Amen.

St. Lazarus

Oh Blessed Saint Lazarus, Patron of the Poor, I believe in you and call on your most holy spirit to grant me my favor. In The Name Of the Father, the Son, and the Holy Spirit. I trust in your infinite goodness to intercede for me through Jesus Christ, Our Lord to grant me this petition (mention petition). Amen.

Miraculous Mother

Oh, Miraculous Mother! With inspired confidence I call upon thee to extend thy merciful, loving kindness so that thy powers of perpetual help will protect me and assist me in my needs and difficulties. Please grant me my desire. Amen (make your petition).

St. Michael

Oh Glorious Archangel St. Michael, watch over me during all my life. Defend me against the assaults of the demon. Assist me, especially at the hour of my death. Obtain for me a favorable judgment and help me in all my needs. Amen.

Our Lady of Perpetual Help

O Mother of Perpetual Help, grant that I may ever invoke thy most powerful name. O purest Mary, O sweetest Mary, let thy name henceforth be ever on my lips. Delay not, O Blessed Lady, to help me whenever I call on thee. For in all my needs, in all my temptations, I shall never cease to call on thee, ever repeating thy sacred name, Mary, Mary. I will not be content with merely pronouncing thy name, but let my love for thee prompt me ever to hail thee, Mother Of Perpetual Help. Amen.

Seven African Powers

Oh, Seven African Powers, who so close to Our Divine Savior, with great humility I kneel before you and implore your intercession before the Almighty. Hear my petition that I may glory in your powers to protect me, to help me and provide for my needs. Amen.

The Psalms

A European magickal tradition adopted into hoodoo was the use of the biblical psalms as spells or conjurations. This was in part due to the publication of a text called *Secrets of the Psalms: A Fragment of the Practical Kabala* by Godfrey Selig (1982). Selig's book described the Kabbalistic philosophy that the psalms (especially those attributed to King David) contain hidden "seed syllables" that will produce magickal effects if pronounced aloud.

> **"For every man, on every occasion, can find in the psalms that which fits his needs, which he feels to be appropriate as if they had been set there just for his sake . . . "—Martin Luther**

The Book of Psalms consists of 150 psalms, each of which constitutes a religious song; one or two are atypically long and may constitute a set of related chants. When the Bible was divided into chapters, each psalm was assigned its own chapter.

The use of psalms in hoodoo magick is much like the conjurations of the Solomonic tradition. The magickal effect produced by the scripture is directly related to the subject matter of the passage. For instance, if one wants to bring fortune to his home, one might recite Psalm 61, which says:

Thou hast been a shelter for me, and a strong tower from the enemy. I will abide in Thy tabernacle forever, I will trust in the covert of Thy wings.

If one has need to travel by night, one might invoke protection via Psalm 121, which says:

I will look up mine eyes unto the hills, from whence cometh my help.

For headaches or backaches, one can recite Psalm 3 (traditionally used in exorcism), which contains the line:

Thou, o Lord, art a shield for me; my glory, and the lifter of my head.

In this manner, the psalms have numerous uses—they can help with release from prison, business success, safe childbirth, success in court, defeat of enemies, general protection from evil, and more.

In the previous version of the *Voodoo Hoodoo Spellbook,* I indicated that you can't be a true conjurer if you don't incorporate psalms in your work. This statement is misleading, though I did not intend for it to be when I first wrote those words. I realize that there are people who want to practice hoodoo but who are not Christian, because I received many letters about this issue following the release of the first edition. I am not a Christian myself, so I understand these concerns and should have discussed the issue further. Since I did not address it then, I will now.

The psalms are obviously a later addition to the original religion. The incorporation of the psalms and other Christian elements reflects the fact that not only were the Africans (as well as Native Americans) colonized, but the religion was as well. I am not one to judge a person's religious preferences, and I will not impose my beliefs on you. What I will say is that the psalms can be used as conjurations in and of themselves, and you do not have to be a Christian to employ them in your work. The ultimate Bon Dieu of your understanding can be the one who is referenced in the psalms, and you can use the words according to your understanding. Or, you can just skip this part and not incorporate the psalms in your work at all. The choice is yours. Christianity was not a part of African Voodoo or any of the indigenous religions on first contact. That said, the influence of Catholicism in New Orleans Voodoo in particular cannot be ignored. Thus, I have provided a list of some of the psalms commonly used in Southern-style conjure and their purposes below for those of you who would like to incorporate them in your work. The list is compiled from a combination of Selig's *Secrets of the Psalms* and the *Book of Psalms.* Hey, maybe those years being forced to go to catechism did pay off.

Table 2: Psalms

Purpose	Psalm	Purpose	Psalm
Accidents, to avoid	64	Court cases, for favorable outcome in	5
Actions of grace	18, 32, 56, 95,116	Blasphemy, against	14, 23, 113
Adversity, to cope with	33, 101	Blessed oil	103
Afflictions, to heal from	56	Blessings, to receive holy	62
Air travel, for protection with	138	Blood, diseases of	6, 123
Alliances, to gain	107	Body odor, to remove . . . as a result of illness	84
Ambitions, achieve	100	Bones, diseases of	6, 21, 33, 101
Anemia, for	21, 37, 72	Broken limbs	37
Anger, for	4, 36, 37	Cancer	37
Animals, protection of	35, 134	Cattle	49, 113
Attacks, to prevent . . . from robbers	18	Character, good	20, 21
Back ache, for relief from	3	Charity	11, 14, 32
Bad dreams, for	90	Chastity, purity of life	11, 23
Bad language, evil talk	5, 63, 90, 119	Chest, diseases of	21, 72
Beasts, domestic	103, 106	Child	36, 101, 112, 126
Beasts, savage	57, 90, 123	Child, retarded	15
Beasts, to be safe from	90	Child, sick	8
Beloved, to make yourself . . . by others	47	Children, protection of	35, 70, 113, 114, 126, 147
Binding, for opponents in court cases	20, 93	Children, to keep alive	33
Black magick and sorcerers, against	140	Choice in life	24, 142
Blessings, for home	23, 62	Clouds (against)	103
Business, for success	8, 63	Cold	147
Business, to overcome trouble and loss frompartners	63	Community, for the welfare of . . . and congregation	85
Boys, where medicine fails to make healthy	9	Crossed conditions, protection from	7
Cocks	21, 31	Danger, at sea or storm	3

Purpose	Psalm	Purpose	Psalm
Danger and suffering, to become free from	20	Fear and persecution, to overcome and stop	11
Danger, from fire and water	76	Fever, to overcome . . . in a family member	49, 50
Death, to protect from violent, sudden, and unnatural	13	Floods, to escape danger of	24, 25
Demons, to exorcise	29 (verse 1)	Fortunate, to be . . . in any of your undertakings	5, 7
Depression, to overcome	15	Friend, to reconcile differences with	85
Disease, to heal from . . . of the eye	6	Gossip and slander, to stop	14, 31, 120
Disease, to heal from incurable	91	Grace, love, and mercy, to receive	32
Dog, to protect from harm when a vicious . . . attacks	58	Hatred, to remove growing . . . between man and wife	140
Dreams, to receive guidance from	23	Headache, for relief from	2, 3
Dreams, to receive information in	23, 42	Health, for good	81
Drunkenness, to keep safe from	37	Hex, to break	7 (verses 1-10), 91
Economic relief, for	127	Home, to make your . . . lucky	61
Enemies, protection from	44, 64	Hospitality, to receive . . . in a strange city	27
Enemies, to change into friends	16	Illness, to keep a family member or friend from wasting away from	89
Enemies, if . . . have made you lose money and caused you to be mistrusted	41, 43	Imprisonment, for severe . . . and fever caused by evil influence	67, 68
Enemies, to conquer and make suffer	69, 70	Influential people, to be received favorably by	34
Enemies, to get rid of troublesome	35, 102	Jinxes, to stop	91, 120
Evil spirits, to drive away	10, 19	Judge, to sway	7
Evil spirit, to cast out	29	Justice, for . . . to triumph	94
Evil spirits, to free yourself from	40	Law, is the . . . is taking measure to punish you	38, 39
Evil spirit, when possessed by	66	Lawsuits, to win	23, 35, 120
Evil, to stay safe from	17, 30, 140		
Evil, to make yourself safe from being possessed with	59		

Purpose	Psalm
Libel, against all	36
Love, to attract	67, 111 (verse 4)
Luck, for . . . in all one's affairs	4, 65
Mental illness, against	15
Misfortune, to keep away all	22
Mistrust, become free from	14
Money, to attract	119 (verses 17-24), 85:12, 84:11
Money, to get quick	81
Natural disasters, to stop	119
Neighbor, to get rid of troublesome or meddling	74, 101, 109
Newborns, to prevent sickness	136
Oppression, escape from	129
Passion, to free yourself from the influence of	56
Peace, to make . . . between man and wife	45, 46
Persecution, to stop	11, 12
Poverty, to be free from . . . forever	72
Pregnancy, to prevent premature birth	1
Prison, for early release from	26
Prison, to receive power of release from	71
Prosperity, at home and work	126, 118:25, 35:27
Rebellions, to stop	119
Reconciliation, with your enemy	28

Purpose	Psalm
Redemption	130
Revenge, against open and secret enemies	53 - 55
Robber, to find out name of	16
Safety, from all evil	17
School, to pass exams	111
Sensuousness, to free yourself from the slavery of	69, 70
Sickness, recovery from	30 (Verses 11-12)
Sin, to receive grace after committing a heavy	51
Sin, to be forgiven from	74
Slander, to become free from	4, 14, 31, 37, 39, 51, 52, 56, 62, 71, 108, 118, 120, 139, 140
Soldiers, to keep safe from injury	60
Sorrow, to turn into joy	16
Storm, for protection from	29 (verses 3-4)
Success, for general good fortune	57, 74
For employment	92
For money	28, 119
Terror, to strike . . . in your enemies	48
Traveling, for those . . . at sea to make safe from accident	64
Uncrossing	7 (verses 1-10), 91, 120
Worldly goods, to acquire	132 (verse 12-18)

CHAPTER FIVE

PREPARE TO MESMERIZE: TOOLS, MATERIA MEDICA, AND CURIOS

It would be impossible for anyone to find out all the things are being used in conjure in America. Anything may be conjure nothing may be conjure, according to the doctor, the time and use of the article.

—*Zora Neale Hurston*

Now that you have a basic understanding of the color symbolism, the role of the saints and psalms, and the deities of Voodoo and hoodoo, you can see the kinds of tools and supplies you will need to perform rituals and rootwork. You will need to have a supply of certain incenses, oils, stones, and curios on hand to grab as the need arises.

Following is a list of some basic tools needed for spellcasting and rootwork.

Tools and Supplies

1. Baskets for harvesting.

2. Bottles and jars. I encourage recycling bottles and jars of all kinds—perfumes, pickles, baby food, etc.

3. Cauldron. A cast iron pot or Dutch oven will suffice.

4. Charcoal blocks. This is the best way to burn loose incense, but avoid those that contain saltpeter, as it is toxic. Pure bamboo charcoals from Japan are preferable.

5. Chimnea. This is a miniature fireplace. They come in a variety of sizes and are great for rituals and burning incense.

6. Droppers. These are essential for dispensing droplets of essential oils.

7. Funnel for ease of transfer of liquids, oils, and powders.

8. Kettle for heating water.

9. Measuring spoons, preferably stainless steel.

10. Mortar and pestle for hand grinding herbs, resins, tough spices, and roots.

11. Plastic bags for storage.

12. Paper bags for drying herbs and disposing ritual remains.

13. Pruning shears for harvesting plants and herbs.

14. Scissors for cutting twine, string, cord, and material.

15. Straining device, such as stainless steel sieve or cheesecloth.

16. Storage containers for herbs such as brown paper bags and dark glass containers.

17. Twine or hemp cord for tying herbs, gris gris, doll babies, and mojo bags.

18. Red, green, yellow, and black flannel (purple flannel, chamois, and leather are also good to have on hand).

Incenses and Resins

In addition to the aforementioned supplies, it is also good to have a supply of certain incenses, herbs, plants, stones, minerals, and other items on hand. Here is a list of some frequently used incenses and resins in New Orleans Voodoo, Southern-style conjure, and rootwork.

"Your plants are an orchard of pomegranates with choicest fruits, with henna and nard, nard and saffron, calamus and cinnamon, with every kind of incense tree, with myrrh and aloes [aloeswood] and all the finest spices" [Song of Songs 5:13-14].

Table 3: Incense

Incense or Resin	Purpose
Aloeswood	Burned as spiritual incense, just as it was in biblical times. Wards off evil spirits; can also attract, renew, and enhance love relationships. To dispel evil spirits, it can be combined with sandalwood, myrrh, and dragon's blood resin and burned on charcoal to fumigate the area in need of cleansing. It can be used in combination with Black Arts Oil to invoke the aid of evil spirits
Alum	Enhance talismans and amulets, for cleansing, can be added to powdered incenses and floor washes, ancestor worship
Amber	Sweet, woodsy aroma, used for love
Benzoin (Styrax benzoin, Sumatran Styrax)	This resin has sweet scent of vanilla. Drives away evil, brings good luck, blesses the home, is often used with camphor in home cleansings
Camphor	Purifying incense, dream incense
Cedar	Blessing, purification
Copal	Fumigant, holy incense that comes as a resin or in cones and sticks. Used in love spells, blessings; healing from respiratory ailments
Dragon's blood	Resin or powder, used as luck charm, for warding off evil, brings luck in money and love
Frankincense	Fumigant, spiritual incense that comes as a resin or in cones and sticks. May be used for protection, blessing, consecration, intensifying concentration, summoning spirits
Jasmine	Fumigant, spiritual incense that comes as dried flower tops or in cones and sticks. Associated with Yemayá
Lavender	Fumigant, spiritual incense that comes as loose flowers or in cones and sticks. Used to attract the same sex
Myrrh	Fumigant, holy incense that comes as a resin or in cones and sticks. Used for peace, healing, relaxation, restoring health, stimulating sensual love, blessing, anointing, protection, blessing, purification
Patchouli	Fumigant, spiritual incense that comes as loose leaves or in cones and sticks. Used for protection, blessing
Sage	Makes space sacred, burned when invoking Black Hawk
Sandalwood	Fumigant, holy incense that comes as chips, powder, or in cones and sticks. Used as an aphrodisiac. Also used for protection, safety, peace, health, blessing, purification, wish-making, and happy home spells

Herbs, Plants, Roots, and Spices

Along with a variety of incenses and resins, you will need a supply of herbs. Here I have provided a list of some of the commonly used herbs and plants and their magickal properties that you should have on hand for your blends, mojo hands, and gris gris. Note that many can be used for more than one purpose, depending upon the properties of the other herbs and plants they are blended with.

Table 4: Herbs

Herb, Plant, or Root	Purpose
Adam and Eve root	Strengthens love between two people
Allspice berries	Good fortune in games of chance and business; relieves psychological stress, health, general good luck
Alfalfa	General good luck; luck in gambling; business success; financial security, prevents poverty and money troubles
Alkanet root	Good fortune in games of chance, money matters, and business, source of red d
Allspice	General good luck; luck in gambling; health
Aloe Vera	Protection
Angelica root (Holy Ghost root, Archangel root, Dong quai)	Protects children; empowers women
Anise	Protection; general good luck; luck in gambling; increases psychic abilities; protects against evil eye
Asafoetida	Also referred to as Devil's Dung due to its nasty small. Has the dual power to protect and to curse
Barbiron moss	Ingredient in cure-alls
Basil	Love, protection, happiness, peace, money, success, associated with Erzulie Freda and Vishnu
Bay leaves	Protection, health, success; enhances spiritual gifts, increases wisdom, clarity of thought, wards off evil and evil eye, drives away enemies; victory
Birch	Protection
Black mustard seed	Causes disturbance and strife
Black pepper corns	Prevents unwanted visitors, causes pain and sorrow to an enemy, revenge
Cactus	Protection, spines used for jinxing

Herb, Plant, or Root	Purpose
Catnip	Love, makes women attractive to men
Cayenne pepper	Jinxing enemies, driving enemies away, causes confusion in enemy household
Cedar	Protection, cleansing, blessing, health, source of benevolent power
Chamomile	General good luck, luck in gambling, protection, removes money jinxes
Cinnamon	Protection, health, spicing up love, brings good fortune in business and games of chance
Cloves	Love, money, friendship
Clover	Love
Cypress tree roots	Ancestral work, works of protection, defense
Damiana	Draws a new lover, intensifies sexual passion, brings back a straying lover
Dandelion	Grants wishes, increases psychic visions
Devil's shoestring	General good luck, luck in gambling, can also be used to trip up enemies
Dill	Love, protection, breaks love jinx, restores sexual feelings, luck in court cases, wards off illness
Egyptian paradise seed, guinea grains, guinea peppers (Amonium Melegrcta)	Success food for the saints
Eucalyptus	Protection from jinxes, casts off evil, breaks bad habits
Fennel	Protection, keeps the law away, wards off troublesome and meddling people
Five finger grass	Protection, health, gaining favors, gambling luck, traveler's protection, money drawing, uncrossing
Galangal (Little John to Chew, Chewing John)	Used to win court cases and gain favor of the judge, chewed up and spit out on the floor
Garlic	Protection, wards off evil
Ginger	Fiery protection, heats up love, gambling luck
Ginger root	General good luck, luck in gambling, heats up love works, adds the needed fire in sex
Ginseng	Protection
grapevine	Used to entangle an enemy or causes them to lose the use of their arms
Guinea paradise seed (see Egyptian paradise seed)	Success food for the saints

Herb, Plant, or Root	Purpose
Guinea pepper	Used for feeding saints, also for breaking up homes or protecting one from conjure
Holly	General good luck, protection of the home
High John the Conqueror root	Love, protection, health, luck in gambling and games of chance, brings great strength, success, personal power, money
Irish moss	Good fortune in money, business, and gambling
Ivy	Protection
Jasmine	Love
Juniper	Love, protection, blessing, cleansing, healing, berries bring good luck in sexual relations
King of the Woods (Aralia racemosa)	Success, conquering
Lavender	Love, protection, peace, promotes passion, cooperation
Lemon balm	Clears away bad luck in love, draws in new lover, cleansing, health
Licorice root	Commanding, controlling, dominating
Lilac	Protection
Lucky hand root	Protection, general good luck, luck in gambling
Magnolia leaves	Protection, keeps a lover faithful
Mandrake root	Love, protection, made into a doll for love or to conjure wealth
Marigold	Protection
May apple	General good luck, luck in gambling
Mimosa	Protection
Mint	Protection, repels enemies, uncrossing, enhances psychic abilities, wards off unwanted spirits
Mistletoe	Protection from enemies, evil, and love jinxes
Mugwort	Burned and inhaled for psychic abilities and also made into tea to wash amulets and crystals
Mustard seed (white)	For protection against harm, love, restore males sexual energy, general good luck, wards off evil, luck in gambling
Nutmeg	Love, general good luck, luck in gambling
Oak	General good luck, luck in gambling, uncrossing, removes unwanted spirits from home or place of business

Herb, Plant, or Root	Purpose
Orange peel	General good luck, luck in gambling
Onion	Protection
Orris root (Queen Elizabeth root)	Attracts men
Parsley	Protection, love, fertility, death
Patchouli	Protection, draws love and money, uncrossing
Peppergrass	Used as a laxative
Pine	General good luck, luck in gambling
Raspberry	Leaves bring good luck and fidelity
Roses	Love, luck, romance, attraction, protection, pink roses are associated with Erzulie Freda, red and yellow for Erzulie Dantor
Rose Otto	Very expensive, used in love workings. Associated with Oshun
Rosemary	Empowers women, powerful guardian, protection, wards off evil, brings good luck in family matters, brings good dreams
Sage	Protection, cleansing, blessing, wisdom, gives strength to women
Samson Snakeroot (Psoralea pedunculata)	Used to rejuvenate lost manhood, can be used in sweetener spells to soften a person up to you
Sasparilla	Conquering and success
Sassafras root	Used as a folk medicine to treat eye problems
Snakeroot	General good luck, luck in gambling, protection, health, domination, virility, money
Spanish moss	Stuffing Voodoo dolls, jinxing, money drawing
Spearmint	Love
Star Anise	General good luck, luck in gambling, lucky dreams, wards off envy
Ten Fingers	Dominance and control
Thyme	Peace of mind, increases and protects money, stops nightmares
Toadstools	Protection from conjure
Vanilla	Love
World wonder root	Used in treasure hunts. Bury a piece in the four corners of the field, also hide it in the four corners of your house to keep things in your favor
Yarrow	Courage, bravery, divination, protection

Stones and Minerals

In addition to incenses and resins, herbs and roots, you will need to have a selection of stones and minerals on hand. Here is a suggested list of some stones and minerals and their properties to get you started.

Table 5: Stones and Minerals

Stone or Mineral	Purpose	Stone or Mineral	Purpose
Agate	Health (lighter shades), luck, gambling luck (darker shades)	Opal	Love
Amber	Love, luck, gambling luck	Pearl	Protection, good luck, gambling luck, love
Amethyst	Health, spiritual protection	Petrified wood	Protection, health
Apache tears	Protection, facilitates grief, comfort	Pyrite	Gambling luck, money
Aquamarine	Love	Quartz crystal	Protection, blessing, peace, health
Aventurine	Luck, gambling luck	Red coral	Protection, love
Gold	Good luck, gambling luck, money	Rose quartz	Love
Hematite	Health, grounding	Ruby	Protection
Flint	Protection, health	Sapphire	Health
Jade	Protection, health	Sodalite	Health
Jasper	Protection	Sulphur	Kill an enemy, crossing, move someone away, make an enemy your friend
Lapis lazuli	Protection, health, love		
Malachite	Protection, love		
Moonstone	Protection, love	Tiger's eye	Protection
Mother of pearl	Protection	Topaz	Protection, health
Obsidian	Protection	Turquoise	Protection, health

Common Household Items

Necessity is the mother of invention, and nowhere is this truer than in hoodoo. Many ingredients used in magickal works consist of common household items due to their affordability and availability.

Table 6: Common Household Items

Household Item	Purpose
Ace of diamonds	Luck in gambling
Alum	Enhances talismans and amulets, for cleansing, can be added to powdered incenses and floor washes, ancestor worship (Santería influence)
Ammonia	Spiritual cleanser and purifier, also used for protection and uncrossing, can be a replacement for urine
Beer	Common ingredient in all sorts of works, particularly to remove the evil eye or to remove negative energy from your home or place of business when used in floor wash
The Bible	Talisman used for blessing, consecration, and adding power to a work
Bluestones (see laundry bluing)	Traditionally, bluestone was used for gambling luck, drawing good spirits, warding off evil spirits, as well as for protection and success. Due to its toxicity, however, laundry bluing has replaced it as an ingredient in conjure in later years
Brick dust (red)	Protection scrub for home, gambling luck, business money scrub. Believers usually spread the powder on or near the thresholds of their homes to keep evil out
Broom	Protection, cleansing
Camphor	Purifying incense, dream incense
Chalk	Used for drawing sigils, symbols, marking crosses
Epsom salts	Disarm enemies, purification bath and floor wash
Laundry Blueing (see bluestones)	Used for gambling luck, drawing good spirits, warding off evil spirits, as well as for protection and success
Molasses	Used as a sweetener in love works, also as an offering to ancestors, in séances, to treat eye problems
Olive oil	Protection, used as a base for blessing oils
Magnets	Draw luck, attract
Pins	Used in bottle spell conjure, and to write on wax candles
Playing cards	Used in spells, divination
Pound cake	Offering to St. Expedite, used in good luck charms
Rum	Used to feed the mojo, offering to spirits
Saints medals	Various blessings according to saint
Salt	Protection, blessings, cleansing, good luck, uncrossing, purification, uncrossing, changing luck
Saltpeter	Is dissolved in water and sprinkled about to ward off conjure.
Sugar cane syrup	Drawing love, attracting customers and money to business, developing goodwill, manipulation in matters of love
Sugar	Drawing love, attracting customers and money to business, developing goodwill, manipulation in matters of love
Whiskey	Recharging gris gris and mojo bags

Zoological Curios

Below are some animal-dervied items for use in Voodoo and hoodoo practice.

Table 7: Zoological Curios

Zoological Ingredient	Purpose
Alligator (teeth, feet)	Carried as good luck charms and protective amulets
Bat	Substitute bat nuts (devil's pods) as bats are endangered, gambling charm, luck, happiness, to kill
Black cat bone (PLEASE do not sacrifice cats for this purpose. Many hoodoo supply stores that currently sell black cat bones are in reality selling chicken bones painted black)	Good luck, gambling luck
Black cat hair	Gambling luck, break up a couple
Black dog hair	Break up a couple, bring trouble to a couple, drive enemies away
Congo snake (in reality, not a snake at all but a species of salamander found in the South)	Dried and used in enemy works
Crab shells	Powdered and used in reversing spells . . . as the crab walks backwards, so does the work
Dirt dauber nests	The mud and insect parts from the nest of the dirt dauber wasp is powdered and used in gris gris and works to improve business, drive away enemies, break up relationships, do battle, reverse crossed conditions, ensure fidelity, and control people, places, and things
Eel	Cures alcoholism
Jellyfish	Dried and powdered can be used in enemy works
Pigeon manure	Used in jinxes
Snake sheds	Healing and renewal (shedding of skin), works of revenge and righteous retribution
Spiders and spider webs	Confusion, binding, and enemy works

Assorted Nuts, Seeds, and Other Objects

Below are some other commonly used elements to have on hand for rootworking, spells, and mojo bags.

Table 8: Nuts and Seeds

Nuts, Seeds, Other	Purpose
Arrowhead	Protection, love
Black beans	Protection
Black-eyed peas	Good luck
Black salt	Evil purposes, drive away evil, get rid of unwanted guests
Buckeye nut	Enhance male virility, gambling charm, improve business sales, gaining employment
Chain	Protection
Coffin nails	Used in spells of malice, cause illness, break up couples
Copper coins or medals	Health
Coins	Money
Cotton	Associated with Obatalá, used to stuff doll babies
Cotton seeds	Wish granting, good luck
Cowrie shells	Used in divination and jewelry, represents female genitalia and used in love and jinxing spells, typically used as a doll or on a Voodoo doll
Crosses	For luck and spiritual protection
Crucifix	Protection, blessing
Dice (pair)	Good luck, gambling luck
Dollar sign	Good luck, gambling luck
Egyptian Ankh	Good luck, gambling luck
Flowers from a wedding	Love
Four leaf clover	Luck, gambling luck
Glass eye or marble	Health
Gold	Money, prosperity
Goofer dust	Jinxing an enemy in family, job, money, and health, killing powder, evil workings
Graveyard dirt	Protection (blessed with holy water), cause unnatural illness in enemies, gaming luck
Holy water	Blessing, protection

Nuts, Seeds, Other	Purpose
Job's tears	Wishing, gambling luck
Keys	Removing obstacles, opportunities, opening doors, love
Lodestones with fillings	Protection, good luck, gambling luck, attract power, favors, gifts
Magnetic sand	Drawing love and money
Mustard seed	Health
Nails	Protection
Needles	Carving names on candles for spells, used for focusing intent in Voodoo doll magic
Scapular	For protection
Pink candles	Love
Prayers to the Saints	Various
Rain water	Protection
River water	Protection
Silver	Money
Tonka beans	Love, luck
Vinegar	Curse and enemy, drive away enemies, love drawing douche, protection, cause discord among enemies
Wedding ring	Love
Witch hazel	Used in potions

While these lists are not exhaustive, they are characteristic of the ingredients you will encounter in New Orleans Voodoo and Louisiana hoodoo spellwork, and form a good foundation for your understanding of why certain elements are called for in spells and conjuring. You may consecrate any of these items if you will be using them as talismans or amulets by following the instructions in the chapter on talismans.

CHAPTER SIX

CANDLE MAGICK

"All the darkness in the world cannot extinguish the light of a single candle."

—*St. Francis of Assisi*

The practice of using candles, oil lamps, or a flame of some sort to accompany prayer is accepted by most religions. While candles are used in many traditions, the act of burning a candle as a focusing tool in prayer is nothing more than an act of devotion.

Candle magick is a primary activity in New Orleans Voodoo hoodoo. However, the intermingling of Catholic, Spiritualist, and African traditions in New Orleans resulted in an evolving form of candle magic that incorporated the saints, psalms, devotionals, and vigils, along with making gris gris, doing séances, performing rituals, and laying tricks. Eventually, the New Orleans style of candle magick spread to other areas of the South to the degree that it became a standard among practitioners.

Candle Colors

Candles are available in all kinds of colors, types, and shapes. Some of the hoodoo candles are multicolored; some are one color or specialized, such as the green lucky lottery candle. Some of these candles are made for specific orishas and saints. The most common candles are the seven day glass-encased candles, self-standing candles, and figural candles. Thanks to Henri Gamache's 1942 classic book *The Master Book of Candle Burning*, the use of small altar candles and setting lights rose in popularity in the 1940s, and their use by rootworkers has remained popular to this day.

Color Symbolism

One of the basic areas of knowledge necessary for conducting effective Voodoo hoodoo rituals is understanding color symbolism. Practitioners must choose the correct colors when purchasing candles, making mojo bags and oils, creating altars, performing ritual bathing, and otherwise pleasing the loas, orishas, saints, and numerous divine entities. This is necessary for what is referred to as "working the rainbow" in New Orleans Voodoo. For a more in-depth discussion about working the rainbow, I highly recommend Luisah Teish's book, *Jambalaya: The Natural Woman's Book of Personal Charms and Practical Rituals.*

Here is a breakdown of the basic colors used in New Orleans Voodoo hoodoo rituals and rootwork and what they mean.

White. White is associated with subtle energies and is used for devotions in remembering, contacting departed souls, and for blessings, purity, healing, and cleansing.

Red. The color red represents love, passion, romance, affection, energy, lust, fertility, attention, libido, victory, and sexuality. Red candles are used in love spells and charms, fertility spells, sex magic, and seduction.

Purple. Works using the color purple are typically concerned with power, psychic ability, commanding, compelling, controlling, mastery, ambition, prophetic dreams, or bending others to one's will. Purple may also be used for peace, protection, and abundance purposes.

Green. The color green is associated with money spells, wealth and prosperity spells, gambling luck, general good luck, fertility, bountiful gardens, and business success. When you want to influence anything to do with money and prosperity, you will use the color green.

Black. The color black can be used to remove evil or send harm. For example, black is used to repel negativity, for protection, or to banish negative people from your life. Another way of using the color black is in inflicting harm or destruction on another. Binding spells, hexes and jinxes, curses, enemy tricks, coercive magic, and summoning dark spirits will often be associated with the color black. Black can also be used in grieving rituals.

Yellow. The color yellow is associated with mental agility and clarity, communication, fast action, success, happiness, money (gold), court cases, and excelling at school or in an academic setting.

Pink. The color pink is used to draw love, success, friendships, romance, and attraction.

Blue. For health, peace, harmony and abundance. Blue is associated with Marie Laveau and St. Joseph in New Orleans, and also with séances and love spells when harmony and peace in a love relationship are desired.

Brown. The color brown is associated with practical and material blessings, court cases, and neutrality.

Orange. This color is associated with recognition, control, changing plans, and creativity. It is also linked to strong or gentle energies, and can be coercive or subtly suggestive.

Red and black (double action). These colors in conjunction are used to remove a love jinx or obstacles and to open the path for opportunities.

White and black (double action). These colors in conjunction are used to remove negative energies and draw positivity and blessings, and to reverse a curse by sending evil intentions back to the sender.

Green and black (double action). Together these colors are used to remove money jinxes, to eliminate debt, and to draw money, wealth, and abundance. Can also be used to reverse infertility and to bring new growth during a drought.

Types of Candles

The most popular types of candles used in New Orleans are the nine day Catholic novena candles, votive candles (also used in novenas), and the seven day glass-encased hoodoo candles with pictures of saints and angels on the front labels and prayers on the back. Seven day hoodoo candles measure about 8.5 by 2.25 inches in diameter and are designed to burn for seven days. There are also candles shaped in human, devil, cross, and other forms and figures that are used in sympathetic magic. Sympathetic magic is based on the principle of like attracts like, so a candle in a shape that closely represents the desired intent is used. For example, fertility spells have long been associated with penis candles; black cat candles are associated with gambling luck.

Double action and reversing candles are 9-inch jumbo candles that attract and repel. One half of the candle is associated with the usual color correspondence; the other half is black for removing negative conditions or reversing troubles. These candles are popular because you get two bangs for your buck. The black side is usually burned first to get rid of the negative influence, leaving the best to burn last. This is done by *butting* the top of the candle—this simply means cutting off the top of the candle so that it is flat and can stand on its own when turned over. The black side is then carved to a point, which reveals the wick, and is burned first. For example, if you get a green and black double action candle, you can use the black half to get rid of debt and the green half to attract money and economic stability.

Following is a table of some of the common figural candle types and what they are used for.

Table 9: Common Types of Figural Candles

Shape	Purpose
Adam and Eve	Strengthen, passion
Black cat	Gambling luck
Coiled snake	To bind or control
Crucifix altar	For divine assistance
Devil	For commanding lust and sex
Seven-knob	For seven-day workings
Male/Female image	To work in a person or relationship
Man and woman back to back	To break up a couple and cause discord in a relationship
Genitals (penis, vagina)	For faithfulness and purity
Penis	For attracting a new or unknown male lover
Skull	To invoke help of deceased spirits, for death and ruin, or gambling luck
Marriage	To work a marriage or lover pair

Seven day glass-encased candles come in a variety of colors and are imprinted with images representing an intent. There is a large selection of candles bearing the images of the various saints and angels. These are typically used in candle spells, when you are seeking the help of a particular saint. Special prayers for the particular saint are typically printed on the back. Sometimes, a candle bearing the image of a saint that corresponds to a particular Voodoo loa will be used in works invoking the assistance of that loa. For example, a candle of El Niño de Atoche can be found on altars for Papa Legba or Ellegua; a candle of Our Lady of Mercy can be used when working with Obàtálá; and St. Joseph can be used when working with Ogun.

Below is a list of some of the seven day candles that include the color, purpose, best day to burn, and associated astrological sign.

Table 10: Seven-Day Hoodoo Candles

Color	Purpose	Day	Astrological Sign
White	Used for spirit, clarity, guidance, for devotions in remembering, contacting departed souls, and for purity and cleansing	Monday but should also be used before doing any candle work	Aries and Pisces
Blue	Ancestors, spirit guides, calming	Monday and Thursday	Gemini and Libra
Green	Money, prosperity, healing, abundance	Friday	Cancer and Aquarius
Red	Courage, love, anger, victory	Tuesday and Saturday	Taurus and Capricorn
Purple	Royalty, healing	Thursday and Saturday	Not applicable
Pink	Unconditional love of self and others, miracles	Any	Any, Aries
Orange	Success, especially in legal matters, joy	Sunday	Not applicable
Yellow	Communication, energy, laughter	Wednesday and Sunday	Taurus
Brown	Problem solving, animal magick, protection for attack	Any	Cancer and Capricorn
Black	Removal of negativity, protection	Saturday	Virgo and Scorpio
Gold	God force, confidence, wealth	Sunday	Virgo and Sagittarius
Silver	Goddess energy, moon magick	Monday	Cancer and Libra
Seven African Powers/ Rainbow	Works on all things at same time	All	All

How to Fix or Dress a Candle

"As above, so below" . . . this is the phrase to remember when dressing your candles with ritual oils. "As above" refers to the act of anointing the top half of the candle first, while "so below" refers to anointing the bottom half of the candle last. To begin, place a few drops of oil that is consistent with your intent on your palm and coat your fingertips generously. Start at the center of the candle and go upwards, sending your prayers and intention upwards to the universe. If you are using a votive candle, place a couple of drops of oil on your fingertips and rub around the surface of the candle outside of the wick in a clockwise fashion. Take some more oil and coat the bottom half of the candle, starting in the center and rubbing the candle downwards, drawing the answer to you. Image candles are dressed the same way as other candles: from the middle and away from you if you want to get rid of the person; from middle and towards you if you want to draw the person close. For a lover, you can spend some time caressing the candle while whispering sweet nothings as you fix the spell and focus your intentions.

To dress a glass-encased candle, make three small holes with a nail or large needle around the candle wick on top of the candle. Fill the holes with a few drops of oil and spread in a circular motion around the top of the candle. Then sprinkle with the appropriate sachet powder or herbs. Be careful not to make the holes too close to the wick or the candle may not burn well.

How to Dispose of Candle Wax Remains

To dispose of candle and other ritual remains, put leftover wax, ashes, etc. in a plain paper bag and leave at a crossroads. I keep a pack of those small brown paper bags around for this reason, as they are the perfect size for candle wax and spell remains. Remains can also be thrown into a running stream or river, or even a creek if it is moving. Burial is another way to dispose of ritual remains. Where to bury the remains will depend on the work, but a simple rule of thumb is keep it close to you if it is something you want drawn to you, and as far away as possible if it's something you want taken away.

Simple Candle Spells

Candle magick was the first thing I learned as a young child of about five or six on the Mississippi bayous, where we would go every weekend to visit my mother's side of the family. My auntie first taught me the ins and outs of conducting séances and communicating with the spirits using candles and nothing more. I had no idea at the time that my auntie was a Spiritualist—it was just something we did. It wasn't until much later that I realized people called what we were doing Spiritualism, hoodoo, and rootwork.

The basic practice of candle magick in hoodoo is fairly simple. First, a candle is chosen of a color that matches the specific need. Then, it is then anointed with appropriate dressing oil (Money Drawing Oil, Fast Luck Oil, etc). It can be rolled in special herbs or sachet powders to enhance the desired effect. The final step is lighting the candle while reciting the appropriate psalm or statement of intent. Always pinch out a flame or use a candle snuffer—never blow it out.

Burning candles while reciting specific psalms is a form of very simple, yet effective candle magick. Before beginning, be sure to be in a quiet place where you will not be disturbed. Focus your mind on your intent, and speak the words from your heart. Wash your candle with blessed salt and holy water, and allow it to dry before lighting. To enhance the spell even further, you can anoint your candle with an appropriate conjure oil, such as any of the ones listed in chapter 7.

Following are a few examples of simple candle spells. Some require only an anointed candle and the recitation of a psalm. You will need the 4-inch self-standing altar candles, figural candles, or seven day candles for these works.

For an in-depth information on working with candles, see Henri Gamache's *The Master Book of Candle Burning.* For working the candles with the saints and psalms, read *The Magical Power of the Saints: Evocation and Candle Rituals* by Ray Malbrough.

White Candle Spell for Clarity

To fix a clarity candle, use a 4-inch, free-standing white altar candle and anoint with Clarity Oil. Roll in powdered abre camino herbs, and say Psalm 134 seven times. Then pray for what you need. A yellow candle can also be used for this work.

Seven-Knob Wishing Candle

Using a white seven-knob candle, inscribe one wish per knob with a brand new nail. You can write the same wish on each knob if it is something you really want to focus a lot of energy on, or you can write seven different wishes to stretch the spell. Dress the candle with Aunt Annie's Wishbone Oil. Every night for seven nights, burn through one of the knobs. Pinch out the flame once the knob is gone.

Seven-Knob Jinxing Candle

Using a black seven-knob candle, scratch seven words, one per knob, that describe what you want to happen to your enemy (i.e. fail, sick, unemployed, debt). Write their name with Dragon's Blood Ink on a piece of brown paper, such as a piece torn from a brown paper bag, and set it under the candle. Dress the candle with Destruction Oil. Every night for seven nights, burn through one of the knobs. Pinch out the flame once the knob is gone. Place the ritual remains in a brown paper bag and leave at a crossroads.

Adam and Eve Candle Spell

Burn an Adam and Eve Lover's Candle to strengthen the passion and to bind your love with another. Write your petition with Dove's Blood ink on a piece of parchment paper and place under the candle. Dress the candle with a mixture of Fire of Love Oil and Adam and Eve Oil. Say the following prayer every day for seven days, or until the candle burns all the way down.

May the power of the symbolic love of Adam and Eve make me strong, attractive, and desirable so that I may enjoy your acts of love and kindness and make your joyful powers of love everlasting.

Place the ritual remains in a brown paper bag and leave at a crossroads.

Black Blessed Candle

To remove negative energies and to reverse bad luck into good luck and happiness, dress a black seven day candle with Curse Reversal Oil and read Psalm 9 daily until the candle burns all the way down. Place the ritual remains in a brown paper bag and leave at a crossroads.

Man and Woman Back to Back Break Up Candle Spell

To separate two people who are causing you and your family problems, burn a black Break Up candle. This is good for those times when your lover may be having an affair and you want to bring your family back together again. Anoint the candle daily with Break Up Oil and say the following Break Up prayer daily until they are no longer together.

I invoke and offer this prayer in the name of the Holy Spirit of hate: To the Guardian Angel of (his name and her name), inspire in these two people a hate so powerful that they can never remember each other's names without feeling hate. Turn all their joyful memories into painful nightmares. If they ever meet and want to see each other, I invoke the spirit of all roads to separate their pathways. Amen.

Curse Reversal Spell

Set a black and white double action reversal candle on a mirror, white side down (butt the white side and carve the black to a point, revealing the wick). Make a circle of powdered crab shells going counterclockwise around the candle. Recite Psalm 48. It is said that your enemy will be seized with fear, terror, and anxiety and will never attempt to harm you again. Place the ritual remains in a brown paper bag and leave at a crossroads.

Blue Blessed Candle

To create peace and blessings in the home, anoint a blue candle with Peaceful Home Oil and light. Read Psalm 32 and you will receive grace, love, and mercy. Place the ritual remains in a brown paper bag and leave at a crossroads.

Purple Blessed Candle

To dream prophetically, carve the holy name "Jah" on a purple free-standing candle and anoint with Aunt Sally's Dream Oil. Light the candle and recite Psalm 23 seven times. After each recitation, follow with this prayer:

Lord of the World! Notwithstanding thy unutterable mighty power, exaltation, and glory, though wilt still lend a listening ear to the prayer of this humblest creature, and wilt fulfill his desires. Hear ye prayer also, loving Father, and let it be pleasing to thy most holy will to reveal unto me in a dream, whether (state what you want to know) as thou didst often reveal through dreams the fate of our forefathers. Grant me my petition for the sake of thy adorable name, Jah. Amen—Selah!

Perform this spell right before going to sleep, and you should have your answer in your dreams.

Vagina Ritual Candle

If your woman is not showing sexual desire for you, purchase a red vagina candle. Write your woman's name with Dove's Blood ink to which you have added a drop of oil of cinnamon on a pretty piece of floral stationery. Then, write your name directly on top of her name and draw a heart around your names. Dress  the paper with French Love Powder and draw a heart in the powder using the finger or fingers you would normally use to stimulate her vagina. Anoint the candle with one of New Orleans' most exotic love fragrances, Cleopatra Oil, taking care to gently stroke the clitoris area as if you are bringing your woman to orgasm. Set the candle on top of the paper and light the candle. Masturbate while the candle burns, visualizing your woman's desire growing for you and she is begging you for sex. When you come, ejaculate all over the vagina candle. Allow the candle to burn all the way down. Place the ritual remains in a red cloth and tie closed with red thread, yarn, or string. Bury the ritual remains in your front yard (or garden if you have one) along with three pieces of cinnamon candy. On the way home, send your woman some pretty red roses and tell her how much you love her and want her.

White Blessed Candle

For a basic blessing for purity and cleansing, dress a white seven day candle with Abramelin Oil, light, and say Psalm 112 seven times every day for seven days.

CHAPTER SEVEN

CONJURE, SPIRITUAL, AND ANOINTING OILS

New Orleans Voodoo hoodoo not only utilizes roots, herbs, and candles in its spells; it also uses conjure oils, spiritual oils, anointing oils, incenses, floor washes, sprays, waters, and powders. Many spells are candle-oriented for added power. The color of the candle is always in sync with the nature of the spell. By dressing the candles with oils and rolling them in powdered herbs, you are amplifying the power of your candle, making it that much more effective.

This chapter reveals an extensive selection of conjure, spiritual, and anointing oils used in New Orleans Voodoo and hoodoo. Most traditional rootworkers make their own, although modernization of the practice and the Internet has made it easier for folks to purchase what they need. Do whatever you want; there is no law that says you have to make your own oils. The advantage of making your own, however, is that you know exactly what goes into the product, and you can charge it with the desired intent yourself. I carry all of the oils in my own botanica. You can refer to the list of suppliers in the back of the book for more resources.

In addition to the obvious African and Indian influences on New Orleans formulary, many of the recipes commonly found in hoodoo today actually derive from the French perfumers. The first full-time *parfumeur* in New Orleans was August Doussan. Doussan came from France to New Orleans in 1843, when he established the Doussan French Perfumery in the Vieux Carré. Doussan catered to Creole high society with his exotic perfumes. He went into business with a young chemist named J.H. Tindel, who had learned perfumery in Europe. Together, they successfully marketed their secret formula, *Eau de Cologne,* and a variety of other scents—traditional ones brought from Europe and the Orient, and many new fragrances developed from local ingredients. When Doussan retired, the perfume shop passed to Tindel's care. Eventually, he changed the store's name to the Bourbon French Perfume Company.[51] Some of the popular formulas developed in New Orleans by this line of French perfumers include Voodoo Love, Kus Kus and Eau de Cologne. At the time of this writing, the Bourbon French Perfume Company is a thriving business in the heart of New Orleans.

Perfumed oils made their way into New Orleans formulary with the commoditization of hoodoo that occurred in the 1930s. There is a subtext to this influence that has implications of race, class, age, gender, and sexuality that is typically overlooked but deserves exposure. But hey, that's another book . . .

Many traditions of magic work with plant materials, and most assign some symbolic meanings to these ingredients. Many hoodoo and Voodoo spells require certain blends of oils and powders to accomplish a particular work or to enhance a spell. Always use a natural carrier oil to blend your magickal oils, as unblended oils can burn the skin. You should only use a drop or two at a time on the skin. I use grape seed oil and almond oil for blending magickal oils, and olive oil for blending holy oils. Jojoba oil is a good alternative because it won't go rancid, although it is more expensive than the others. Mineral oil is good for negative works and oils using magnets, minerals, and lodestones as ingredients. You should always add tincture or liquid resin of benzoin or vitamin E oil to prevent the oils you create from going rancid. This additional ingredient is not needed if you are using mineral oil or jojoba as the carrier.

Carrier Oils

Essential oils do not go rancid, but carrier oils do—unless they are fixed with a natural preservative. Below you will find a list of carrier oils that can be used to make magickal anointing oils. This is important information when considering how often you will use the particular oil you make.

Grape Seed Oil

Shelf life is approximately three to six months. Solvent extracted grape seed oil has a shelf life of nine months. Keep refrigerated.

Jojoba Oil

Indefinite shelf life.

---

51 *www.neworleansperfume.com/about.htm*

Olive Oil

Shelf life is approximately twelve to eighteen months if stored properly in a cool dark place.

Sweet Almond Oil

Shelf life is approximately three to six months if not refrigerated. If refrigerated, the shelf life can be increased to twelve months.

Sunflower Oil

Sunflower oil doesn't get the attention it deserves. It is one of my favorite oils because it has a light texture, is odorless, and is easily absorbed in the skin, making it ideal for wearable oils. Sunflower oil is naturally rich in vitamins A, D, and E, which gives it a shelf life of about eight months without the addition of an additional preservative. Look for the sunflower oil with a high oleic formula—this will extend its shelf life. Natural preservatives such as additional vitamin E, rosemary extract, or grapefruit extract go well with sunflower oil because they will further slow down the oxidation process, helping the mixture last significantly longer.

Mineral Oil

Simply put, mineral oil is liquid petroleum. It is not used in conjure as it is in the cosmetic industry. It is used for anointing objects, but not people.

Tropical Oils

Some conjure oil formulas call for the use of tropical oils such as coconut, palm, and palm kernel oils. These oils are inexpensive and have a long shelf life.

Making Magickal Oils

As a general rule, you can use the following method for creating magickal anointing oils. In a mortar and pestle, pour two ounces of your base oil (olive, almond, grape seed, etc.) and then add the herbs and other ingredients. Gently crush the ingredients and transfer the mixture to an airtight container. Store in a dark place. After four days, check the oil to see if the fragrance is to the desired strength. If it is, you can either strain the oil with cheesecloth into your final container, or simply leave everything together. Store in a dark place. If you do not have the right aromatic strength, then strain the oil in cheesecloth back into your mortar, add enough of your base oil to bring it back to 2 ounces, and repeat the process of adding your ingredients, crushing them into the oil, and storing away for three days at a time. Repeat this as many times as necessary to achieve the desired strength.

Some herbs and resins are more readily absorbed than others. If you have an essential oil of an herb used in a recipe, you can add some to the recipe to enhance the aroma. Be sure to add a few drops of tincture of benzoin or vitamin E oil to your formulas or they will go rancid (unless you are using jojoba oil as a base).

Precautions

Please note that it is always possible to have an allergic reaction to any oil or oil blend. A skin patch test should be conducted prior to using any essential oil that will have contact with the skin. This is to determine if you may be allergic or have a sensitization reaction to the oil. Other precautions include:

1. Keep all essential oils out of the reach of children and pets.

2. Pregnant women and persons with health problems must consult a doctor before using essential oils.3. Essential oils should never be used undiluted on the skin.

4. Essential oils should not be taken internally.

5. Products made with natural ingredients may still cause allergic reactions in some individuals.

When using oils on skin, be aware of any reactions that seem to be happening, and take first aid measures immediately. Flush the area with a lot of clean water and seek medical attention. Take the same steps (flush with clean water, seek medical help) if you spill undiluted essentials on yourself, or get them in your eyes, nose, mouth, or an open wound.

Working with essential oils requires knowing the properties and safety issues associated with the oils you use. For your convenience, I have compiled a list of essential oils based on information from *The Illustrated Encyclopedia of Essential Oils: The Complete Guide to the Use of Oils in Aromatherapy and Herbalism* by Julia Lawless. I encourage you to purchase the book and study it to gain the in-depth knowledge required to master the art of apothecary.

Hazardous Oils: Bitter Almond, Arnica, Boldo, Broom, Buchu, Calamus, Camphor, Cassia, Chervil, Cinnamon (bark), Costus, Elecampane, Fennel (bitter), Horseradish, Mugwort, Mustard, Oregano, Pennyroyal, Pine (dwarf), Rue, Sage (common), Santolina, Sassafras, Savine, Savory, Tansy, Thuja, Thyme (red), Tonka, Wintergreen, Wormseed, and Wormwood.

Toxicity: Essential oils that should be used in moderation (only in dilution and for a maximum of two weeks at a time) because of toxicity levels are: Ajowan, Anise Star, Basil (exotic), Bay Laurel, Bay (West Indian), Camphor (white), Cassie, Cedarwood (Virginian), Cinnamon (leaf), Clove (bud), Coriander, Eucalyptus, Fennel (sweet), Hops, Hyssop, Juniper, Nutmeg, Parsley, Pepper (black), Sage (Spanish), Tagests, Tarragon, Thyme (white), Tuberose, Turmeric, Valerian.

Dermal/Skin Irritation: Oils that may irritate the skin, especially if used in a high concentration: Ajowan, Allspice, Aniseed, Basil (sweet), Black Pepper, Boreol, Cajeput, Caraway, Cedarwood (Virginian), Cinnamon (leaf), Clove (bud), Corn mint, Eucalyptus, Garlic, Ginger, Lemon, Parsley, Peppermint, Thyme (white), and Turmeric.

Sensitization: Some oils may cause skin irritation only in those people with very sensitive skins or can cause an allergic reaction in some individuals. Always do a patch test before using a new oil to check for individual sensitization. Oils that may cause sensitization include: Basil (French), Bay Laurel, Benzoin, Cade, Canagaa, Cedarwood (Virginian), Chamomile (Roman and German), Citronella, Garlic, Geranium, Ginger, Hops, Jasmine, Lemon, Lemongrass, Lemon Balm (melissa), Litsea Cubeba, Lovage, Mastic, Mint, Orange, Peru Balsam, Pine (Scotch and long-leaf), Styrax, Tea Tree, Thyme (white), Tolu Balsam, Turmeric, Turpentine, Valerian, Vanilla, Verbena, Violet, Yarrow and Ylang Ylang.

Phototoxicity: Some oils are phototoxic, meaning they can cause skin pigmentation if exposed to direct sunlight. Do not use the following oils either neat or in dilution on the skin, if the area will be exposed to the sun: Angelica root, Bergamot (except bergapten-free type), Cumin, Ginger, Lemon (expressed), Lime (expressed), Lovage, Mandarin, Orange, and Verbena.

High Blood Pressure: Avoid the following oils in cases of hypertension: Hyssop, Rosemary, Sage (Spanish and common), and Thyme.

Epilepsy: Fennel (sweet).

Diabetes: Hyssop, Rosemary, Angelica, and Sage (all types).

Homeopathy: Homeopathic treatment is not compatible with the following: Black Pepper, Camphor, Eucalyptus, and Peppermint.

Storage: Essential oils should be stored in dark glass bottles or vials. However, essential oils can be packaged in clear glass bottles or vials if they are stored in a box or dark carrying case. All essential oils should be kept at a moderate to cool temperature and away from children and pets.

Formulas

Making conjure oils and potions is like being a Creole cook: you use a little bit o' dis and a little bit o' dat until you get one tasty gumbo that does the trick (figuratively and literally). Formulas vary from rootworker to rootworker, and while the main ingredients may be the same for a "standard" formula such as Van Van, one person might use more lemongrass while the next may go heavier on the vetivert. Both formulas contain similar ingredients, but the exact formulas are proprietary and are not typically shared. Let your knowledge, intuition, and the sprits be your guide.

For formulas that tend to get a lot of use, like Van Van or Fiery Wall of Protection, you may want to create a mother bottle. This is a large bottle that holds the herbs and oils. You can transfer the oil into smaller dram bottles from the mother oil, and strain the oil through cheesecloth to keep the herbs from entering the smaller bottle, unless you prefer to have herbs in the small bottles. Just remember to top the mother bottle off with more oil as you use it, and use dried herbs instead of freshly picked, green herbs. I leave some of the herbs and roots in each bottle I make, as the old-timers I knew and know don't concern themselves with straining out the herbs. I was taught that a spiritual union occurs between the oils and the herbs; all of the ingredients combine to create one oil that is comprised of the many spirits of the little sisters (plants and herbs). As such, to remove the plant materials would break the spirit of the magick you created and lessen the effectiveness of the oil—or even render it ineffective. This is what I was taught; however, I am aware that other folks like to strain the herbs from their oils for their own reasons.

Following are formulas for making magickal oils. The specific ingredients are listed, but suggested ratios are not provided for all of them. Trust your intuition and knowledge of the magickal properties of each ingredient to guide you to the formula you need. In the meantime, here are some basic guidelines to go by when the precise measurements are not provided for a particular formula.

Anointing Oil

Anointing oils can be made using different concentrations of essential oils. Add 60-75 drops of essential oil or essential oil blend to approximately 1 ounce of carrier oil.

Perfume

Add up to 20 drops of essential oil to ⅓ ounce of carrier oil. There are two types of carrier oils that work well for perfumes: jojoba oil and fractionated coconut oil. These carrier oils have a long shelf life and are nearly odorless.

Spray

Add 30-50 drops of an essential oil or essential oil blend to an 8-ounce spray bottle. Fill the remainder of the bottle with distilled water. Most spray bottles of this size will be plastic; remember the oils will erode the plastic bottle in time.

Bath Oil

Add 5-7 drops of essential oils or essential oil blend to one ounce of carrier oil. Pour a small amount of the blend into a tub of running water. Stir the water and oil together before getting in the tub.

Following are some recipes for a variety of oils and potions for use in your magickal works. Anointing oils may be used for general purpose prayer or other applications, except for the Holy Anointing Oil, which is reserved for consecration and blessing purposes only.

Abramelin Oil

Abramelin Oil, also called Oil of Abramelin, is a ceremonial magical oil blended from aromatic plant materials. Abramelin Oil became popular in the Western esoteric tradition in the twentieth century after its description in a medieval grimoire called *The Book of Abramelin* by Abraham of Worms, a fifteenth-century Jewish Kabbalist. The recipe is adapted from the Jewish Holy Oil of the Tanakh, which is described in the Book of Exodus attributed to Moses.[52]

The original biblical recipe contains olive oil, calamus (sweet flag), cinnamon, and myrrh. Olives are one of the seven "native" fruits with which the land of Israel is blessed.[53] In the Jewish tradition, the olive is a symbol of peace, hope, and steadfastness. The word "calamus" in Hebrew is *qaneh*, which means "a stalk or aromatic reed." Calamus is a sweet-smelling herb that is associated with moral uprightness and humility in the Bible. Magickally speaking, it is often associated with male fertility and virility because of its phallic shape. Cinnamon is exceptionally fragrant and aromatic and is favored for its warming ability.

Biblically speaking, myrrh symbolizes luxury and beauty, equal in weight value to gold. It is associated with love and the death of Christ, embalming and anointing the dead, and was used as a perfume, cosmetic, and medicine.[54] The Hebrew

---

52 *en.wikipedia.org/wiki/Abramelin_oil*
53 Rabbi Jo David (1999-2002) *Gems in Israel*, Yael (Zisling) Adar . Retrieved January 9, 2011 from *www.GemsinIsrael.com*.
54 King & Stager, 2001.

word for myrrh is *mowr*, meaning "distilled," and comes from the root word *marar*, which means "bitterness." Myrrh is extracted by piercing the tree's heartwood and allowing the gum to trickle out and harden into bitter, aromatic red droplets called "tears." Thus, myrrh tears are also associated with the suffering of Christ.[55] Interestingly enough, myrrh essential oil contains a high amount of sesquiterpenes, organic compounds that directly affect the parts of the brain (hypothalamus, pituitary, and amygdale) considered to be the seat of our emotions.

The symbolism of the four spices is a bit different when viewed from a hoodoo perspective. Myrrh's correspondences are similar to its biblical correspondences in that it is associated with love and is considered holy. It is also used to create an atmosphere of peace and serenity and is often mixed with other resins for specific purposes. Olive is used as a carrier oil for many conjure oils because of its pure nature. Cinnamon is used for money, good fortune in business, luck in games of chance, and to "heat up" spell works. Calamus is used for uncrossing and breaking jinxes, as well as dominating and controlling others.

The four ingredients listed by Mathers in his translation of *The Book of the Sacred Magic of Abramelin the Mage* are myrrh, cinnamon, galangal, and olive oil. The word that he translated from the French as "galangal" is actually the word "calamus"—other existing manuscripts list calamus as the ingredient. In hoodoo, galangal root is used in protective work, especially work involving court cases.

Following are several recipes for making Abramelin Oil. One method employs the maceration (crushing and soaking) of herbs, and another employs the blending of essential oils. Which recipe and method you choose is purely a matter of personal preference.

Macerated Abramelin Oil

- 4 parts powdered cinnamon bark
- 2 parts finely ground myrrh resin
- 1 part calamus chopped root, reduced to powder
- 7 parts olive oil

Gently macerate the resins and spices with a mortar and pestle, cover with olive oil, and allow to sit for a month. Then transfer to a bottle. This method produces a fragrant oil suitable for use as an anointing oil on any portion of the body, and will not burn the skin. It may be applied liberally, after the manner of traditional Jewish

---

55 From Rebecca Park *Totilo Spiritual Significance of Myrrh in the Bible.* Retrieved January 9, 2011 from *searchwarp.com/swa478654-Spiritual-Significance-Of-Myrrh-In-The-Bible.htm*

holy oils, such as the one that was poured on Aaron's head until it ran down his beard.[56] Store this oil under the altar.

Mathers' Macerated Abramelin Oil

The following recipe for Abramelin Oil substitutes galangal root for calamus root.

- 4 parts cinnamon bark quills, reduced to powder
- 2 parts myrrh resin tears, finely ground
- 1 part galangal sliced root, reduced to powder
- 7 parts olive oil

Gently macerate the mixture, cover with olive oil, and allow to sit for one month. Then, strain the oil through cheesecloth and bottle for use. The result is a fragranced oil suitable for anointing any portion of the body. It will not burn the skin. Store the oil under the altar.

Abramelin Oil Made with Essential Oils

- Half part cinnamon essential oil
- 1 part myrrh essential oil
- 1 part calamus essential oil
- 1 part cassia essential oil
- 7 parts olive oil

Keep this mixture in a clean container until you need it. This highly fragranced oil may be applied to the skin liberally; it is a close, modern approximation of the oil described by Abramelin to Abraham of Worms. Store this oil on or under the altar.

Crowley's Holy Oil of Aspiration (Oil of Abramelin)

British occultist Aleister Crowley had a different symbolic view of the ingredients that he found in the Mathers translation.[57] According to Crowley:

> This oil is compounded of four substances. The basis of all is the oil of the olive. The olive is, traditionally, the gift of Minerva, the Wisdom of God, the Logos. In this are dissolved three other oils; oil of myrrh, oil of cinnamon, oil of galangal. The Myrrh is attributed to Binah, the Great Mother,

---

56 *en.wikipedia.org/wiki/Abramelin_oil*
57 Crowley, A. (1997). *Magick : Liber ABA, Book Four, Parts I-IV.* York Beach, ME : S. Weiser.

who is both the understanding of the Magician and that sorrow and compassion which results from the contemplation of the Universe. The Cinnamon represents Tiphereth, the Sun—the Son, in whom Glory and Suffering are identical. The Galangal represents both Kether and Malkuth, the First and the Last, the One and the Many, since in this Oil they are One. [. . .] These oils taken together represent therefore the whole Tree of Life. The ten Sephiroth are blended into the perfect gold.[58]

Crowley's recipe is as follows:

- 8 parts cinnamon essential oil
- 4 parts myrrh essential oil
- 2 parts galangal essential oil
- 7 parts olive oil

Crowley's recipe has a much higher concentration of cinnamon than the Mathers version. Since cinnamon can be an irritant in high concentrations, this recipe is not for liberal use on the skin. Rather, it is designed for the consecration of ritual tools.

According to the Ordo Templi Orientis, Crowley's Holy Oil of Aspiration should undergo a special consecration. The ideal time for a consecration ceremony is during the Equinox. It may also be consecrated with the following suggested ceremony:

1. Place the vial of oil on the Altar between the symbols of the four elements.

2. Banish.

3. Purify the oil with water and salt.

4. Sanctify the oil with fire and air.

5. Circumambulate the oil thrice, reciting:

   "O Lion and O Serpent, etc."

6. At your altar, invoke with the first section of the anthem.

7. Raise the vial of oil to the Stele in the east and say:

   Thou that art One, our Lord in the Universe the Sun, our Lord in ourselves whose name is Mystery of Mystery, uttermost being whose radiance enlightening the worlds is also the breath that maketh every

---

58 Crowley, 60.

God even and Death totremble before thee—by the Sign of Light
appear thou glorious upon the throne of the Sun.
Make open the path of creation and of intelligence between us and
our minds. Enlighten our understanding.
Encourage our hearts. Let thy light crystallize itself in this oil, for the
accomplishment of Thy Will, which is mine.
A ka dua
Tuf ur biu
Bi a'a chefu
Dudu nur af an nuteru!

8. Pause in silence. Replace the vial on the altar. Banish.[59]

Absinthe Conjure Oil (Green Fairy Oil)

Absinthe is a potent alcoholic beverage made from select herbs and a large percentage of the purest alcohol. In French, the word *absinthe* means "wormwood." Accounts in ancient texts dating as far as 1500 BC mention wormwood's medicinal as well as religious significance. The original recipe was simply wormwood leaves soaked in wine.

Absinthe was also known as the "Green Fairy" during its heyday in France in the 1800s. The Green Fairy is the English translation of La Fee Verte, the French nickname given to absinthe in the nineteenth century. The nickname stuck, and over a century later, the concoction is still called "absinthe," "Green Fairy," "Green Goddess," and "Madness in a Bottle."

According to some accounts, absinthe was first formulated in the 1790s by Dr. Pierre Ordinaire, a French doctor living in Switzerland. He made it by combining wormwood with other herbs such as hyssop, coriander, anise, and melissa, with 68 percent alcohol. He created the amazing elixir to treat his patients and patented it as a "cure-all," guaranteed to heal what ails you.

The legacy of absinthe as a mystifying, addictive, and mind-altering elixir continues to this day. Absinthe has been incorrectly portrayed in fine art, music, literature, and the media as an unnaturally glowing green liquid that causes over-the-top hallucinations and madness.

In truth, modern-day absinthe is an anise-flavored liquor or spirit that is

---

59 Consecration of the Oil, Prepared for the use of E.G.C. clergy by T. Apiryon (1997) Ordo Templi Orientis Retrieved from *hermetic.com/sabazius/oil.htm*

made by steeping wormwood (wormwood has been defined as the quinine of the poor) and other aromatic herbs (hyssop, lemon balm, and angelica) in alcohol. The drink is distinguished by its dazzling emerald blue-green clarity, due to its chlorophyll content. When mixed with water, the liquor changes to cloudy white. The drinking of absinthe was exported to New Orleans and the French Quarter, where the Old Absinthe House has been a tourist attraction for more than a century. Absinthe appeared in New Orleans liquor advertisements as early as 1837, but its popularity didn't take off until the later half of the nineteenth century with the opening of the barroom that would become the Old Absinthe House in 1874.

The classic French absinthe ritual involves placing a sugar cube on a flat perforated spoon, which rests on the rim of the glass containing a measure or "dose" of absinthe. Iced water is then very slowly dripped onto the sugar cube, which gradually dissolves and drips, along with the water, into the absinthe, causing the green liquor to louche ("loosh") into an opaque opalescent white as the essential oils precipitate out of the alcoholic solution. Usually three to four parts water are added to one part of 68 percent absinthe.[60]

The people of the Czech Republic have a different absinthe-drinking ritual. They set it up similar to the traditional way, with a slotted spoon and sugar cubes, but they soak the sugar directly in the absinthe, then set it on the spoon and put a match to it. The absinthe in the glass and the sugar both ignite, and the sugar melts and drips down into the glass. The remnants of the cube are eventually dropped into the absinthe, and the fire is blown out. The warm absinthe is now ready to drink. This method of absinthe preparation is obviously dangerous, and is not recommended.[61]

Aleister Crowley wrote about the spiritual/metaphysical function of water in the making of absinthe in 1917: "Here, too are marble basins hollowed—and hallowed!—by the drippings of the water which creates by baptism the new spirit of absinthe."

Absinthe conjure oil is used to enhance psychic visions and create unusual spiritual clarity and heightened clarity of mind and vision. This oil will produce vivid dreams and is a powerful aphrodisiac.

Like the absinthe ritual for creating the beverage, conjuring the magickal oil also involves a ritual of baptizing the spirit of absinthe into being. Make sure your herbs are fresh and green, though dried. This is extremely important for the final product. Here is the formula for making absinthe:

---

60 The Virtual Absinthe Museum, (2002-2008). Retrieved, July 27, 2010 from *www.oxygenee.com/absinthe-ritual.html*
61 Earl, J. (2008). *A Brief History of Absinthe.*

Herbs:

- Cardamom
- Lemon balm (Melissa)
- Hyssop
- Common wormwood (*Artemesia absinthium*)
- Petite absinthe (*Artemesia Pontica*)
- Green anise or Spanish anise, powdered
- Whole and powdered fennel
- Calamus, powdered (minor ingredient)
- Fennel, powdered
- Peppermint

Essential Oils:

- Oil of wormwood
- Anise essential oil
- Peppermint essential oil

Additional ingredients:

- Base alcohol (beet alcohol or grape alcohol are traditionally used, but you can substitute everclear)
- Distilled water
- Sugar cube

If you have gathered your own wormwood, you will need to strip the leaves from the stems—you only want to use the leaves. Combine all of the herbs in a mortar. Gently macerate the herbs together until they are well-mixed and the fragrance is strong. Pour a quantity of base alcohol in a copper pot and dilute with distilled water to about 85 percent. Add the herb mix and allow to steep in the alcohol overnight. In the morning, add a little more water and heat over the stove on low heat for about an hour. Keep the pot covered, and periodically stir the mixture and collect the condensation from the lid of the pot. Take off of the stove and allow the liquid to cool. Strain the alcohol out of the herbs and do a second maceration with the artemesia, hyssop, and lemon balm, using about half of the strained liquid. You can either add the herbs in loose, or put them in a tea bag to make the straining process easier later. Warm over the stove until hot, but do not allow the liquid to boil. Remove the mixture from the stove and allow it to cool. This mixture should be a bright emerald green. Strain the liquid again. Filter through cheesecloth into a clear bottle until clear of herbs and sediment. Add the first liquid to the bottle and cover tight. Allow this mixture to sit for a couple of weeks to allow all of the fine sediment to settle to the bottom of the container. When the liquid appears very clear, you are ready to make your smaller bottles of Absinthe Conjure Oils.

For a one-dram bottle of Absinthe Conjure Oil, take about ten full droppers of the Green Fairy liquid and put in the bowl. Add one full of dropper each of the oil of wormwood and the anise essential oil. To this, add about half a dropper full of peppermint. Gently stir the oils and liquid. Now, fill your smaller dram bottle about three-quarters of the way full with the Green Fairy liquid. Place a funnel into the top of the smaller one-dram bottle and put a sugar cube into the funnel, so that the distilled water you will add has to pass through the sugar. This is the actual baptism of the Green Fairy. Using an eye dropper, slowly add the distilled water, drop by drop, on the sugar cube until the bottle is full. The final mixture should be a milky green.

You should have enough extra absinthe elixir to last a long, long time. It will not go bad so long as you store it in a cool dark place, in a dark amber bottle (or other dark-colored glass). Do not refrigerate your absinthe elixir, because some of the chemical constituents can crystallize and may not remix with the other ingredients when it reaches room temperature.

Most folks who make the Green Fairy Oil will simply blend the essential oils in a base of grape seed oil, perhaps with a sprig of wormwood added to the bottle. This is certainly a less complicated method. However, as you can imagine, the effect is not nearly the same on a magickal level. You don't have the intimate relationship with the herbs, the same kind of power of intent from the whole process, and you don't have the baptism of the spirit of absinthe. The technique I have described here really is a fabulous process and you will feel ecstatic when you get it right.

The base absinthe formula is a vintage recipe for the absinthe brew, and so it can technically be consumed as an alcoholic beverage. Please exercise caution when consuming absinthe, as it is an extremely powerful spirit.

Here are a couple of vintage New Orleans recipes for drinking absinthe. While drinking absinthe is not a hoodoo activity, it is decidedly New Orleans, and so I have included them as a little lagniappe for their historical value.

Green Fairy Frappe (lagniappe recipe)

- 1 ounce base Green Fairy formula
- ½ ounce simple syrup
- 7 fresh mint leaves
- 1 ounce soda water

Combine mint leaves and simple syrup in a tall glass. Add crushed ice. Place an absinthe spoon over the top of the glass and place a sugar cube on top of it. Add the absinthe by carefully pouring it through the sugar cube into the glass. When all of the absinthe has been poured into the glass through the sugar cube, cover with a cocktail shaker and shake vigorously. Top off the drink with soda water.

Absinthe Cocktail (lagniappe recipe)

- 1 jigger absinthe
- 1 teaspoon sugar syrup
- 1 dash anisette
- 2 dashes Peychaud's Bitters
- 2 ounces charged water

Fill a highball glass a little more than half full with cracked or crushed ice. Pour in the absinthe, sugar syrup, anisette, and bitters, and then squirt in carbonated or other live water. Jiggle with a bar spoon until the mixture is well frapped. Strain into cocktail glasses that have been iced ahead of time.[62]

Absolute Absinthe Perfume Oil

This mesmerizing and hypnotic oil can be worn by both men and women and its scent will be unique to the body's chemistry. It triggers the release of pheromones.

- Black Chinese tea
- Bergamot
- Galbanum
- Lily of the valley
- Lotus flower
- Jasmine
- Ylang ylang
- Nutmeg
- Ceylon cardamom
- Sandalwood
- Musk

Blend in a base of almond oil that has been fixed with benzoin or vitamin E.

---

62 From *Famous New Orleans Drinks and how to mix'em* by S.C. Arthur, 1937.

Abundance Oil

This highly fragranced conjure oil is used to bring abundance in all things. It can be used to anoint candles for rituals, worn as a supercharged magickal fragrance, or added to your bath water.

- Spruce
- Myrrh
- Patchouli
- Cassia
- Orange
- Clove
- Ginger
- Frankincense

Blend equal parts in a base of almond oil that has been fixed with benzoin or vitamin E.

Adam & Eve Oil

Adam and Eve Oil is designed to intensify the love between two people of either sex. Conversely, you can use it to bring your lover back to you if you have drifted apart or fought.

- Rose geranium
- Musk oil
- Melissa
- Apple blossom
- Pair of lodestones
- Magnetic sand
- Adam and Eve root

Blend equal parts in a base of almond oil that has been fixed with benzoin or vitamin E.

African Ju Ju Oil

African Ju Ju Oil is an exceptionally potent oil that is used to cross enemies and uncross clients. It can also be used in protective works and to anoint candles for rituals, worn as a supercharged magickal fragrance, or added to your bath water.

- Myrrh
- Mimosa
- Jasmine
- Patchouli
- Galangal

Blend equal parts. Suggested use: When using African Ju Ju oil, recite Psalm 23, and pray intently on your need. For best results, use during a waxing moon phase.

All Night Long

A dual action aphrodisiac lover's oil said to eliminate sexual tensions and problems and to reignite passion. It is reported to enhance and lengthen lovemaking and to help improve sexual relationships in marriages that have lost their fire and fun.

- Almond
- Jasmine
- Liquid benzoin

Blend equal parts. Wear as a perfume or anoint red candles in love works.

Altar Oil (See Holy Spirit and Van Van)

Altar Oil is one of the holy trinity of altar formulas used by New Orleans practitioners when working for positive purposes such as healings and blessings (these are: Altar, Holy Spirit, and Van Van). It is used to anoint candles for beginning and ending candle magic spells, and to summon helpful spirits for assistance with the work to be done. Because the ingredients used in the formula are all highly positive energies, this oil should never be used to anoint candles or other ritual objects for left-handed or sinister purposes. Altar oil is designed for blessing oneself or another, ritual objects, or anything that resides on the altar.

- 40 drops frankincense
- 20 drops myrrh
- 10 drops cedar

Blend with 2 ounces of olive oil to which a small amount of vitamin E has been added as a preservative. Add a piece of frankincense and a piece of myrrh gum to each bottle.

Amor Oil

In 1925, French perfumer and couturier Jean Patou (1887–1936) presented the first of his trilogy collection of love perfumes. Each of the perfumes was designed for women with a particular hair color. The perfume assigned to brunettes was called *Amour*. It was followed by *Que Sais-Je?* (What Do I Know?) for blondes, and *Adieu Sagesse* (Farewell Wisdom) for redheads.

A hoodoo version of Patou's Amour oil has become a classic New Orleans love oil, with a spicy hot and sweet fragrance.

- Orange
- Almond
- Cinnamon
- Balm of Gilead
- Apple blossom
- Ambergris
- Piece of coral

Blend equal parts in a base of almond oil that has been fixed with benzoin or vitamin E. Add a piece of coral to each bottle.

Angel/Archangel Oil

This is a beautiful, powerful, and sacred fragrance. It has a multitude of uses, including breaking curses, protecting from evil spirits, and invoking the help of benevolent angels and spirits. This oil is particularly useful in ancestral works for remembering and honoring the dead. Carve the name of the one in need of protection or the name of the angel being invoked in an Angelic Alphabet (see the chapter on gris gris) on a white or blue candle and anoint with Angel Oil.

- Lavender
- Sandalwood
- Holy water
- Spring water
- Angelica root

Blend equal parts with 2 ounces of olive oil to which a small amount of vitamin E has been added as a preservative. Add a piece of angelica root to each bottle.

Anointing Oil

Here is a very basic formula for anointing oil that is perfect for acts of consecration and blessings.

- 35 drops frankincense
- 35 drops myrrh

Blend with one ounce of extra virgin olive oil that has been fixed with benzoin or vitamin E.

Apricot Oil

Apricot oil is believed to be a powerful and effective aphrodisiac within the New Orleans tradition. It is used in works associated with love and the protection of love. Use pure apricot oil to anoint red, pink, or yellow candles. You may add a few drops of rose or jasmine oil for added fragrance if you desire.

Arabian Nights Oil

This classic love and attraction oil is very popular in New Orleans. The formula comes from the ancient Persian mystics (sans the opium and powdered lizard, of course) and is reputed to be an incredibly powerful aphrodisiac.

- Chinese cubebs
- Cinnamon
- Cloves
- Cardamom
- Ginger
- White pepper
- Coriander
- Male frankincense (called zakana, which is deep yellow or reddish in color)
- Honey
- Honeysuckle

Blend equal parts in a base of olive oil that has been fixed with benzoin or vitamin E.

Attraction Oil

Here is a general hoodoo attraction oil for drawing money and love.

- 2 parts allspice oil
- 2 parts white musk oil
- 1 part orange oil
- ½ part sweet pea oil

Blend equal parts in a base of almond oil that has been fixed with benzoin or vitamin E. Add a coriander seed to each bottle.

Attraction Love Oil

Use this oil to attract love, success, passion, or luck, and to amplify any attraction spell. If it is a lover you are attracting, rub a small amount on a piece of wood, such as a door, trim, wall, or chair, while facing your bedroom and calling out your lover's name. If it is something else you want, stand outside of your home and go to the nearest tree in your yard. Place a little oil on your fingertips and rub the oil into the tree in the direction of your home while stating your desire.

- Frankincense
- Sandalwood
- Myrrh
- Cinnamon
- Orris

Add to a base of almond oil that has been fixed with oil of benzoin or vitamin E.

Aunt Anna Wishbone Oil

This is probably the most popular wishing oil in the New Orleans repertoire. Use this oil to anoint photos or images of something you want or need; anoint yourself to help you stay focused on your wish.

- Sandalwood
- Orris
- Allspice
- Musk

Add equal amounts to a base of almond oil that has been fixed with oil of benzoin or vitamin E.

Aunt Sally's Dream Oil

This is another popular New Orleans conjure oil. In New Orleans hoodoo, dreams are believed to be prophetic—a means of learning lucky numbers for gambling and making decisions about the future.

- Anise
- Cinnamon
- Cardamom
- Coriander

Add equal amounts to a base of almond oil that has been fixed with oil of benzoin or vitamin E. Anoint your forehead or a light a blue candle prior to going to sleep. If you have a particular concern, write a petition on parchment paper and place underneath the candle before burning.

Azalea Oil

To make this naturally magnetic attraction oil, pick some small pink wild azalea blossoms from the Southern Gulf Coast and cover them with almond oil. Use the oil immediately if using fresh flowers. To make oil that will last, place the blossoms in a brown paper bag and allow them to dry. This time-tested method was taught to me by my mother; it dries herbs and flowers very quickly and effectively. Then cover the dried blossoms with almond oil. You can also add a drop of magnet oil or other oil with attraction properties to the Azalea Oil to enhance its potency.

Balm of Gilead (populus balsamifera)

According to an old Black spiritual, "There is a balm in Gilead to soothe the sin-sick soul." Cultivated in Judea on Mt. Gilead, this balm was presented as a gift to Solomon.

Balm of Gilead comes from cottonwood poplar trees in the United States. These trees produce a resinous, sticky, and tight bud that is highly aromatic. The dried, unopened buds of the poplar tree have been used in ointments and skin treatments for at least three thousand years. Balm of Gilead has been effectively used in compounds for its antibacterial and anti-inflammatory actions. Balm of Gilead buds are added to ointments, typically in a ratio of 1 part buds to 5 parts cream.[63]

As in the Bible, Balm of Gilead buds are used in hoodoo works for love, protection from the malicious meddling of others, and comfort. If there are problems with sexual relations, Balm of Gilead buds can be placed in pairs in the four corners of the bedroom and under the bed to foster compatibility and resolution.[64]

---

63 Caring for Burns, Cuts, Drowning, and Minor Accidents. (n.d.). Retrieved from *www.ssrsi.org/Onsite/backwoodsdoc2.htm*
64 Yronwode, C. (2002). *Hoodoo Herb and Root Magic: A Materia Magica of African-American Conjure,* Lucky Mojo Curio Company.

Balm of Gilead can also be used as an oil of consecration. Burn the buds to attract spirits, or carry them to attract a new love. Carrying a mojo bag that contains just Balm of Gilead buds that have been anointed with rose oil will produce a sensation of personal allure that others will find irresistible.

Bend-Over Oil (Essence of Bend-Over)

This extremely potent oil makes other people do your bidding. Use it to break any hexes and to order evil spirits to return to their sender. This oil is suitable for anointing candles and Voodoo dolls.

- Calamus root
- Licorice root
- Bergamot leaf or essential oil of bergamot

Blend equal parts together with a few grains of frankincense in almond oil and a bit of vitamin E oil.

Black Arts Oil

Black Arts Oil is designed to give you complete dominance over enemies. It is one of the more potent black magic oils, and can be used in any enemy work. Because of the ingredients, it is usually brownish in color. Add the following to 2 ounces of mineral oil:

- Oil of patchouli
- 1 pinch graveyard dirt from the grave of a criminal
- Oil of black pepper
- 1 pinch black dog hair
- 1 pinch black mustard seeds
- 1 pinch Spanish moss
- 1 pinch mastic
- Powdered sulphur
- Powdered mud dauber nest, insects and all
- 9 whole black peppercorns
- 9 whole red peppercorns

Add all of the above to a base of mineral oil. Be sure not to get any on you, because the smell is atrocious and hard to get off.

Black Candle Tobacco Oil

This is a very famous New Orleans recipe that is used in seemingly impossible legal situations to influence the judge and jury and to take fire away from your opponent's case. Use with a black candle.

- High John
- Low John
- Clove
- Sage
- Rosemary
- Pipe tobacco
- Leather

Mix everything in a base of olive oil. Add a full dropper of vitamin E oil to keep it from going rancid.

Black Hawk Spiritual Oil

A wonderful spiritual oil for use in battling enemies, and for protection and defense. Use when petitioning the great Indian Spirit Guide and he will fight your battles for you.

- Anise seed
- Star anise
- Celery seed
- Mugwort
- Sage
- Indian tobacco (*Nicotiana rustica*), just a pinch
- Oil of benzoin
- 1 pinch of dirt from a sweat lodge or from the banks of the Illinois River, where Black Hawk lived and fought his great battles

Native Americans believe that tobacco is one of the most sacred gifts that the Great Spirit gives to the people. It is used for prayer, protection, respect, and healings, and is considered a sacred medicine. This oil can be added to an olive oil lamp on which an arrowhead has been placed, and burned continuously until the desired outcome is achieved. Say the prayer to Black Hawk over the lamp every day upon rising and right before going to bed.

Blessed Oil

This is the kind of oil that you should have on hand and ready for positive situations. It is also the oil to use when working with angels and saints. Blessed Oil is used to give blessings, expand protection from compassionate spirits during disquieting times, and for blocking enemy attacks. Blessed Oil can also be used to draw good things to yourself or others.

- Lavender essential oil
- Angelica essential oil
- Ylang ylang essential oil
- Rue
- Silver magnetic sand
- Piece of agrimony

Mix everything in a base of olive oil. Add a full dropper of vitamin E oil to keep it from going rancid. Anoint a white candle on a Sunday during a waxing moon and pray for the blessings you need.

Boss Fix Oil

Tremendously popular in the Vieux Carré, Boss Fix Oil is perfect for handling problematic employers. Because Boss Fix is a duel action conjure oil, you can use it to compel your employer to agree with you. Stealthily place a tiny bit under your employer's desk, or anoint an orange candle representing him/her. Boss Fix Oil is used for creating harmony in the workplace, stopping a supervisor from harassing you, or drawing a promotion or raise. Write your supervisor's name on brown paper, turn the paper ninety degrees, and cross with your name and intention. Then, anoint the four corners of the paper with this oil. Wear it in your right shoe to "walk on" your boss. Anoint your employer's office or paperwork where he/she will walk in it or touch it. This works well with Pay Me, Do As I Say, and Crown of Success products, and a host of others.

- Tobacco
- Sage
- Chili
- Gravel root

Mix everything in a base of olive oil. Add a full dropper of vitamin E oil to keep it from going rancid. Add a piece of master root to the bottle for its dominating effects, and a pinch of sugar for its sweetening effects.

Camellia Oil

Just as Marie Laveau is the Queen of Voodoo; Camellia Oil is the Queen of New Orleans money oils. It has the ability to bust away all obstacles, draw in great riches, and enhance cash flow in all areas.

- Vetivert
- Cinnamon
- Patchouli
- Sugar cane syrup

Mix the above ingredients with one ounce of camellia oil to which a full dropper of vitamin E has been added.

Citronella

Citronella is used to draw friends to your life and success to your business. To make, blend a half ounce of pure citronella essential oil to one ounce of carrier oil that is fixed with vitamin E oil. Use with yellow and green candles during a waxing moon for the best effect.

Cleo May

Cleo May products are based on an old-time New Orleans recipe designed for prostitutes seeking to attract high-end clientele with the ability to pay large sums of money in return for sexual favors. This way, the working girl didn't have to service as many men in one day. Today, Cleo May products are still used with similar intent—to draw men with money. The difference is that it is not used solely by prostitutes anymore; Cleo May products are used by all women interested in securing a man with means.

- Jezebel root
- Magnolia
- Carnation
- Rose
- Orange
- Vanilla

Blend the above ingredients in a base of almond oil that has been fixed with vitamin E or benzoin.

Cleopatra Oil

A sexy and exotic fragrance, Cleopatra Oil is one of New Orleans' most attractive love fragrances. Its intricate formula is beyond compare for inviting sensual and sexual encounters into your life. To draw love, use with red or pink candles.

- Lotus
- Sandalwood
- Ylang ylang
- Honeysuckle
- Balm of Gilead
- Musk
- Orange
- Frankincense

Blend the above ingredients in a base of almond oil that has been fixed with vitamin E or benzoin.

Come to Me Oil

To draw the one you desire closer to you, use this magickal oil.

- Magnolia oil
- Vetivert oil
- Rose oil
- Gardenia oil
- Catnip
- Lodestone
- Honeysuckle blossoms
- Orange blossom oil

To the above formula, add rose petals for enhancing love; cinnamon for enhancing passion; and Queen Elizabeth root for attracting women or gay males. Then, blend the ingredients in a base of almond oil that has been fixed with vitamin E or benzoin.

Commanding Oil

Commanding oils are called *Baume Commandeur* in French and are used to command and influence others. To use, rub a small amount in the palms of your hands before meeting the person you wish to influence. Be sure to touch the person or shake their hand. Look directly into the person's eye while focusing on your will.

- Bergamot
- Bay
- Clover
- Balm of Gilead
- Calamus
- Five finger grass
- High John the Conqueror root

Add the above ingredients to a base of olive oil that has been fixed with vitamin E or oil of benzoin.

Confusion Oil

This oil is used when one wants to impair another person's ability to think clearly.

- Guinea pepper
- Chicory root
- Licorice root
- Spider webs
- Spanish moss

Add a pinch of each to a base of mineral oil to cause confusion in your rival.

Cooling Anger

The classic New Orleans "home sweetener." Use to smooth things over after an argument or quarrel, or to calm the nerves of someone who is quick to snap.

- Wormwood
- Passion flower
- Orris root
- Honey granules
- 1 pinch brown sugar
- Lavender

Add the above ingredients to a base of olive oil that has been fixed with vitamin E or oil of benzoin.

Court Case Oil

When you need to have the upper hand in legal situations or influence mediators, judge, or jury, use this oil. Anoint brown candles with it for court works.

- Galangal (Little John to chew)
- Calendula flowers
- Carnation petals
- Dill seed
- Deer's tongue
- Benzoin
- Frankincense
- Devil's shoestring

Add the above ingredients to a base of olive oil that has been fixed with vitamin E or benzoin.

Crown of Success

This is another New Orleans classic formula for attracting success. It can be used when success is desired in any area, and is particularly suited for success in business, school, and employment.

- Orange oil
- Allspice oil
- Cinnamon oil
- Geranium oil
- Lavender
- Bergamot
- Anise
- Rosemary
- High John the Conqueror root

Add the above ingredients to a base of sunflower oil that has been fixed with vitamin E or oil of benzoin. Add a piece of High John the Conqueror root and a pinch of gold glitter to each bottle.

Curse Reversal Oil

Use to reverse curses, break jinxes and hexes, and change a streak of bad luck into good luck.

- Hyssop
- Camphor
- Agrimony
- Dragon's blood
- Vetivert

Add the above ingredients to a base of olive oil that has been fixed with vitamin E or oil of benzoin.

Cut and Clear Oil

Used in rituals to rid yourself of any remaining link to an ex-lover or ex-partner.

- Rue
- Mint
- Lemon
- Lemon verbena
- Salt

Add the above ingredients to a base of olive oil that has been fixed with vitamin E or oil of benzoin.

D.U.M.E (Death Unto Mine Enemies)

D.U.M.E. is New Orleans hoodoo's answer to a mafia hit man when it comes to getting revenge on an enemy. It can be used offensively or defensively, but given the power and intent of this oil, be prepared for the consequences should you choose to use it offensively and without justification.

- Calamus
- Vetivert
- Licorice
- Guinee peppers
- Black peppercorns
- Black pepper essential oil
- Chicory root
- Devil's shoestring
- Essential oil of capsicum

Add all of the above to a base of mineral oil, being sure to chop up the roots and lightly macerate.

Desire

This oil is designed for lesbians and gay men to inspire sexual desire in a person of the same sex. Wear or use to anoint red or purple candles to draw and influence the one you desire.

- Lavender
- Magnolia
- Almond
- Vetivert

Add the above ingredients to a base of sweet almond oil that has been fixed with vitamin E or oil of benzoin.

Devil's Shoestring Oil

To trip up an enemy, try this simple recipe.

- Devil's shoestring root
- Patchouli
- Vetivert
- Ground chicory root

Chop up a piece of devil's shoestring and add to a base of mineral oil.

Dixie John Oil

Use for help with family, love, and luck. The formula uses Dixie John root, also known as Beth's root, Southern John, and Trillium, as the main ingredient.

- Dixie John root
- Patchouli
- Vetivert

Dry and chop the roots and lightly macerate with a mortar and pestle. Add all ingredients to a base of sweet almond oil that has been fixed with vitamin E or benzoin.

Dixie Love Oil

This is a love-drawing oil that also encourages romance and increases sex appeal for the wearer.

- Beth's root
- Dixie Iris bulb (*iris hexagona*), a native Louisiana iris
- Rose
- Gardenia
- Patchouli
- Cinnamon
- Jasmine

The Dixie Iris is the oldest recognized species in the Louisiana iris group *(Hexagonae)*. It is found in ditches, swamps, and shallow slow-moving streams in either full sun or half shade. Dry and chop the roots and lightly macerate with a mortar and pestle. Add all ingredients to a base of sweet almond oil that has been fixed with vitamin E and benzoin.

Domination Oil

Use in all ways of domination, power, control, and compelling works.

- 4 parts patchouli
- 4 parts vetivert
- 1 part lime
- 1 part frankincense
- 1 part calamus root
- 1 part licorice root

Add all ingredients to a base of sweet almond oil that has been fixed with vitamin E or benzoin.

Dragon's Blood Oil

In New Orleans, Dragon's Blood Oil is considered the most powerful and protective oil, next to High John the Conqueror. It may be used to add power to any positive purpose, from uncrossing to love.

- Dragon's blood resin chunks
- Vetivert
- Alkanet root
- Liquid resin of benzoin

Steep chunks of dragon's blood resin in almond oil and add the additional ingredients. The result is a very powerful oil that should be a very dark red in color.

Dream Potion

For vivid, prophetic dreams, blend the following and anoint the forehead before going to sleep:

- Red wine vinegar
- Red wine
- Handful of rosemary
- Honey

Add all ingredients to a base of grape seed oil that has been fixed with vitamin E or benzoin.

Dryad

Kill two birds with one stone with this oil. A favorite among gay men, Dryad is a classic New Orleans oil to be used exclusively to attract and hold on to a lover.

- Lavender
- Musk
- Oakmoss
- Civet
- Patchouli

Add all ingredients to a base of sweet almond oil that has been fixed with vitamin E or benzoin.

Easy Life

Another classic oil in the class of success formulas. Use when you need to maintain a steady flow of cash or positive energy in your life.

- Cloves
- Lemon
- Ginger
- Orange
- Cassia

Add all ingredients to a base of sweet almond oil that has been fixed with vitamin E or benzoin and store in a tightly sealed bottle at room temperature.

Erzulie Freda Floral Perfume Oil

Use this oil to increase your personal magnetism, and to draw love and prosperity to you.

- ¾ cup jojoba oil
- ½ teaspoon essential oil of rose
- ½ teaspoon essential oil of lavender
- 1 teaspoon essential oil of geranium
- ¼ teaspoon essential oil of ylang ylang

Add all ingredients to a base of sweet almond oil that has been fixed with vitamin E or benzoin and store in a tightly sealed bottle at room temperature. Wear as a perfume or to anoint charms.

Essence of Bend Over

Essence of Bend Over is definitely a commanding formula and is often used with purple candles for such purposes. It manipulates people into being agreeable to you, doing favors for you without complaining, and in general, it makes life easier with regards to difficult people in your life. It can be used to break jinxes and command evil entities to get the hell out. Though its effects are often subtle, do not underestimate the power of this formula.

- Frankincense
- Honeysuckle
- Vetivert
- Calamus root essential oil
- Licorice root
- Bergamot leaf or bergamot essential oil
- Calamus
- High John root
- Rose geranium essential oil

Add all ingredients to a base of sweet almond oil that has been fixed with vitamin E or benzoin and store in a tightly sealed bottle at room temperature.

Essence of Van Van

Essence of Van Van is one of the most popular conjure potions in New Orleans. It is used for success, good luck, and power spells.

- Essential oil of lemongrass
- Alcohol (Everclear or perfumer's alcohol)

Simply add 10 percent oil of lemongrass to alcohol. Use to bless your home by scrubbing your front steps and foyer. Of you need a real good cleaning, wash all of your floors with it and wipe down your furniture and walls.

Eve Oil

One might think of this as the original seduction oil according to biblical legend, but this is not the case. Still, it is fabulous for women who want a powerful formula to get what they want (usually a man) or any kind of "forbidden fruit." This oil is used in New Orleans as a magnetic seduction oil that draws men to the woman wearing it like moths to a flame.

- Apple blossom
- Rose
- Lemon
- Vanilla
- Gold lodestone

Add to a base of sweet almond oil that has been fixed with vitamin E. Wear as a perfume or to dress a red or pink candle onto which you have inscribed your target's name. Set the candle on a bed of sugar and allow to burn all the way down.

Fast Luck Oil

The traditional New Orleans Fast Luck Oil is yellow in color.

- Lemongrass
- Cinnamon
- Bergamot
- 3 juniper berries per bottle
- Small lodestone

Add the above ingredients to a base of 2 ounces of sunflower oil to which a whole dropper of vitamin E has been added.

Fiery Wall of Protection Oil

Fiery Wall of Protection is one of most popular formulas for psychic and spiritual defense and warfare in New Orleans Voodoo and hoodoo. It can be used to deal with every type of threat imaginable, and works well with Commanding, Bend Over, and Uncrossing products. In addition to being used as a means of defense, this formula can be used to help with legal, health, and business problems. Its name is said to invoke the power and protection of Archangel Michael's flaming sword.

If you are in need of protection from an evil perpetrator, anoint the doors and windows of your home with this oil. You can use the oil to dress candles for candle spells as well. It can also be used in tandem with enemy works as a means of protection from potential backlash or counterattack.

- Frankincense
- Cayenne pepper
- Pinch of rue
- Sandalwood essential oil
- Pinch of angelica
- Cinnamon essential oil
- Blessed salt*
- Ginger essential oil
- Bay laurel essential oil
- Chunk of dragon's blood resin

Add the above ingredients to 2 ounces of pure olive oil to which a dropper of vitamin E has been added.

*Ordinary table salt can be blessed by reciting Psalm 23 over it.

Fire of Love

In New Orleans hoodoo, there are two sex magick oils referred to as the Two Fires. These oils are Fire of Love and Fire of Passion. They are similar in formula, but one focuses more on the love and intimacy in a sexual relationship, while the other is about pure passion and sex.

- Saffron
- Damiana
- Musk
- Patchouli
- Cinnamon
- Rose
- Flakes of alkanet

Add the above ingredients to 2 ounces of sweet almond oil to which a dropper of vitamin E has been added

Fire of Passion

The second of the Two Fires, Fire of Passion Oil is strictly about XXX-rated sex and lust.

- Saffron
- Damiana
- Musk
- Patchouli
- Cinnamon
- Flakes of alkanet

Add the above ingredients to 2 ounces of sweet almond oil to which a dropper of vitamin E has been added.

Follow Me Boy

According to tradition, this recipe was created by Marie Laveau. It is formulated specifically for women to get men to follow them around when money, love, sex, or protection are needed. Follow Me Boy makes a wonderful massage oil when diluted further with extra sweet almond oil.

- Orris root
- Dried catnip
- Lavender
- Calamus
- Licorice root
- Damiana leaf
- Jasmine flowers
- Rose absolute
- Vanilla
- Night jasmine essential oil
- Piece of Queen Elizabeth root
- Flakes of alkanet

Mix everything in a base of sweet almond oil to which a full dropper of vitamin E oil has been added. Wear as a perfume.

Follow Me Girl

On the other side of the coin, this oil is designed to be worn by men to attract women.

- Myrrh
- Patchouli
- Vetivert
- Lemon
- Vanilla
- Sandalwood

Mix everything in a base of sweet almond oil to which a full dropper of vitamin E oil has been added.

Flying Devil Oil

Flying Devil Oil is a powerful uncrossing and reversal oil that will undo any negative work or crossing. Use to send malintent back to the sender.

- Cayenne pepper
- Black pepper
- Dragon's blood
- Cassia
- Patchouli
- Dash of tabasco sauce

Use with black and purple candles. Add the above to a base of mineral oil. Do not get this on your fingers and rub your eyes or you will be very sorry!

French Love Oil

A sensual blend of earthy, floral, and spicy ingredients used as perfume oil as well as in magickal works to draw passionate but sweet love into your life.

- Lavender
- Rose
- Dragon's Blood Oil
- Honey
- Musk
- Gardenia
- Vanilla
- Ambergris
- Vetivert

Mix everything in a base of sweet almond oil to which a full dropper of vitamin E oil has been added.

Friendly Judge Oil

This is handy oil to have when dealing with the courts and lawyers. Anoint yourself and your clothing on the day you go to court. Also add 3 drops to the palm of your hand and then rub both hands together briskly before going into the courtroom, shaking hands with your attorney, or signing any legal papers. Anoint all four corners of your legal papers with the oil, and for three days prior to your court date, add a small amount to your bath water.

- 2 parts carnation
- 1 part anise seed
- 1 part cinnamon
- Galangal root

Mix everything in a base of sweet almond oil to which a full dropper of vitamin E oil has been added. Add a small piece of galangal root to the bottle.

Gambler's Luck Oil

Use this oil on all works related to gambling. You can also anoint your palms with the oil and rub them together right before playing games of chance.

- Cinnamon
- 1 carnation petal
- Narcisse
- Ginger

Add the above ingredients to 2 ounces of pure olive oil to which a dropper of vitamin E has been added. Add a piece of High John the Conqueror root to each bottle of oil.

Get a Job Oil

This is a practical magickal oil that can help you get a job. You will have to work hard at keeping it, though. Get your job applications, then anoint the each of the four corners with the oil. If you are applying online, anoint yourself and focus intently on the application screen. Fill it out, and once you have a clear vision in your mind of getting the job, click send.

- 1 part sandalwood oil
- 1 part patchouli oil
- 1 part clove oil
- 1 part frankincense oil
- 1 part nutmeg oil

Blend in carrier oil such as almond, olive, or grape seed that has been fixed with vitamin E.

High John the Conqueror Oil

Probably the most famous of all roots used in New Orleans Voodoo hoodoo. It is considered most powerful and often used in commanding works and uncrossing. It's also useful for drawing luck and success in any area of your life.

- High John the Conqueror root
- Vetivert oil
- Peony root
- Guinea pepper

Chop up the roots and gently macerate with a mortar and pestle. Steep in almond oil to which you have added vitamin E oil or benzoin and add the other ingredients.

Holy Spirit Oil

This is another of the New Orleans Holy Trinity of Blessing oils, the others being Altar Oil and Van Van. As with Altar Oil, Holy Spirit Oil is used for highly positive works and summoning helpful spirits. Holy Spirit Oil is designed for blessing oneself or another, ritual objects, or anything else that needs special blessings.

- Lily of the valley
- Basil
- Hyssop
- Lavender

Combine the above ingredients in a base of pure olive oil from Israel. Add a little vitamin E to the bottle to keep it from going rancid.

Hoodoo Love Drawing Oil

- Patchouli
- Dried orange rind
- Oil of jasmine
- Rose petals

Blend in carrier oil such as almond, olive, or grape seed. Add rose petals for enhancing love, and patchouli leaves for enhancing passion.

Inflammatory Confusion Oil

To create chaos and confusion between couples, cause extreme confusion in the mind of an enemy, or make a rival business fail, use this powerful oil on red or black candles.

- Vetivert essential oil
- Patchouli essential oil
- Black pepper essential oil
- Cayenne pepper
- Black mustard seeds
- Black peppercorns
- Dried jalapeno pod
- Oak ashes
- Fennel
- Musk

Blend equal parts of the oils and add the peppers and mustard seeds to the bottle. Top off with almond oil that has been fixed with vitamin E.

Join Together Drops

Get together with the one you desire with this traditional New Orleans oil.

- Vanilla
- Night jasmine
- Adam and Eve root
- Pair of small lodestones (male and female)

Blend in carrier oil such as almond, olive, or grape seed that has been fixed with vitamin E.

King Solomon Oil

King Solomon oil is one of those classic oils with a legend behind its purported power. According to the story, a secret formula for a powerful and sacred annointing oil was revealed to King Solomon. Apparently, whoever wore the sacred oil would receive infinite wisdom, intuition, and power. The secret formula was only known by King Solomon, the Queen of Sheba, and select magicians in Africa.

Somehow the secret got out—and here it is. In addition to the above uses, use King Solomon Oil when you need to solve problems quickly and think clearly.

- Solomon's Seal
- Hyssop
- Rose
- Benzoin liquid resin

Combine the above ingredients in a base of pure olive oil from Israel.

Kiss Me Quick

A popular love and attraction perfume oil.

- Cassie
- Ambergris
- Narcissus
- Tonka
- Orris root
- Civet
- Rose
- Citronella
- Lemongrass

Blend in carrier oil such as almond, olive, or grape seed that has been fixed with vitamin E.

Kus Kus (Khus Khus)

This 160-year-old original scent of New Orleans is a soft powdery spice created in 1843 by August Doussan. Use this oil to attract the love of others and to enhance self love. It smells so divine you won't be able to resist it!

- Magnolia
- Vetivert

Add to a base of jojoba oil.

Law Keep Away Oil

To keep the police from knocking on your door, avoid an IRS audit, or to keep others from testifying against you in a court case, mix up a batch of this oil.

- Anise
- Dragon's blood chunks
- Licorice root

Blend in carrier oil such as almond, olive, or grape seed that has been fixed with vitamin E.

Legba Oil (St. Anthony)

Use Legba Oil to create opportunities and clear away obstacles.

- Pinch of coffee grounds
- 3 drops avocado oil
- 3 drops coconut oil
- Palm kernel oil
- Pinch of sugar
- Dropper of rum
- Abre camino herbs

Blend the above to two ounces of almond carrier oil and a full dropper of vitamin E.

Lodestone Oil

Lodestones are described in the old hoodoo catalogues as being "alive with magnetism." As such, they are considered the preeminent drawing curio. To make lodestone oil, pick out a small pair—male (pointed and angular) and female (round in shape)—to have a balanced dynamic, and baptize them in Hoyt's Cologne or whiskey. To do this, brush off any magnetic sand that may be sticking to the lodestones and wash them with either of the aforementioned liquids. Set aside and allow to air dry, which should be fairly quickly, given the fact that both Hoyt's Cologne and whiskey are alcohol-based. Once they are dry, drop them in a small bottle and sprinkle just a pinch of magnetic sand, then cover them with mineral oil. Voilà! Now you have a wonderful bottle of lodestone oil with which you can draw luck in love and money.

Louisiana Van Van Oil

Louisiana Van Van Oil is the third of the holy trinity of all-purpose blessing oils in New Orleans. It is the basis for the quintessential New Orleans conjure drug, Lucky New Orleans Van Van Wash. This oil can be used to boost any type of spell. It has multiple uses in New Orleans Voodoo. Its popularity has spread to other regions of the country, where most hoodoos keep a supply of it on hand. Like vetivert, Van Van is a multipurpose oil that is used for uncrossing, clearing, drawing love and success, and just about anything else you can think of. It can also be used by itself as an anointing oil and in a number of floor washes. It helps clear away negativity, changes bad luck to good, uncrosses crossed conditions, brings luck in love and business, and functions as a road opener to new opportunities. Following are three formulas for Van Van Oil.

Formula 1:

- Lemongrass essential oil
- Citronella essential oil
- Vetivert essential oil
- Palmarosa essential oil
- Lemon verbena essential oil
- Gingergrass essential oil

Blend equal parts of the above oils to a base of sunflower, sweet almond, or grape seed oil that has been fixed with vitamin E.

Formula 2:

Add 2 tablespoons of lemongrass herb and 2 drops of lemongrass oil to 2 ounces of base of sunflower, sweet almond, or grape seed oil. Add a piece of rock salt that has been blessed to the mixture.

Formula 3:

- 1 part lemongrass essential oil
- Cinnamon essential oil
- 1 part vetivert essential oil
- 1 part rosemary essential oil
- 1 part palmarosa essential oil

Blend equal parts of the above oils to a base of sunflower, sweet almond, or grape seed oil that has been fixed with vitamin E.

Lucky Hand Oil

Lucky Hand Oil is so called because the main ingredient in the formula is an orchid root that is shaped like a hand. For luck in the lottery, at the casino, and in all games of chance, anoint your money and place a few drops in your palms and rub together briskly. This oil may also be used with green and gold candles. When combined with the following ingredients, its effectiveness is said to be unsurpassed.

- 1 lucky hand root
- Five 3 drops patchouli
- Piece of John the Conqueror root

Blend the above with 2 ounces Lodestone Oil for one powerful lucky conjure oil.

Luv Luv Luv Oil

Luv Luv Luv Oil is an all-purpose love and attraction oil designed to change your luck in love. If you do not have any particular person in mind, you can use this oil to bring you your ideal mate.

- Rose oil
- Angelica
- Clove oil
- Honey
- Honeysuckle blossoms

Blend in carrier oil such as almond, olive, or grape seed that has been fixed with vitamin E.

Lucky Nine Oil

This oil is said to bring luck to your door. Add 9 drops to your bath water to get a job.

- Musk oil
- Rose geranium oil
- Sandalwood oil
- Frankincense oil
- Myrrh oil
- Bergamot oil
- Citrus oil (orange, lemon)
- Allspice oil
- Vervain

Blend in 2 ounces of almond oil that has been fixed with vitamin E.

Magnet Oil

Magnet Oil is an all-purpose attraction oil that is prepared in a special way. It is ideal for dressing candles to increase their magnetism, and can be added to gris gris or mojo bags.

- Lodestone or magnet
- Magnetic sand
- Bible
- Mineral oil

Place your Bible under the light of the full moon. Place the bottle you will be using to hold the oil on top of the Bible. Add the lodestone or magnet followed by a pinch of magnetic sand. Using a dropper, add one drop of oil for every year of your life plus one into the bottle. Repeat every full moon and use sparingly until you have a full bottle.

Magnolia Oil

Magnolia (*Magnolia grandiflora*) was named after French botanist Pierre Magnol. It is believed to be one of the most ancient flowering plants and is the official state flower of both Mississippi and Louisiana.

In the New Orleans tradition, Magnolia Oil is synonymous with fidelity. Its one primary purpose is to keep your partner faithful.

Magnolia Oil is only available as a synthetic. It should be cut with a carrier oil along with a ½ dropper of benzoin. If your partner has been deceitful, gather some magnolia leaves and anoint with the oil. Make two doll babies stuffed with damiana leaves and Dittany of Crete (one red to represent the faithful partner, and one purple to represent the unfaithful partner). Tie the two dolls together with a red cord in nine knots. With each knot, say "You are tied to me and only me" or something to that effect as you anoint the knot with some of the oil. Anoint the dolls as well. Get one red candle to represent the faithful partner, and one purple candle to represent the unfaithful partner. Inscribe each party's name on their respective candle. Lay the dolls on the magnolia leaves and set the candles on either side of the dolls. Light the candles and allow to burn all the way down. Wrap the dolls in red cloth and hide under your mattress. Take the wax remains and magnolia leaves and dispose of them at a crossroads. If you are a woman, wear some of the oil daily. If you are a man, give some to your woman as a gift. I have yet to know a woman who does not absolutely love the fragrance of magnolia flowers.

Master Key Oil

As its name implies, Master Key Oil is used to master and gain expertise in any area. It is often used to succeed in school or in a profession.

- Master root
- Galangal
- Frankincense
- Myrrh
- Mimosa
- Patchouli
- Jasmine
- Cinnamon

Blend in carrier oil such as almond, olive, or grape seed that has been fixed with vitamin E.

Ogun Oil (St. John the Baptist Holy Oil)

Use Ogun Oil for protection from enemies, defense from evil influences, and to remove barriers.

- Eucalyptus leaves
- Rosemary leaves

Add 2 tablespoons of each herb to 2 ounces of olive oil that has been fixed with vitamin E. Add a piece of rock salt to the final mixture to honor the orisha Ogun.

Oshun Oil (Caridad del Cobre Holy Oil)

Use Oshun Oil to honor the river goddess and draw love and prosperity. Use the following essential oils to create this holy oil:

- Sweet orange
- Rose scent, which can be one or more of these:
  Essential oil of roses (rose otto)
  Essential oil of rose geranium
- Cinnamon
- Magnolia
- Benzoin liquid resin

Blend in a base of grape seed oil to honor the love goddess Oshun. To the above formula, add rose petals for enhancing love, and cinnamon chips for enhancing passion.

Peace Oil

- Rosemary leaves
- Basil leaves
- Lavender flowers
- Sandalwood oil

Blend in a carrier oil such as almond, olive, or grape seed.

Peaceful Home Oil

This is one of the most popular oils in New Orleans. It's used to promote peace, harmony, and love in the home. It is also very effective for creating a barrier of protection to keep conflict, agitation, and other negative influences out of the home.

- Pennyroyal
- Rosemary
- Lavender

Blend in a base of organic extra virgin olive oil from Israel to which a full dropper of vitamin E has been added.

Protection Oil

Wear this oil as a perfume or anoint charms to protect from evil and negativity.

- Few drops of sandalwood oil
- Frankincense resin
- Few drops of sage oil
- Patchouli leaves
- Gardenia petals

Blend equal parts of the leaves into two ounces of olive oil that has been fixed with vitamin E.

Power Oil

A subtle, yet extremely effective New Orleans commanding oil. It is used to force success in any given situation. Use with a purple candle to reap the best benefits.

- Lemon essential oil
- Grated lemon rind

- Patchouli
- Vetivert

Blend the above ingredients in a base of almond oil to which a full dropper of vitamin E has been added to prevent rancidity.

Queen Esther Perfume Oil

Queen Esther is a beautiful, exotic anointing oil that is a blend of sweet odors extracted from plants, trees, and flowers found in biblical days. It has an elegant scent and a sweet, fragrant aroma. Queen Esther is revered in Spiritualist churches in New Orleans. In preparation to see the king, Esther went through a purification using oil of myrrh for six months and sweet odors for six months.

This formula is based on the biblical formula.

- Rose
- Amber (Bdellium)
- Sandalwood
- Lilly of the valley
- Pomegranate
- Honey
- Coriander
- Myrtle
- Myrrh
- Frankincense
- Spikenard essential oil

Blend equal parts of the above oils in a base of organic extra virgin olive oil from Israel to which a full dropper of vitamin E has been added.

Red Fast Luck Oil (Algiers Formula)

This recipe is decidedly New Orleans in origin and is a triple luck formula used for quick success in gambling, luck, love, and sex.

- Oil of cinnamon
- Oil of vanilla
- Oil of patchouli
- Oil of wintergreen
- Flakes of alkanet

Blend equal parts of the leaves and add to two ounces of olive oil that has been fixed with vitamin E.

Anoint your money before you spend it, or rub the Red Fast Luck Oil on the doorknob at your place of business. It can also be used as a floor wash to bring luck and harmony to the home or at a place of business to draw customers in.

Revenge Oil

Revenge Oil is used to seek revenge against one who has done you a great wrong.

- Red pepper
- Sulfur
- Wormwood
- Ground ivy root

Add equal amounts of each to 2 ounces of mineral oil base.

St. Anthony Spiritual Oil

To receive the blessings of St. Anthony, to open roads, and to protect enemies from steering you in the wrong direction, conjure up a batch of this oil.

- Coffee
- Coconut
- Sugar
- Rum

Add equal amounts of each to 2 ounces of avocado oil to which oil of benzoin has been added.

St. Jude Spiritual Oil

St. Jude is the patron saint of lost causes and is considered the miraculous saint for this reason. To create St. Jude Oil, simply use the highest grade of olive oil you can afford and recite the prayer to St. Jude over it. This blessing invokes God's protection from evil and deceit, and brings his blessings for health of mind and body.

Merely touch the area of your body in need of healing and say the St. Jude Prayer. Then, be sure to publicly thank St. Jude by posting in a blog or newspaper the positive effects you experience, especially if your prayers are answered.

Prayer to St. Jude

O most holy apostle, St. Jude, faithful servant and friend of Jesus—People honor and invoke you universally, as the patron of hopeless cases, of things almost despaired of. Pray for me, for I am so helpless and alone. Please help to bring me visible and speedy assistance. Come to my assistance in this great need that I may receive the consolation and help of heaven in all my necessities, tribulations, and sufferings, particularly (state your request) and that I may praise God with you always. I promise, O blessed St. Jude, to be ever mindful of this great favor, to always honor you as my special and powerful patron, and to gratefully encourage devotion to you by publishing this request. Amen.

St. Joseph's Oil

St. Joseph is the patron saint of families, travelers, realtors and working people. Make this oil to receive his blessings.

- Buds from the garden of Gilead
- Berries of the fish
- Wishing beans
- Juniper berries
- Japanese scented lucky beans
- Large star anise
- Lily of the valley

Blend in a base of organic olive oil from Israel to which a full dropper of vitamin E has been added. When making this oil, say the following prayer to empower it with St. Joseph's blessings.

Prayer to St. Joseph

O Glorious St. Joseph, faithful follower of Jesus Christ, to thee do we raise our hearts and hands, to implore thy powerful intercession in obtaining from the benign Heart of Jesus all the helps and graces necessary for our spiritual and temporal welfare, particularly the grace of a happy death, and the favor we now implore (Say intention, then say the following seven times): O Glorious St. Joseph through the love thou bearest to Jesus Christ and for the glory of His Name. Hear our prayers and obtain our petitions. Jesus, Mary and Joseph, assist us. Amen.

Three Jacks Oil

For the upper hand in games of chance, add a few drops to the palm of your hand before going gambling. You may also anoint your wallet and money, and any gambling paraphernalia such as dice and cards.

- Galangal
- Vetivert
- Patchouli
- Cardamom

Blend in a base of almond oil to which a full dropper of vitamin E has been added.

Three Kings Oil

This is a great oil for anointing items on your altar and dressing altar candles. Three Kings Oil and incense are said to be very lucky formulas. Not only is this a wonderful blessing and consecration oil; but it smells absolutely divine!

- Frankincense
- Myrrh
- Sandalwood
- Amber

Blend in a base of organic olive oil from Israel to which a full dropper of vitamin E has been added.

Thrifty Oil

No practitioner should be without this oil, particularly if you have a tightwad in your midst. If you know someone who is miserly and greedy and won't come off of their money for anything—someone who expects you to always pick up the bill and provide the tip when going out (if you can get them to go out at all)—then try whipping up a batch of this oil and watch a miracle occur. Not only will your friend spend money on you; but he or she won't have to be asked! This oil can be used with purple, yellow, or green candles, depending on your intention.

- Orris
- Sage
- Lavender

Blend in a base of almond oil to which a full dropper of vitamin E has been added.

Tranquil or Tranquillo

This oil is from the Santería tradition and is used for gaining control of chaotic conditions and situations. It is designed to restore peace and harmony and to facilitate calm, cool-headed conversations between those who may be prone to bickering.

- Balsam
- Lavender
- Rosemary
- Thyme

Blend in a base of organic extra virgin olive oil from Israel to which a full dropper of vitamin E has been added.

Van Van Oil (see Louisiana Van Van Oil)

Vetivert Oil

No serious New Orleans rootworker or conjurer who blends their own magickal oils would be without this one. A clear influence from the French perfumers, it is the original main ingredient in Doussan's 1843 New Orleans Kus Kus blend. Its use as an additive in perfumes is based on perfumery formulations, but it also serves as a powerful oil in and of itself. A great New Orleans secret (well, not anymore) is that using it as an additive to almost any conjure oil will give a hefty boost to the power of the oil. It is also used for protection against theft and in works concerning money, love, luck, and uncrossing. This is the kind of oil that you will not be able to make yourself, as it is extracted from the washed, chopped, dried, and soaked roots and rootlets by steam distillation. Invest a little money to get a nice quantity of pure vetivert oil to add to your other oils to enhance their effectiveness. Be aware, however, that although vetivert is characterized as an earthy, musty scent, there will be differences between suppliers. The difference is marked enough that if you are sensitive to scent, you should be certain to find a brand you like and stick with it. If you are not concerned so much about the fragrance of the oil, then any vetivert will do.

Voodoo Oil

Voodoo oil is not the same as Voodoo Nights Oil or Voodoo Nights Perfume Oil. This is a downright powerful conjure oil.

- Patchouli essential oil
- Vetivert essential oil
- Pine essential oil
- Black pepper
- Pinch of ground mullein

Create this oil at midnight during a full moon. Blend equal parts of the above oils to a base of almond oil that has been fixed with vitamin E. Voodoo Oil can be used to anoint charms and supercharge Voodoo dolls. It will bring success to your magickal endeavors.

Voodoo Nights Oil

Not to be confused with Voodoo Oil, this is a deep, powerful, resonating magickal oil that should be blended at midnight to unite the powers of the spirits with the energy of ecstasy. There are two formulations or versions of this oil. This one is geared for use by men to wear on their person to attract women or men. The second version is formulated for women to attract men or women. Both are Voodoo Nights Oil, but the addition of "perfume" in the title indicates the one created for use by women. As you will see, they are two different formulations that are designed to have a similar effect. I personally love both of these fragrances and find most women will like both formulations and use them according to their moods. Men usually find the perfume oil blend to be a little too flowery to wear themselves, but love its scent on their partners.

- Myrrh
- Patchouli
- Vetivert
- Lime
- Vanilla
- Pine
- Almond
- Clove

Blend the above to 2 ounces of sweet almond carrier oil and fix with a full dropper of vitamin E oil. Use to anoint purple, red, and pink candles in love and sex spells, or anoint your clothing and body. You can also make a cologne spray for your bed sheets. Trust me on this one—it smells divine! Simply get a 4-once spray bottle and fill with one ounce of pure grain alcohol (like Everclear) or perfumer's alcohol. Add the above oils and fill to the top with distilled water. Shake well before each use.

Voodoo Nights Perfume Oil

Here is the second formulation of Voodoo Nights, designed for women, though it can be used by men as well. It is used as a powerful sexual attraction scent that, when breathed in by another, will fill them with intoxicating passion for you.

- Jasmine
- Vanilla
- Honeysuckle
- Wisteria
- Gardenia
- Lilly of the valley

Blend the above with 2 ounces of sweet almond carrier oil and fix with a full dropper of vitamin E oil and liquid resin of benzoin. Use as above.

Uncrossing Oil

A staple oil in any rootworker's repertoire, Uncrossing Oil is used to break curses, hexes, and jinxes and to clear away evil and negative energy.

- Hyssop
- Bay
- Rue

Blend in a base of organic extra virgin olive oil from Israel to which a full dropper of vitamin E has been added.

War Oil

This extremely potent oil is used in a variety of ways. It can be employed in enemy works, to protect oneself from psychic and spiritual attacks, to stop gossip and slander, and to cross an enemy. Because of the number and size of some of the ingredients, you should use a mason jar and keep some extra on hand for use at a moment's notice.

- 3 rusty nails
- Dragon's blood chunk or powder
- Oil of tar
- Gunpowder
- Thorns from a rose bush or honey locust bush
- Stinging nettle
- Bergamot essential oil
- Graveyard dirt
- Black pepper essential oil
- Dirt dauber nest
- Cayenne pepper
- Patchouli essential oil

Using a new nail, write Psalm 119 on the lid of the jar. Add all ingredients to the jar and cover with mineral oil.

XXX Algiers Oil

For expediency in works of success, luck, love, gambling, and money, use this triple-strength formula. Like Fast Luck oil, it works in a hurry but is short in duration. Thus, any work in which it is used should be repeated as needed.

- Vanilla
- Patchouli
- Cinnamon
- Wintergreen
- Red sandalwood
- High John the Conqueror root
- Nutmeg
- Devil's shoestring
- Gold lodestone

Add the above to a base of almond oil to which oil of benzoin has been added.

Yemayá Oil (Mary, Star of the Sea Holy Oil)

To honor the Mother of the Seven Seas and draw love, fertility, and family connection, use this special oil.

- Verbena leaves
- Basil leaves
- Anise seeds

To each ½ ounce of oil, add a small clear quartz crystal or an uncultured pearl. Blend in grape seed oil that has been fixed with liquid benzoin to honor the mother of all orishas, Yemayá.

Zorba Oil

In New Orleans hoodoo, Zorba Oil is used to restore a man's nature. Rub on genitals prior to a sexual encounter, or in a solo love session.

- Burdock root
- Sweet almond oil

Simply add a piece of burdock root to a bottle of sweet almond oil and allow it to steep for a couple of weeks before using. You may leave the root in the bottle.

Note that there are a number of formulas out there called Zorba. The ingredients in these formulas would not be safe for rubbing on your genitals, so pay attention to how you use them should you decide on a different recipe.

....

MAGICKAL VOODOO INKS

Many spells and rituals require the use of special ink. Early varieties include Egyptian ink and various natural dyes made from metals, the husk or outer covering of beans or seeds, and sea creatures like the cuttlefish (this ink is known as sepia). India ink is black and originated in Asia. Iron gall ink was used by many of the old masters for drawing. Early cultures developed many colors of ink from available berries, plants, and minerals. Scribes in medieval Europe (about 800 to 1500 AD) wrote on sheepskin parchment. One twelfth-century ink recipe called for hawthorn branches to be cut in Spring and left to dry. Then the bark was pounded from the branches and soaked in water for eight days. The water was then boiled until it thickened and turned black. Wine was added during boiling. Then the ink was poured into special bags and hung in the sun. Once dried, the mixture was mixed with wine and iron salt over a fire to make the final ink. Approximately five thousand years ago, an ink for blackening the raised surfaces of pictures and texts carved in stone was developed in China. This early ink was a mixture of soot from pine smoke, lamp oil, gelatin from animal skins, and musk.

As an alternative to making your own inks or using the suggested ink, you can take a regular pen in the required color and consecrate it for use in ritual. Here is a ritual that was adapted from the Key of Solomon the King that will prepare your pen for ritual use.

Holding your pen up in front of you, recite the following:

ADRAI, HAHLII, TAMAH, TILONAS, ATHAMAS, ZIANOR, ADONAI, banish from this pen all deceit and error, so that it may be of virtue and efficacy to write all that I desire. Amen.

Smudge the pen with pleasant-smelling incense such as sandalwood. Sprinkle the pen with holy water, and place it aside in a silken cloth of any color except black or gray.

Let a woman write her sweetheart's name with some of her menstrual blood, and he will fall in love with her.

For those who are so inclined (meaning you have patience and time), I have listed some recipes for a few different inks below.

Formulas

Bat's Blood Ink

- High quality red ink
- Cinnamon essential oil
- Myrrh essential oil

Blend together and use as ink for writing spells.

Bat's Blood Ink (Slater's Formula)

- Dragon's blood
- Myrrh resin
- Cinnamon oil
- Indigo color (synthetic)
- Alcohol
- Gum arabic

Steep the ground resins in the alcohol until dissolved. Then add the cinnamon oil, indigo, and ground gum arabic. Filter and bottle.[65]

Dove's Blood Ink Easy Formula

- High quality red ink
- Essence of rose

Blend together for writing love spells and drawing love talismans.

---

65   from "The Magickal Formulary" by Herman Slater, 1999.

Dove's Blood Ink (2)

- 1 part dragon's blood resin
- 2 drops cinnamon oil
- 2 drops bay oil
- 10 parts alcohol
- 1 part gum arabic
- 2 drops rose oil

Steep the dragon's blood resin in the alcohol till dissolved, then add the cinnamon oil, bay oil, rose oil, and ground gum arabic. Filter and bottle.

Dragon's Blood Ink

"Dragon's blood" refers to the bright red gum resin of the dragon palm tree. The red resin was used in ancient times as varnish, medicine, incense, and dye. It was also used in medieval ritual magic and alchemy. It continues to be employed for the aforementioned purposes by some. In hoodoo and New Orleans Voodoo, it is used in mojo hands for money drawing or love drawing, and is used as incense to cleanse a space of negative entities or influences. It is also added to red ink to make Dragon's Blood Ink, which is used to inscribe magical seals and talismans.

To make your own Dragon's Blood Ink, you will need:

- High quality red ink
- Dragon's blood resin

Blend together for writing luck or protection talismans.

Dragon's Blood Ink (2)

- 1 part dragon's blood resin
- 15 parts alcohol
- 1 part gum arabic

Steep the dragon's blood resin in the alcohol until dissolved. Then add the gum arabic and bottle.

Invisible Ink

To make an ink that enables you to write invisibly, combine some alum with a bit of water until you have a watery paste. Write your petition with the paste. Allow to dry. This can only be read by steeping the paper in clear water.

Lampblack Ink

This is a time-consuming way of making ink, so only use this recipe if you won't be needing very much, have hours to spare, and really need to focus your energy in the work in a super-amplified way. Light a beeswax candle and hold a spoon over the flame until black soot forms on the spoon. Scrape this off with another spoon until you have a small pile of it. Add an equal amount of gum arabic and mix carefully and thoroughly. Add water a few drops at a time until the mixture has the consistency of ink. Bottle it up and it's ready to use.

Purple Pokeberry Ink

Since purple is the color used for works of domination and control, you may want to have some purple ink on hand to write your commanding petitions. Pokeweed or pokeberry (*Phytolacca Americana*) and Indian pokeberry in particular (*Phytolacca Acinsoa*) have been used in production dyes, so they make great agents for the creation of purple magickal ink. Indian pokeberry is a perennial herb that grows clusters of purple berries and small white flowers. When the purple berries are crushed, they produce a natural purple dye and ink. Gather a cupful and crush them, removing the seeds from the berries. Add some gum arabic to thicken the liquid to the consistency of ink. The seeds and the roots are poisonous, so keep this ink out of the reach of children.

Pokeberry has some magickal properties, including uncrossing and breaking jinxes. When the poisonous parts are dried and powdered (seeds and roots), they make for a great crossing agent when added to other ingredients in foot track magick.

Indian pokeberry has been used in Native American medicine as an emetic, a laxative, and for rheumatism, among other things. Scientists are now discovering why. Apparently, the plant contains chemicals called pokeweed mitogens that are being studied for use in the treatment of autoimmune diseases including AIDS and rheumatoid arthritis.

CHAPTER NINE

FLOOR WASHES

The cosmic element of water has been used across cultures and over time for purifying, cleansing, baptizing, scrying, and a variety of magickal purposes. It is an important tool for hoodoo and Voodoo, and is considered powerful and transformative. Through the addition of special flowers, herbs, sticks, and other natural ingredients, ordinary water becomes spiritually charged floor wash, cologne/perfume, and spiritual water.

If you sweep trash out of the house after dark, you will sweep away your luck.

Many of the spiritual waters used in hoodoo were originally created as colognes or perfumes. They gained special symbolism in the spiritual world because of their natural ingredients. Added to floor washes, they provide an effective means of cleansing away negativity and crossed conditions, drawing in good luck and prosperity, and purifying one's space. Following is a nice selection of recipes for floor washes to help you achieve luck, prosperity, better business, health, blessings, and success.

General Guidelines for Making Floor Washes

Use these guidelines to make any of the following floor washes for storage in a bottle. Unless otherwise noted, combine the ingredients in one quart of water and bring to a boil. Allow the concoction to boil for twenty minutes. Allow the mixture to cool, and add one cup of ammonia to the liquid. Add ½ to 1 cup of the spiritual water or cologne, depending on the desired strength. Pour the mixture into a plastic spray bottle for use at a moment's notice. I keep a bottle of Chinese wash at my desk, where the majority of my work is done. I can easily reach for it and cleanse my space with it, giving me a clean slate from which to work and create.

For any of the ingredients listed in these recipes, consult the resource section in the back of this book.

Formulas

In addition to the following formulas, you can use any of the formulas for spiritual waters and colognes in the next chapter in your floor wash.

Babalú-Ayé Protection from the Evil Eye Floor Wash

For protection against jealousy, envy, and coveting, or to ward off the evil eye, use the following formula as a floor wash.

- 2 drops eucalyptus oil
- 3 drops lime oil
- 2 drops myrrh oil
- 3 drops wintergreen oil
- 1 tablespoon buffalo ammonia

Add the above to a bucket of hot water. Start by scrubbing the back of the house, making your way out to the front step to banish the effects of the evil eye. It is best to start before dawn. Throw the remaining water to the east at or before sunrise.

Chango's Victory Floor Wash

This floor wash draws on the powers of the orisha Changó, who rules over fire, thunder, lightning, and victory. Use it to overcome all obstacles, ensure victory against enemies, and for protection from psychic and spiritual attacks. Best used as a preventative. Use this wash on a Friday, or on the fourth day of any month. You can use either the herbs or the essential oils.

- 1 cup Palo vence batalla (short sticks that are used in Palo and Santería . . . they can be found at any botanica)
- 1 cup heather flowers
- 1 cup lavender flowers
- 1 cup sasparilla
- 1 cup cedar
- Voodoo Mama's Cologne de Chàngó

Start by scrubbing the back of the house, making your way out to the front step to drive away evil spirits, anger, or general negative energy. It is best to start before dawn. Throw the remaining water to the east at or before sunrise.

Chinese Wash

This is a great all-purpose floor wash. Use to clear away negative energy, to draw luck and clarity, and to keep your home and space open to receiving new opportunities.

- Louisiana Van Van Oil
- Broom straws
- Piece of blessed rock salt or frankincense
- Murphy's Oil Soap

Dilute with water.

Dragon's Blood Floor Wash

This floor wash is used to drive away negative energy, banish evil spirits, and eliminate anger directed at you. It also creates a barrier of protection.

- 1 cup dragon's blood powder
- 1 cup High John the Conqueror root
- 1 cup quinta maldicion herb
- 1 cup kosher rock salt
- 1 cup espanta muerto herb
- Florida Water

Start by scrubbing the back of the house, making your way out to the front step to drive away evil spirits, anger, or general negative energy. It is best to start before dawn. Throw the remaining water to the east at or before sunrise.

Fast Scrubbing Essence

Fast Scrubbing Essence is a mixture of thirteen oils and is used for business success. It can also be used in initiation baths.

- Cinnamon essential oil
- Wintergreen essential oil
- Geranium essential oil
- Bergamot essential oil
- Orange flowers essential oil
- Lavender essential oil
- Anise essential oil
- St. Michael conjure oil
- Rosemary essential oil

Start by scrubbing the front doorstep. Go from the front to the back to draw in business. It is best to start before dawn. Throw the remaining water to the east at or before sunrise.

Fast Luck Floor Scrub

This is a very simple but effective recipe. Add a tablespoon of oil of citronella to a bucket of hot water and scrub the floor. This floor wash brings luck in business, pulling customers into a store. Start by scrubbing the front doorstep, and go from the front to the back. Throw the remaining water to the east at or before sunrise.

Red Fast Luck Floor Scrub

Add the following oils to a bucket of hot water. Use as above to bring good luck to the premises.

- Cinnamon essential oil
- Vanilla essential oil
- Wintergreen essential oil

Essence of Van Van

Used for luck and power of all kinds. This is considered by many to be the most popular conjure drug in Louisiana.

- 10 percent oil of lemongrass
- Grain alcohol

Start by scrubbing the front doorstep, and go from the front to the back to draw in business. Throw the remaining water to the east at or before sunrise.

Floor Wash for Fidelity

To keep your lover faithful, prepare the following floor wash and scrub the entire house, paying extra attention to the bedroom.

- 9 large magnolia leaves
- 1 large magnolia blossom
- Brown sugar
- Florida Water
- Rain water or river water

Soak 9 large magnolia leaves and one large magnolia flower blossom in a bucket of rain water or river water overnight. Use spring water if you don't have access to rain or river water, but be sure to pray Pslam 23 over the water (or recite a comparable prayer in a tradition comfortable for you). In the morning, pour the water into a large pot and heat it up to just before boiling. Remove it from the stove and pour the water back into the bucket. Add one cup of brown sugar and some Florida Water, and scrub your entire home, starting from the front doorstep and going inward, front to back, to draw fidelity to your relationship. While you are scrubbing your home, you should be focusing on what you want, and claiming that which is yours. Throw the remaining water to the east at or before sunrise.

Marie Laveau's Floor Wash for Business Success

Here is a formula allegedly used by Marie Laveau for washing the floors of a business to bring in customers. It smells divine.

- Ammonia
- 1 cup sugar
- 1 cup powdered cinnamon
- 30-40 drops cinnamon essential oil
- 1 cup nutmeg
- 1 cup cloves
- 1 cup mint leaves
- 20 drops mint oil
- Pint of whiskey

Add the above dry ingredients to a bucket that you have filled 3/4 full with hot boiling water. Stir well, then add the oils. Stir again and add the whiskey. Stir again. Pour some of the mixture into the four corners of your place of business; then mop the floors with it. Throw the remaining water to the east at or before sunrise.

Peaceful Home Floor Wash

This floor wash is used to restore harmony, eliminate conflicts, and bring peace and tranquility to a home.

- 1 cup gardenia flowers
- 1 cup violet flowers
- 1 cup lilac flowers
- 1 cup sea salt
- Florida Water

Add the above ingredients to a bucket of hot water and wash your home real good with it. Leave some for your front porch if you have one, or for right outside your door. Throw the remaining water to the east at or before sunrise.

Seven African Powers Floor Wash

This floor wash calls on the blessings of the Seven African Powers to bring success, protection, luck, love, and money.

- 1 cup abre camino herb
- 1 cup gardenia flowers
- 1 cup violets
- 1 cup rosemary
- 1 cup peppermint
- 1 cup anise
- 1 cup brown sugar
- Florida Water

Add the above ingredients to a bucket of hot water and wash your home real good with it. Leave some for your front porch if you have one, or for right outside your door. Throw the remaining water to the east at or before sunrise.

CHAPTER TEN

SPIRITUAL WATERS AND COLOGNES

Spiritual waters, or *eaux* in French perfumery, are solutions of fragrant essential oils combined with distilled water and some degree of perfumer's alcohol or grain alcohol, with or without the addition of other fragrant substances (i.e. Eau de Cologne). Often they are charged with odorous principles of flowers (i.e. Eau de Rose). They originated in the South of France or Italy, and were transported to New Orleans with the earliest perfumers.

Spiritual waters can be blended with ingredients such as water from specific sources, essential oils, tinctures, herbs, and so on. They are used as offerings to the spirits or added to floor washes and spiritual baths. The importance of water from different sources is a key part of the hoodoo body of knowledge. In New Orleans, we have numerous sources of water, from swamp water to river water and sea water. When you are familiar with the various associations, the potential for their use in potions and blends is limitless.

Spiritual waters are used in home protection rituals and spiritual cleansings. They can be used on the altar as an offering, as a floor wash for blessings, or on the person to receive the special benefits they possess. These spiritual waters are readily available in pharmacies and botanic and magic shops in most areas, and are relatively inexpensive. They can also be made from scratch with the right formulas. They are not very difficult to make, though they do require some investment in the essential oils and access to the right herbs for sufficient fragrance.

Following is a selection of formulas for the most common of the commercially available *eau spiritueuse,* or spiritual waters and colognes, as well as some of the more obscure ones.

Formulas

Angel Water (Portugal Water)

Angel Water, also called Portugal Water, is said to have its roots in Portugal. It first made its appearance in hoodoo during the eighteenth century. The most popular recipe for this water is in Henri Gemache's 1942 *The Magic of Herbs*, where he describes how it is made according to H. W. Leyell, a supposed authority on the subject:

> Shake together a pint of orange flower water, a pint of rose water, and half a pint of myrtle water. Add 2/3 of distilled spirit of musk and 2/3 ambergris. Heat spoils it and cold imprisons its perfume.[66]

I have been unable to locate a H.W. Leyell in any literature of note. However, I did find a recipe in a 1901 formulary for *Eau de Ange*. The ingredients and portions are as follows.

Eau d' Ange

- ½ pint Eau de Rose
- ½ pint Eau de Fleur d' Oranges
- ¼ pint Eau de Myrtle
- 2 fluid drams essence of ambergris
- 1 fluid dram essence of musk
- ½ dram of violet, rose, or verbena (as an alternate for the musk)[67]

Agitate the ingredients together in a bottle briskly for some hours. Do this frequently for a few days, keeping the bottle (closely stopped) in a warm room. After repose, decant the clear portion, and if necessary, filter the fluid through white bibulous paper. The mixture should be nearly colorless.[68] Almost miraculous virtues are attributed to this delicious water.

Compound Spirit of Rosemary (Eau d' Hongrie, Hungary Water)

This water can be used by itself as a magickal aid for women in need of empowerment. It can also be worn as cologne or sprayed about the home for protection, to ward off evil, and to bring good luck to family matters. It is called for as an ingredient in *Eau de Paris*.

---

66 Gemache, 1942, p. 28.
67 Sturgis and Walton Co., 1913.
68 *The Scientific American Cyclopedia of Receipts, Notes and Queries* edited by Albert Allis Hopkins, 1901.

- 2 pounds rosemary tops in blossom
- ¼ pound fresh sage
- 3 quarts grain alcohol
- 1 quart distilled water
- ½ pound table salt
- 1 ounce Jamaica ginger (bruised)

Combine all ingredients except for the distilled water and Jamaica ginger. Let sit for a few days and either decant or filter the plant matter from the liquid. Add the distilled water and then the Jamaica ginger.

Creole Water

This is traditional spiritual water that can be used when working with New Orleans-specific spirits.

- 6¾ ounces orris root
- 1½ pints French brandy
- 3 drams oil of orange blossoms
- ¾ fluid ounce oil of geranium
- Essence of cumerin

Cut the orris root into small pieces and add to the French brandy. Allow to sit for two weeks, gently swirling the mixture daily. After two weeks, you can either strain the brandy or keep the orris root pieces in the brandy—I like to keep the herbal matter in my mother oils and waters, but this is a matter of personal preference. Then, add the oil of orange blossoms and the oil of geranium. Finally, add the essence of cumerin—the amount is up to you, and depends on how you want the final product to smell.

Eau de Cologne

Eau de Cologne is a spirit-citrus perfume launched in Cologne in 1709 by an Italian perfumer. The original recipe remains a secret to this day. Nonetheless, the ingredients are known—just not the exact measurements of each. In a base of dilute ethanol (70 to 90 percent), Eau de Cologne contains a mixture of citrus oils, including oils of lemon, orange, tangerine, bergamot, lime, grapefruit, and neroli. It can also contain oils of lavender, rosemary, thyme, orange leaf, and jasmine. Some recipes call for the inclusion of Eau de Portugal (Angel Water). You'll have to experiment to get the fragrance that appeals to you. It can be worn on the person, used as a floor wash, or to bless ritual items.

Here is one suggested formula for the preparation of a concentrated Eau de Cologne that dates back to 1821. It can be diluted with ten times its volume with grain alcohol or perfumer's alcohol.

- Oil of bergamot 375 min
- Oil of citron 60 min
- Oil of lemon 60 min
- Oil of lavender 30 min
- Oil of Portugal 60 min (see Angel Water this section)
- Oil of Thyme 4 min
- Oil of neroli 75 min
- Oil of rosemary 75 min
- The best alcohol you can get, perfumer's preferably, or grain alcohol 62 ounces
- Distilled water

Mix and dilute with distilled water, then add 2 ½ ounces of Melissa Water and 5 ounces of orange flower water. Then dilute with distilled water again. Use your nose to determine how diluted you want the fragrance to be.

Eau de Paris

This is the official formula for Eau de Cologne according to the French Pharmaceutical Codex.

- ¾ ounce oil of cinnamon
- 1 ½ ounces oil of lavender
- 1 ½ ounces oil of Rosemary
- 1 ½ ounces neroli
- 3 ounces oil of bergamot
- 3 ounces oil of citron
- 3 ounces oil of lemon
- 1 quart spirit of rosemary (see formula for Compound Spirit of Rosemary)
- 3 pints compound spirit of balm
- 3 gallons rectified alcohol

Combine ingredients and let sit for eight days. Then add to 3 gallons of distilled water.

Florida Water

Florida Water is the American answer to Eau de Cologne, or Cologne Water. It shares the same citrus base as Cologne Water, but has the addition of sweet orange (rather than the lemon and neroli of the original Cologne Water), and adds spicy notes, including lavender and clove. According to the current trademark holders, Lanman & Kemp Barclay, Florida Water was introduced by the New York City perfumer (and founder of the original company) Robert Murray in 1808. The company states that their product, now sold under the Murray & Lanman brand, still uses the original 1808 formula, and that the current label is also a slightly modified version of the 1808 original.

Originally, Florida Water was valued as unisex cologne, suitable for men and women. Victorian etiquette manuals warned young ladies against the "offensive" impression made by a strong perfume, but Florida Water and Eau de Cologne were recommended as appropriate for all, along with sachets for scenting linen. Large quantities were also used by barbershops as cologne and aftershave. In the 1880s and 1890s, Murray & Lanman Florida Water was advertised as "The Richest of all Perfumes" and "The Most Popular Perfume in the World." Although now obscure to most of the general American population, Florida Water remained popular among South American and Caribbean cultures. It was incorporated into magical and ritual traditions, including hoodoo.

Numerous formulas for Florida Water have been published over the years. Here are two.

Florida Water Formula (1)

- 3 fluid ounces oil of bergamot
- 1 fluid ounce oil of lavender
- 1 fluid ounce oil of lemon
- 1 ¼ fluid drachms oil of cloves
- 2 ½ fluid drachms oil of cinnamon
- ½ fluid drachm oil of neroli
- 6 fluid ounces essence of jasmine
- 2 fluid ounces essence of musk
- 8 pints alcohol
- 1 pint rose water

Mix, and if cloudy, filter through magnesium carbonate.[69]

---

69 From "Fortunes in Formulas For Home, Farm, and Workshop" by Hiscox and Sloane, The Norman B. Henley Publishing Co., 1937.

Florida Water Formula (2)

- 3 ounces oil of bergamot Oil of bergamot
- 1 ounce oil of lemon
- 1 ounce oil of English lavender
- 12 drops oil of clove
- 20 drops oil of cinnamon
- Tincture of benzoin
- 1 gallon alcohol
- 1 pint rose water [70]

Follow Me Water

This is an old formula said to be invented by Marie Laveau to make a man follow a woman. Back in the day, this formula was popular among prostitutes, who used it as a lure for customers. The water was placed on a handkerchief and waved in the face of the man who the woman desired. Since we don't really use handkerchiefs like this anymore, mix up a batch of Follow Me Water in a spray bottle and use like cologne water or perfume right before you go to meet the person you want. Or, if the man is coming over to your home, spray some Follow Me Water in the doorway, and spray your bed sheets. It is said that this is very powerful stuff, and that the man will not leave you unless you fix him with Go Away Powder (see chapter 13).

- 1 pint rose water
- 7 drops vaginal fluids after masturbating
- Pinch dried catnip
- Lavender essential oil
- Calamus essential oil
- Licorice essential oil
- Damiana essential oil
- Jasmine flowers
- Rose absolute
- Vanilla essential oil
- Night jasmine essential oil
- Piece of Queen Elizabeth root

---

70 Adapted from "American Druggist and Pharmaceutical Record."

- The dried rind of a whole pomegranate
- 10 percent everclear or perfumers' alcohol

Combine all ingredients in a glass container and allow it to sit for seven days. The number seven represents the union of the male and female principles (see chapter 12). Then strain through cheesecloth into a spray bottle and return the piece of Queen Elizabeth root to the bottle.

Ghost Water

To make spiritual water specifically for communing with the dead, go to a cemetery at midnight and bring a bottle of spring water. Place the bottle of water on the grave of a person who represents the deceased you wish to speak with. For example, if it is a child, place the bottle on a child's grave. If you are seeking assistance from the dead for a particular purpose, such as protection, then place the bottle on the grave of a known police officer. Allow the water to stay on the grave until just before dawn. When you remove the bottle, be sure to pay the spirit with a small bottle of rum and three pennies before you leave.

Hoyt's Allegedly German Cologne

One of the most popular of the cologne waters for drawing luck in games of chance is Hoyt's Cologne. Developed by Eli Waite Hoyt, Hoyt's cologne was first made for sale in his apothecary shop. The designation "German" (Hoyt's German Cologne) was added to the name in 1870 as a marketing ploy—not because the formula came from Germany or bore any resemblance to German cologne. Hoyt was born in New York, and his apothecary shop was located in Lowell, Massachusetts.

While the exact proprietary blend is unknown, there are some close approximations. Following is one such formula according to the *American Pharmaceutical and Druggist Record*, Volume 33.

- 1 dram oil of rose geranium
- 2 drams oil of lemon
- 30 mm oil of patchouli
- 1½ ounces oil of bergamot
- 2 drams oil of lemon
- 4 drams oil of lavender
- 60 mms oil of sandalwood

- 60 mms oil of snakeroot
- 30 mms oil of neroli
- 1 ounce tincture of storax
- 1½ ounces extract of orris root (fluid)
- 12 grams musk
- 30 fluid ounces alcohol

Combine the above ingredients and let sit for sixty days, shaking the solution daily. The result resembles Hoyt's Cologne.[71]

Iron Water

Iron water can be used as an offering to Joe Feray or Ogun. It can be used in any works where you need protection and defense. To make, put 3/4 pound of new iron nails in a large glass bottle with ½ pint of water. Let sit for eight days, then add one more quart water. Replenish the bottle with water as it is used.

Jockey Club Cologne

Jockey Club is unquestionably the most famous New Orleans gambling recipe. Its origin actually lies with the famous French perfumer, Jean-Baptiste Rigaud. In 1852, Rigaud began his career in the world of perfumery with a renowned pharmacist, Monsieur Grimault, and opened his perfumery in the rue Vivienne with the name Parfumerie Victoria as a tribute to the Queen of England. This was a calculated business move, as the French aristocracy in Paris was infatuated with anything English at the time.

> "A great perfumer … is not only the one who succeeds in creating a fine perfume, but who also manages to transform into fragrance some of life's most poetic manifestations."
>
> —Jean-Baptiste Rigaud

Guided by his imagination and fueled by unbridled enthusiasm, Rigaud decided to travel the world in search of new scents from exotic lands. He quickly realized the fascination and emotion these provocative new scents could awaken in Europe's fine ladies.

The names of the scents he supplied to his clientele had a decidedly English sound: "Kiss Me Quick," "Jockey Club," "Bouquet Victoria." He explained his approach in these terms: "In founding a perfumery house, my aim was higher than simply to engage in the ordinary commerce of perfumery. . . . I therefore hit upon the idea that

---

71 *American Pharmaceutical and Druggist Record*, Vol. 33, American Druggist Publishing Co., 1898.

introducing a new aromatic plant would be like adding a new note to my keyboard, as it were, and that only on that condition would I be able to create new products bearing the stamp of originality."[72]

Later, these names became exploited by the hoodoo marketeers and fast became staples for believers. Jockey Club was adopted for use in hoodoo for luck at the race tracks and other games of chance. It is also used for good luck and success in money matters. It is considered by many to be the definitive, old-time barber shop scent. As with many of the colognes, there are a number of formulas available. Below are two, according to Askinson.

Jockey Club (French Formula)

- 1 ounce oil of bergamot
- 3 pints extract of jasmine
- 2 quarts extract of rose
- 1 quart extract of tuberose
- ½ pint tincture of civet
- 1 ounce oil of mace

Use the above ingredients in the strength that suits you. Mix with distilled water to make a wonderful cologne.

Jockey Club (English Formula)

- 1 pint extract of jasmine
- ¾ pint tincture of ambergris
- 1 ½ pints extract of rose
- ¾ pint extract of tuberose
- 3 pints tincture of orris root
- 1 ½ pints essence of rose (triple)
- ¾ ounce oil of bergamot

Use the above ingredients in the strength that suits you. Mix with distilled water to make a wonderful cologne.

---

72 See *www.rigaud-paris.com/history* for more information about Jean-Baptiste Rigaud.

K Water (Bouquet Canang)

Another exotic flower essence was added to Jean-Baptiste Rigaud's innovative accomplishments—the Kananga flower of Japan, more commonly known as ylang ylang. Charmed by the mysterious legend of this flower, Jean-Baptiste made it a brand in its own right, symbolized by a Japanese girl holding a Kananga branch in her right hand. Eau de Kananga, created in 1869, quickly became a great sensation throughout Europe and the United States.[73]

Formula for Bouquet Canang:

Note that one minim equals 1/480 fluid ounce.

- 45 minims ylang ylang oil
- 15 minims rose oil
- 5 minims cassie oil
- ½ minim almond oil
- 1 fluid ounce tincture of orris rhizome
- 3 fluid drachms tincture of storax
- 3 grains grain musk
- 1 grain civet
- 3 (chopped) tonka beans
- 9 fluid ounces alcohol

Mix, digest one month, then filter. The result will be a very delicious perfume.

Formula for Kananga Water:

- 10 minims oil of ylang ylang
- 5 minims oil of neroli
- 5 minims oil of rose
- 3 minims oil of bergamot
- 10 ounces alcohol
- One grain of musk (optional)

Dilute with distilled water to make a toilet water.[74]

---

73 Ibid.
74 From "Manual of Formulas, Recipes, Methods, and Secret Processes" edited by Raymond B. Wailes, Popular Science Publishing Co., New York, 1932.

Four Thieves Vinegar

Four Thieves Vinegar is a classic formula for use in banishing people, sending people away, or making family members fight amongst themselves. One trick is to dab a little on the doorknob of someone you want to go away.

- 1 gallon cider vinegar
- 1 ounce rosemary
- 1 ounce wormword
- 1 ounce lavender
- 1 ounce powdered camphor
- 1 ounce sage
- 1 ounce peppermint
- 1 ounce lemongrass
- 1 ounce rue

Mix everything in an airtight jar and set aside for six weeks. Strain the liquid into another container to bottle your homemade Four Thieves Vinegar.

Rapid preparation: Mix everything in an airtight container and heat in boiling water for four minutes for four days, beginning on a Monday. On the fourth day, strain the liquid and bottle your Four Thieves Vinegar.

Magickal Gypsy Water

Here's a recipe for Gypsy Water, which was used as a cure-all for just about anything, from mouthwash to hair rinse to astringent to foot soak. It also works nicely as spiritual water for blessing your sacred space. It calls for lavender or rose essential oils. I prefer rose for this recipe, and since rose essential oil is cost-prohibitive, rose absolute does the trick very nicely. Put the following in a large mason jar:

- 6 parts lemon balm
- 4 parts chamomile
- 1 part rosemary
- 3 parts calendula
- 4 parts rose
- 1 part lemon peel
- 1 part sage
- 3 parts comfrey leaf
- Vinegar to cover

- Rose water or witch hazel to cover
- Rose absolute
- Sage essential oil

Use fresh herbs if you can get them. If not, dry will do. Then cover the mixture with the vinegar. Let it sit in a warm spot for two to three weeks. Then strain the liquid and add one cup of rose water per one cup of vinegar. Add several drops of rose absolute until you get the strength of the fragrance you like. I also add a few drops of sage essential oil. Keep the jar sealed tightly when not using, and the fragrance should last indefinitely. Put some in a spray bottle for misting your sacred space.

Marie Laveau's Peace Water or Five Holy Waters

Marie Laveau's Peace Water is said to be the combination of water from five sources. The sources of water she may have used can be determined with some degree of accuracy given the geography of New Orleans and the bodies of water in the surrounding area, and the areas in which she is said to have performed her rituals. The following recipe is an educated guess based on this reasoning. If you do not live in the New Orleans area, I have provided a more generic formula as well.

Marie Laveau's Peace Water

- Holy water from a Catholic church
- Water from Bayou St. John
- Water from Lake Ponchartrain
- Water from the Mississippi river
- Rain water

Blend the five waters altogether, with no fragrance and no oil.

Five Holy Waters

- River water
- Rain water
- Ocean water
- Spring water
- Holy water

Blend the five waters altogether, with no fragrance and no oil.

Sea Water

Some conjure works in the South call for salt water, which is readily available in the Gulf of Mexico. If you do not live close to the sea, here is a recipe for sea water that so closely resembles actual sea water that it will actually support marine life in an aquarium.[75]

- 81 grams table salt
- 7 grams epsom salts
- 10 grams magnesium chloride
- 2 grams potassium chloride
- 3 to 4 liters of water

Spirit Water (Eau Spiritueuse d' Anis)

This traditional water is used for ancestral works, for summoning spirits of the dead, and in Spiritualist work such as when performing séances. A clear glass of crystal is filled with the water and placed on the altar or medium's table. The proportions are according to an official formulary and will have to be reduced to suit your needs. You will have to do the math. Here is the original formula and proportions.

- 16 ounces angelica seed
- 6 ounces anise
- 8 pounds brandy

Bruise the seeds, and combine with the brandy for a few days, taking care to gently swirl the solution daily. Add to distilled water to dilute. The resulting liquid will be cloudy upon blending the water and alcohol.

War Water or Water of Mars

For a potent weapon for battling enemies, mix up a batch of this old-time traditional New Orleans War Water recipe.

- Oil of tar
- Rusty nails
- Swamp water

---

75 *The Scientific American Cyclopedia of Receipts, Notes and Queries* edited by Albert Allis Hopkins, 1901.

Combine all of the above ingredients in a wide-mouth mason jar and shake up the mixture. Let it sit for a couple of weeks, periodically opening the jar to encourage oxidation and further rusting of the nails in the water. After a period of time, the water will get rustier and blacker, making it all the more potent.

Water of Notre Dame

Water of Notre Dame can be sprayed about the home to make peace and bring blessings. It can also be used to in spells to summon spirits, cleansing spells, and uncrossings spells.

- Holy water
- White rosewater
- Violet hydrosol
- Little John the Conqueror root

Mix the above ingredients and add to a spray bottle. Keep the bottle on your altar or on or near your Bible.

CHAPTER ELEVEN

SPIRITUAL BATHS

Spiritual or ritual bathing is a good way to cleanse not only your physical body, but your spiritual body as well. Ritual bathing is recommended whenever you expect to encounter negativity, fatigue, depression, anxiety, or fear of any kind. It can also be performed to fortify the spirit following a negative experience. Often, spiritual baths take place before other works, and they can be taken every season to refortify and rebalance your spirit.

Ritual bathing is done with any number of washes and bath salts made with special herbs and colors specific to the purpose at hand. There are a couple of things that are important to do when preparing a ritual bath. Some of these are discussed on the following section.

Preparing the Ingredients

There are a few guidelines for preparing herbs and other ingredients for ritual bathing. First, *herbs are never boiled*. Rather, they are placed in a bowl and hot water is poured over them. They are allowed to steep for fifteen minutes, and the water is then strained and allowed to cool. The cooling down period is when the water becomes "charged" with its medicinal powers.

Secondly, *roots, nuts, barks, and beans are boiled for about thirty minutes in a cast iron pot*. Be sure not to use aluminum or metallic pots for this purpose. The wash should be brownish in color.

To prepare flowers and fresh herbs, gently tear, rub in the palms, and place in cool water. While doing this, you should be praying for the desired effect. The herbs and flowers are then strained from the water, which should have a green tint. This wash is referred to as the Green Blood of the Earth, which refreshes and revitalizes all that comes in contact with it.

Basic Guidelines for Taking a Spiritual Bath

Guidelines for ritual bathing are as follows:

1. Wake up before dawn and draw your water. Fill the tub with warm water, not hot.

2. Always bless the water before getting into the tub. You can do this through prayer or invocation of the loas, saints, and orishas of the healing waters in a manner that is meaningful to you.

3. As you get into the tub, soak yourself from head to toe while naming your problems. To remove negativity or crossed conditions, pour the water over your head so that the water runs down your body while you are standing. If drawing something to you, such as love, success, or luck, rub your body in an upward direction only.

4. Spend at least fifteen minutes soaking in the healing water for a ritual bath. You may meditate, visualize a resolution of your problem, sing, or sit in silence. Do whatever feels comforting to you.

5. Save all or a portion of the water for proper disposal.

6. As you let the water go down the drain, visualize your problems washing away. With the last drop of water, say, "So be it."

7. Always clean your tub with saltwater afterwards. Sea salt is best, though regular salt will also do, so long as you have prayed over it. Also, be sure to clean any objects used in the tub with saltwater.

8. Take the leftover water and dispose of it in the direction of the east at or before sunrise.

9. As part of preparing your ritual bath, you may light your favorite incense and light a candle in a color appropriate for the purpose to make the experience especially comforting, effective, and enjoyable.

10. Always take a soap bath prior to a ritual bath. Never use soap, oils, or anything else. Never stay in a ritual bath longer than thirty minutes. Allow your body to air dry to achieve the full effect. Always dress in fresh, clean clothes and sleep on clean, preferably white sheets (see Luisah Teish's *Jambalaya* for more great information about spiritual bathing).

Spiritual Bath Recipes

Three-Ingredient Bath

For relief from bodily aches and pains, try this bath recipe that comes straight from the Louisiana plantation slaves.

- Red oak leaves
- Red brick dust
- Handful of salt

Add ingredients in a large pot and fill halfway with water. Boil these ingredients for three minutes, then add the solution to a warm bath. Soak for thirteen minutes. Throw the remaining water to the east at or before sunrise.

Thirteen-Herb Bath

Use this bath for uncrossing, purification, and protection.

- Five finger grass
- Althea
- Hyssop
- Rue
- Basil
- Angelica
- Mint
- Patchouli
- Lemon verbena
- Dill
- Peony
- Eucalyptus
- Sage

Pour the water over your head thirteen times if removing a crossed condition or general negativity. Rub the water in an upward direction if in need of protection. Repeat this bath daily for thirteen days. Throw the remaining water to the east at or before sunrise.

Basic Spiritual Bath

Add 2 to 4 ounces of Florida Water Cologne to the bath water.

Basic Hoodoo Bath

To make a simple bath for any condition, simply add a handful of epsom salts and a handful of blessed salt to your bath water. Then add a few drops of a conjure oil consistent with your intent.

Blue Bath for Protection

This is good for when you are feeling nervous, stressed out, highly anxious, or paranoid. It will help you feel protected and calm.

- Blue food coloring or indigo laundry bluing balls
- Lavender and rosemary herbs
- Wash with sea shells
- Blue or white candle
- Peace or watermelon incense

Green Bath to Heal Bodily Aches and Pains

This is a recipe my mama would make for us when we were little and sick with cold and flu symptoms. She would go outside and "pick a mess of greens," tie them up in a bundle, and throw the bundle in the bathtub. The bundle consisted of three herbs: plantain, pokeweed, and peppermint. I still remember how refreshing the smell of the peppermint was when I got into the tub. This is an invigorating and healing spiritual bath.

Green Bath for Health and Wealth

This is good for maintaining optimal health.

- Green food coloring
- Heal-all or comfrey herbs
- Wash with white sage leaves or flowers
- Green or brown candle
- Myrrh or bayberry incense

Lucky Gambler's Seven Herb Hand Wash

If you are a regular gambler, you can make up a gallon of this hand wash and keep it in your refrigerator to use right before you go gambling. Wash your hands in the solution to empower your hands for winning.

- Allspice
- Five finger grass
- Peppermint
- Chamomile
- Cinnamon chips
- Irish moss
- Alfalfa

The easiest way to use this hand wash is to fill up your wash basin with enough water to wash your hands. Then add a cup of this mixture to the water and proceed with washing your hands. Do not use soap when doing this. You should wash your hands with soap and water prior to washing your hands with your Lucky Gambler's Seven Herb Hand Wash. Allow your hands to air dry for a lasting effect.

Magickal Bath to Promote and Foster Love

Make a bath with rose blossom cologne, orange blossom cologne, and a cup of yarrow tea.

Magickal Baths to Wash Away Negativity

The following baths are used to rid you of unwanted negative energies. They vary in complexity, some using a single ingredient and others using multiple ingredients.

Bath (1)
- Hyssop
- Rosemary
- Rue
- Rock salt
- Consecrated or holy water
- 1 tablespoon Florida Water Cologne

Bath (2)

- Sweet basil
- 1 tablespoon powdered eggshell
- Consecrated or holy water

Bath (3)

To be used when a person's life and safety are in danger due to a hex or curse. This bath is said to remove very powerful negative spells.

- Blessed thistle
- Boneset
- Clover
- Hyssop
- ¼ teaspoon myrrh
- Vetivert
- 1 cup rock salt
- Consecrated or holy water
- 1 cup goat's milk
- 1 tablespoon powdered eggshell

Bath (4)

To get rid of the negative people in your life, make the following bath.

- 1 teaspoon garlic
- Iron weed
- Rosemary
- Florida Water Cologne
- Consecrated or holy water

Old-Time Conjure Cleansing and Uncrossing Bath

This is a traditional hoodoo recipe to get rid of crossed conditions and remove negativity. It is an extremely simple recipe that uses ingredients readily available from your kitchen, and so it costs only pennies to make.

- ½ cup of blessed salt (table salt or sea salt that has been prayed over with Psalm 23)

- ½ cup of kosher salt
- ¼ cup vinegar

Add the above ingredients to your bath water. Light two white candles on either side of the tub. Stand in the middle of the tub and pray, reciting Psalm 37 or a heartfelt prayer of your own. Using a cup, scoop up a full cup of the water and pour it over your head thirteen times. Each time you do so, say, "Remove this negativity from me." After you have done this, take another cup of the water and set it aside. Drain the rest of the water from your tub and allow yourself to air dry. When you are dry, put on some freshly washed clothes. Then take the water you have set aside and go outside. Facing the east and watching the rising sun, pray again for the removal of the condition. Then, pour the water in that direction.

Purification Bath

Take this bath after you have performed a crossing or other bad work. It must be done in conjunction with Psalm 51.

- Handful of hyssop
- Handful of rue
- Sea salt
- 2 white candles

Stand between the two white candles and light them. Recite Psalm 51 and pour the water over your head. Throw the remaining water to the east at or before sunrise.

Purple Bath for Power

When feeling the need for empowerment or to take control of your life and affairs, take the Purple Bath.

- Blue and red food coloring
- Five finger grass or mustard seed
- Wash with 2 whole eggs (do not break)
- Purple or red candle
- Dragon's Blood or Commanding incense

Red Bath for Courage

This bath is good for when you are feeling tired and lethargic. Do not take a red bath if you are angry, as it will throw you way off balance.

- Red food coloring
- John the Conqueror root or red peppers
- Wash with stones (jasper if available)
- Red or white candle
- Helping Hand or John the Conqueror incense

Road Opener Bath (Abre Camino)

If you have been facing a lot of obstacles in your life and feel stuck and unable to get ahead, then a Road Opener Bath should help. This bath is designed to clear away negative obstructions and open the door for new opportunities. Fill the bathtub with warm water, and add the following ingredients:

- 3 sprigs of rosemary
- 3 cinnamon sticks
- 1 bunch fresh parsley
- Red and white roses
- Coconut oil, Legba Oil, or Road Opener Oil
- White tea light candle

Take this bath every week on a Monday, which is the day sacred to Legba. Burn a white tea light candle each time you bathe.

Simple Ammonia Bath

Add one tablespoon of ammonia to the bath water. This bath should only be used once every three months. You may also add a tablespoon of ammonia to the water you use to wash your clothes on a weekly basis. This insures that your clothing is free from negative energy.

To Remove the Evil Eye

If you have been the victim of someone's jealousy and envy, take the following bath three days in a row. You should feel refreshed, rejuvenated, and fortified immediately afterwards.

- 1 quart of milk
- 3 carnations
- 3 handfuls of blessed salt

Fill your tub with warm water and add the above ingredients. Relax for about fifteen minutes and visualize a fortress of light surrounding you. Allow the water to drain and gather the flower remains. Allow yourself to air dry. Take the carnation remains, along with a small mirror, and bury in your front yard as close to your front door as possible.

White Bath for Purification

This is good for when you feel spiritually dirty, want to cleanse your aura, need spiritual revitalization, or for cold and flu symptoms.

- 2 to 4 cups evaporated milk or powdered milk
- 2 to 4 tablespoons anise
- Wash with sea salt
- White or blue candle
- Coconut or Blessings incense

Yellow Bath for Attraction

This is good for correcting relationships, attracting a lover, or for skin conditions.

- Yellow food coloring
- Parsley and yarrow flowers
- Wash with honey
- Yellow or orange candle
- Patchouli or cinnamon incense

CHAPTER TWELVE

ŊEW ORLEAŊS GRIS GRIS

"The gregories bee things of great esteem amongst them, for the most part they are made of leather of severall fashions, wonderous neatly, they are hollow, and within them is placed, and sowed up close, certaine writings, or spels which they receive from their Mary-buckes, whereof they conceive such a religious respect, that they do confidently believe no hurt can betide them whilst these gregories are about them."

—Richard Jobson, 1623

Gris gris (pronounced *gree-gree*) is a term used to describe the type of religi-omagical system practiced by folks in the New Orleans Voodoo tradition. According to the New Orleans Voodoo Museum, the etymology of the word *gris gris* (gerregerys) derives from the Mande language groups a little to the north of Benin in what are today Senegal and Mali. With the transatlantic slave trade, the term became part of the Louisiana Voodoo lexicon.[76] With its pronunciation so close to the French word *gris* meaning "gray," and given the influence of French on the language and culture in New Orleans, it stands to reason that this is why gris gris is commonly translated as "gray gray." And because gray denotes that which is between black and white, it also refers to the kinds of ingredients used in the creation of gris gris.

The term *gris gris*, like the word *hoodoo*, is a noun and a verb. The gris gris is the magick and the act of creating the charm, which can be in the form of a bag, doll, or powder (among other things). The person doing the gris gris is often called a gris gris man or woman. The resulting object is essentially a portable charm, prayer, or spell. As I explain it in my book, *Voodoo Dolls in Magick and Ritual,* gris gris is a form of talismanic magick and is based on principles of sympathetic and contagious magic. In the case of sympathetic

---

76 *www.voodoomuseum.com/index.php?option=com_content&view=article&id=33&Itemid=29*

magic, an object is created in the likeness of the person for whom the gris gris is intended. Most commonly, this type of gris gris is in the form of a doll. Contagious magick occurs when something belonging to the person for whom the gris gris is intended is added to the gris gris, such as a lock of hair, fingernails, or a piece of clothing. The personal item provides a magical link from the physical to the spiritual world of the person; thus, the gris gris is believed to influence that person's life in a very specific way.

In the New Orleans tradition, there's a gris gris for anything and everything. Usually, gris gris is likened to a mojo bag and that is the extent of it. Most of the time it is mispronounced (please . . . the "s" is silent!). I was always taught that gris gris is whatever mixture of herbs and common household ingredients you concoct and whatever words you write and speak for whatever situation that arises. Gris gris can be a combination of powdered minerals, herbs, graveyard dust, roots, bones, and sacred words and seals written on paper with magickal ink. It can be used as a powder thrown in the path of an enemy, in an amulet or gris gris bag, in a doll, mixed with water and drunk, or used in a magickal bath. In the distant past, gris gris even included lethal powders and poisons. Whatever the form and method of deployment, gris gris is a complete religiomagical system that has remained relatively intact in New Orleans as it came from Africa by the first Senegambian slaves in the early 1720s. This makes it not only a unique characteristic of New Orleans Voodoo, but also an important aspect of New Orleans cultural history.

Between 1726 and 1731, thirteen slave ships arrived in French Louisiana; all but one from Senegambia. The others were from the Congo region and Benin (including Whydah, where the serpent aspect of the New Orleans Voodoo religion originates). Many of the major crops grown in Louisiana in the eighteenth century were brought from the Senegal valley—rice, corn, cotton, indigo, peas, and tobacco, to name a few. While the Africans learned much from the Native Americans about local botany and healing herbs, many of them, especially the Bambaran males, possessed knowledge of the plants, herbs, and roots, and knew how to create poisons, charms, amulets, and wangas.[77] All of the introduced plants were integrated into Louisiana commerce and Cajun and Creole cuisine, as well as in gris gris magick and the New Orleans Voodoo hoodoo formulary. The popular myth that the Africans knew nothing of the botany of the region is debunked by historical evidence.

Some of the Africans who came to Louisiana were actually Muslim, and their religious leaders, called *marabouts*, made their living in Africa by teaching chil-

---

77   Hall, 1992.

dren and making gris gris. Even today, one can find folks wearing gris gris as a sort of amulet that is prepared by the marabout among the Senegalese. It is typically worn around the neck on a leather cord, around the waist in cases of infertility, and around the head, arms, and ankles according to the purpose of the gris gris. It is contained in elaborately etched or plain leather pouches that have either handsewn or handwritten text from the Koran inside them along with special numbers with mystical meanings. They are blessed with holy water and specific prayers are said over them before they are given to the wearer.[78] The marabout directs energy released through the spoken word towards a specific end. This energy is consequently attached to the gris gris amulet which may be held in secret or displayed publicly.

In terms of ethnicity, most (but not all) of the slaves who arrived in Louisiana were Bambara, a Mande people with a strong tradition of oral history. The Bambara resisted Islam and maintained their traditional culture and religion. Among them were the official storytellers, who helped preserve their culture by passing on the myths and legends of their cosmology via oral tradition. Both Muslim and non-Muslim Africans, however, utilized gris gris as part of their religious systems.

References to gris gris used by New Orleans slaves can be found in historical documents dating from as early as 1734. It was observed that when the slaves arrived in Louisiana, they did not want to part with their fetishes, charms, and gris gris. Even as they settled into the camps located in what is now the Algiers section of New Orleans, many of their illnesses could only be cured by African and indigenous healers. Some colonists turned to the Africans for healing certain illnesses; other colonists accused slaves of poisoning their masters and various commanders of the colonies. While the courts would not allow for the "superstitions" of the Africans, they nonetheless punished those believed to be poisoners, stating "perhaps it is poisons that do all the damage attributed to sorcery."[79]

Actually, the colonists had good reason to fear the African's gris gris. It was routinely used as a weapon of war, as well as a protective defense. Because of the marabouts and their occult skills and military traditions, gris gris played an important role in numerous slave revolts as well as in the Haitian revolution.[80] One example of a gris gris poison was described by Dieterlen. Apparently, the Komo would dip the talons of a bird of prey into mud, snake venom, and ground copper. Even a small wound from talons covered with this mixture was reputed to cause death. Wade Davis and Bernard Diederich confirm that slaves in St.

---

78 Walter & Fridman, 2004.
79 Superior Council, 1729.
80 Diouf, S. A. (1998). Servants of Allah: African Muslims enslaved in the Americas. New York: NYU Press.

Domingue (now Haiti) and New Orleans made lethal powders from animal and plant matter during the eighteenth century.[81]

There are a couple of other things to consider about gris gris and why things are done a certain way when it comes to its practice. Numbers and colors are significant. A person skilled in the gris gris tradition should be knowledgable in other occult arts such as numerology, divination, geomancy, astrology, and astronomy. When making gris gris charms, for example, you don't just put any number of things into it (as some purport to do with mojo bags). Everything goes into a gris gris for a purpose, and that purpose is closely related to the original Bambara cosmology and/or Islamic tradition. The number three, for example, is the minimum number of ingredients in a gris gris charm. According to traditional Bambara cosmology, the number three represents the male aspect (two testicles and a penis), while the number four represents the female (the four lips). The number seven is the perfect number, because it signifies the androgynous unity of the male and female principles. According to Islamic tradition, the number five refers to the Five Pillars, the five prayers, and the five holy persons

(Mohammed, Aliu, Fatima, Hasan, and Useyn). The latter is often written to resemble an outspread hand, with each name on a finger, as a gris gris that protects against the evil eye.[82]

Let's take a look at the personal effects that are utilized in gris gris: hair, fingernails, and so on. Hair is not just a "personal effect;" it holds a much deeper significance when it comes to working gris gris. Hair represents an important part of the soul called *ni*. When you take a piece of a person's hair and work gris gris with it, you are working with a sympathetic link to that person's soul. Cowry shells are significant because they were not only used as currency and decoration, but are sacred today because they come from the deep waters from the bed of Faro, the androgynous water spirit whose job it was to reinstate harmony between the sexes. This reverence to the earth as Mother and sacredness is one of many beliefs that were held in common by the Africans and the Native Americans.

The importance of the materials used to write the words of power, seals, or symbols used in gris gris should not be underestimated. The marabout travelled the world in order to obtain the paper and ink that was required for transcribing words of power into their gris gris. Sometimes these words of power were deliber-

---

81 See Wade Davis and Bernard Diederich, 1983.
82 Diouf, S. A. (1998). *Servants of Allah: African Muslims enslaved in the Americas*. New York: NYU Press.

ately written illegibly so that their secrets could be preserved. The adoption of the use of magickal alphabets in the gris gris of New Orleans as a means of cloaking petitions may have developed for similar reasons.

The multitudes of enslaved Africans from the Kongo (called Bakongo) brought with them other spiritual and graphic communication in the form of symbols and traditional graphic writing systems. Over time, these writing systems were reconstructed through the Diaspora experience and seemingly replaced the written Arabic texts. The creation of gris gris can entail the "calling down" of the spirit into the charm through the use of ritual symbols in conjunction with words of power. The sacred ritual symbols of the Voodoo spirits are found in the Vévés of Haitian Vodou and New Orleans Voodoo, the Firmas in the Palo Mayombe religion found in Cuba, and Ponto Riscados of the Kongo and Yoruba-based Umbanda religion in Brazil.

Vévés found in Haitian Vodou and New Orleans Voodoo draw upon cultural components of both Vodún in Benin and Togo and the Kongo in West and central Africa. Vévés are drawn as conduits through which the powers of the various Voodoo spirits are manifested in ritual. Vévés are often added to gris gris in New Orleans Voodoo when the assistance of specific spirits are needed. *Firma* means "signature" in Spanish. Firmas are graphic representations of the individual characteristics of the various spirits, and are used to define sacred space and to call the spirits into that space. They are also used in divination and to communicate with ancestral spirits. In Umbanda, Ponto Riscados define sacred space and the spiritual boundaries of the various spirits, and are a graphic tradition with origins in the Kongo and Yoruba cultures. Each of these symbolic writing systems is evidence of the lasting influence of Bakongo culture in the West.

How to Make a Gris Gris Bag

Gris gris is a system of magick that is on a continuum of intent and purpose. As in the past, gris gris continues to be used to assist in all matters of living and as charms of empowerment, whatever the intent. What follows is just a short primer on the basics of fixing a gris gris bag. Once you know the basics, the rest is up to you.

Traditionally, a gris gris bag is a 2-inch by 3-inch drawstring bag made out of red flannel, chamois, or leather. Special herbs, stones, personal effects, roots, bones, coins, metal lucky charms, crystals, good luck tokens, carved stones, and European seals and sigils that have been written with magickal ink on parchment paper are placed inside the bag. Other colors can also be used, according to their magickal symbolism. You should only put an odd number of items into your gris gris bag; never less than three and never more than thirteen. The items are blessed as they are placed into the bag and the whole bag is dressed with anointing oil or holy water. It is then smudged in incense of some kind, words of power are spoken into it, and it is breathed upon. These rituals are said to activate the magick of the gris gris.

In New Orleans, gris gris is often hidden from public view. It is always ritually prepared in front of an altar and consecrated to the four elements: earth, fire, water, and air. Here are a few rules of thumb to remember when "fixing" a gris gris bag:

1. Gris gris can be created on the cardinal points of the Kongo cosmogram.

2. Color symbolism is important. Choose a color specific to your need.

3. Gris gris must contain an odd number of items: more than three, never more than thirteen.

4. It must be filled with items that are specific to the desired purpose.

5. It must be dressed with a liquid of some kind.

6. Be very careful of the words you speak when making gris gris. Your words create energy that will become a part of the gris gris itself.

7. Each ingredient can be smudged (asperged) or smoked in incense, and so can the final bag.

8. A petition written in a magickal alphabet or a magickal seal or sigil drawn on a piece of parchment paper with a magickal ink is placed or sewn into the bag. Magick squares and other talismans can also be added to gris gris bags.

9. Words of power are spoken over the bag as a means of activating the divine energy.

10. The final act is to breathe upon the gris gris to give it life.

To create a gris gris, you should set up a basic gris gris altar. This altar should contain the four elements already mentioned: a bowl of water to represent the element water, incense to represent the element air, a bowl of graveyard dirt to represent the element earth, and a candle flame to represent the element fire. These elements can be arranged according to the Kongo cosmogram, a powerful symbol in Kongo cosmology. The cross pattern represents the crossroads; the division of the spiritual world from the earthly world at a sacred point which is the center. It is a circular cosmology, reflecting the belief that the journey of life is a continuous process as opposed to a beginning (birth) and an end (death). The four cardinal points of the Kongo cosmogram are read counterclockwise, starting at the bottom or southern point and going east, north, and west. Place the graveyard dirt at the bottom or southern point, which is where birth occurs and also where the container of our ancestors resides; the candle is placed in the east where the transformation of the individual begins as a full member of society; the incense is placed in the northern direction, the point of intellectual power; and the bowl of water is placed in the west, where comprehension, understanding, and the point of departure takes place. The gris gris itself should be placed in the center of the crossroads design and created on the center point of the cosmogram. Note that there are other interpretations of the cardinal points and the one I have given is the one of my understanding.

Magickal Alphabets

While the marabout use passages from the Koran, New Orleans Voodooists will use one of the many magickal alphabets to write a petition to place into a bag of gris gris. Some individuals of Christian persuasion may use passages from the Bible or one of the psalms. The Theban alphabet, also known as the Witch's alphabet, is a particular favorite among New Orleans practitioners. I have provided an overview of several magickal alphabets; the one you choose to use, should you want to use one, is entirely up to you. Do note, however, that some of these alphabets were designed with specific purposes in mind. Consider the intent of your work and the intent of the magickal alphabet you use in order to keep the energy of your work strong and focused.

For a more in-depth discussion on the various magickal alphabets, see my book, *13 Proven Magickal Alphabets*, which is part of Planet Voodoo's *Applied Magick Handbook* series.

Theban Alphabet

Though the Theban alphabet is a writing system with disputed origins, it emerged when Kabalistic studies were prominent in medieval European magic. First published in Johannes Trithemius' *Polygraphia* (1518), the alphabet was attributed to Honorius of Thebes. For this reason, it is also referred to as the Honorian alphabet or the Runes of Honorius, even though the Theban alphabet is not a runic alphabet. On the other hand, Trithemius' student Agrippa (1486–1535) attributed the alphabet to Pietro d'Abano (1250–1316).[83] Despite its unknown origin, it is called the Witch's alphabet because it has been used in various forms of witchcraft as a means of cloaking magickal writings, talismanic inscriptions, and magickal spells.

---

83   Heinrich Cornelius Agrippa (1531). *Three Books of Occult Philosophy.*

This alphabet is ideal for writing on candles, parchment paper, the leaves of herbs, stones, wood, or bark for use in gris gris or mojo bags.

The Theban alphabet is relatively easy to learn because there is a one to one correspondence with the letters of the Latin alphabet with the exception of the letters J, U, and W. To use the omitted letters, use these simple substitutions.

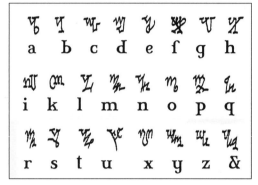

Latin Letter	Theban Letter
J	I
U	V
W	VV

Enochian Alphabet

According to Tobias Churton in his text *The Golden Builders*,[84] the concept of an angelic language was common during the sixteenth century. It was believed that a person could interact with the angels if they could communicate with them through the written word. The court astrologer and magician Dr. John Dee (1527-1608) and his associate, Sir Edward Kelly (1555-1597) claimed that angels revealed to them a special language that they recorded in their journals as an alphabet. This alphabet became known as the Enochian alphabet because Dee claimed that the last human to know the language before he and Kelly was the biblical patriarch Enoch. Apparently, Dee preferred to describe the language in terms other than Enochian, such as First Language of God-Christ, the Holy Language, Celestial Speech, the Language of Angels, or Adamical.

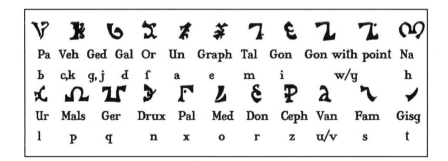

---

84 Churton, T. (2002). *The Golden Builders*. Signal Publishing.

According to Abrahamic traditions, the Adamic language was the language spoken by Adam and Eve in the Garden of Eden. As with all claims of a magickal and mystical nature, linguists have questioned the Enochian alphabet's construction; nonetheless, it has proven to be a workable alphabet for use in magick.[85]

Typically, the Enochian alphabet is used in the practice of Enochian magic on Enochian calls or keys, which are used to call angels. The alphabet can also be used to write petitions designed to invoke the blessings and intervention of angelic beings in the making of gris gris.

Alphabet of the Magi

Another example of an angelic alphabet of the sixteenth century is the Alphabet of the Magi. This alphabet was created by Theophrastus Bombastus von Hohenheim (also known as Paracelsus), who was more than likely influenced by the Hebrew script, as well as the various magickal alphabets from older grimoires of the time. Paracelsus was a Renaissance physician, botanist, alchemist, astrologer, and general occultist.[86] He is said to have engraved the names of angels on talismans for the treatment of various illnesses and for divine protection. Given its original purpose, use this alphabet for gris gris works that involve health and healing, protection, and spiritual defense.

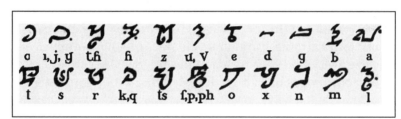

Gris Gris Charms

Following are a few examples of gris gris charms that you can make for a variety of purposes. Because gris gris is a highly intuitive magickal system, you should try a few of these and get the feel for how it is done. Then, use your intuition, along with your knowledge of the plants, herbs, and minerals, for making your own gris gris. Remember, gris gris is not confined to a bag. Some gris gris is merely a powder or a potion. Sometimes it can be made into a doll.

---

85   See Donald Laycock, "Enochian: Angelic language or mortal folly?," 19-64 in *The Complete Enochian Dictionary*.
86   Allen G. Debus, "Paracelsus and the medical revolution of the Renaissance" - A 500th Anniversary Celebration from the National Library of Medicine (1993), p. 3.

Gris gris should be assembled in the middle of your gris gris altar, the ingredients asperged with incense and if made as a bag, tied shut using hemp string, wax thread, or leather cording.

Come to Me Gris Gris

Create this charm to make someone you love return to you, or to draw someone you desire to you.

- 2 x 3 or 3 x 4 red flannel bag
- Pinch of damiana
- Queen Elizabeth root
- Red clover
- Magnetic sand
- Come to Me Oil
- Personal concern
- Handwritten petition of your name and your lover's name written in Theban

During a full or waxing moon, burn a red candle while making this gris gris bag. Burn Come to Me Incense as well. Add each of the ingredients to the red flannel bag, one by one. With each ingredient added, focus strongly on your desire. Sprinkle the magnetic sand over the other ingredients. Add seven drops of Come to Me Oil. Tie up the gris gris with some string. Once you have done this, hold the gris gris bag to your mouth and breathe life into it. This activates the gris gris. For added power, leave the gris gris out under the full moon and allow the candle to burn all the way down. In the morning, retrieve the gris gris bag and keep it with you every day, carrying it on your left side, in your pocket or in your bra. Reanoint the bag every Friday to recharge the gris gris. Discard the remains of the candle wax at a crossroads or in a garbage can that is not your own.

Fast Luck Gris Gris Charm

For this gris gris you will need some Fast Luck Oil. You can use the yellow Fast Luck Oil or the Algiers formula, both of which are provided in the chapter on magickal oils. This gris gris is good for folks playing games of chance, or those who are in need of luck in a hurry. For this charm you will need:

- Red flannel bag
- 1 whole nutmeg
- 1 buckeye nut
- Fast Luck Oil
- Yellow offertory candle
- Green offertory candle
- Five finger grass
- Peppermint
- Cinnamon
- Juniper
- Patchouli
- Personal effect or written petition
- Dollar bill

Anoint the buckeye nut, dollar bill, and the whole nutmeg with Fast Luck Oil. Set these between the yellow and green offertory candles and light the candles. Focus on your intent for thirteen minutes, staring at the candle flame. Let the candles burn out completely and then add the buckeye nut, dollar bill, and whole nutmeg to the red flannel bag along with the other ingredients. Dress the whole bag with Fast Luck Oil. If you are having great financial troubles or are a regular gambler, recharge your bag weekly on Friday by setting the bag on a mound of cinnamon sugar and anointing with Fast Luck Oil. Hang the gris gris above the doorway to bring luck fast into your life. Alternately, you can wear it around your neck from a leather cord, or in your pocket, on the right side if a man and on the left side if a woman.

Get Even Gris Gris Doll

This is an example of how to make and use a gris gris doll. It is a creepy little revenge spell from my book, *The Voodoo Doll Spellbook: A Compendium of Ancient and Contemporary Spells and Rituals, Vol. I.*

Create a small doll baby out of black fabric. Stuff the doll with saffron, salt, gunpowder, graveyard dirt, powdered dog manure, and crumpled newspaper from the obituary section. You can also write your target's name in the Theban alphabet and put it inside the doll. Place the doll near your enemy—under their front porch, in their dresser drawer, in their purse, in the kitchen cabinets. Be sure to be discreet. Your target will surely suffer three times the anguish they have caused you.[87]

Gris Gris Bag for Money Blessings

- 3 x 3 piece of green flannel
- 1 whole nutmeg
- Piece of pyrite
- Magnetic sand
- Fast Luck oil or
  Money Drawing oil
- Allspice berries
- Cinnamon
- Alfalfa
- Irish moss
- Fenugreek seeds
- Pine resin

As you can see from the list above, there are nine ingredients in this gris gris (the anointing oil does not count as an ingredient). If you plan on trying this one, I would encourage you to add two to four more items that belong to you and that

---

87 From *The Voodoo Doll Spellbook: A Compendium of Ancient and Contemporary Spells and Rituals* by Denise Alvarado, 2010.

are related to your finances—for example, a dollar bill and a check that you have filled out for the amount of money you want or need.

Lay out the green flannel square. Light some Money Drawing incense while you fix this gris gris. I like to burn cedar or sage and smudge each item with the smoke before putting it onto the flannel square. The last ingredient to be put into the bag is the magnetic sand—sprinkle it over the other ingredients. Tie up the gris gris with some string. Some folks will use yarn, but yarn is typically found on gris gris bags made for tourists. The last step is to anoint the bag with Fast Luck or Money Drawing Oil and pray Psalm 23 (or substitute another prayer or words of power). Once you have done this, hold the gris gris bag to your mouth and breathe life into it. This activates the gris gris. Then do the following spell.

Simple Money Spell

Light a green candle. Hold your gris gris bag and concentrate on it. Then repeat the following phrase over and over until you feel it starting to work.

> I will the energy contained within this candle and contained in this bag
> to heal, harmonize, and balance my being.
> May the magic of money flow freely through my life.
> I attract money like a magnet.
> I am open and receptive to all prosperity.
> May light and love surround and protect me in all of my endeavors.
> As I will it, so will it be . . .

Remember that the entire ritual is the gris gris, not just the bag. The gris gris is the magick; it is the act of creating the charm; and it is the resulting bag as well.

Gris Gris Charm to Banish Anxiety and Fear

For anyone who is experiencing a lack of confidence or anxiety, try this gris gris charm. It is wonderful for people in new positions of employment, before tests, during life transitions, and during adolescence.

- Yellow flannel
- Gold lodestone
- Magenetic sand
- Orange peels
- Mimosa oil or blossoms
- Lemon balm
- Personal effects

Make this gris gris during a full or waxing moon. Burn a yellow candle that has been anointed with Crown of Success Oil and visualize yourself as strong, confident, and knowing. Repeat this ritual every month on a Sunday, being sure to reannoint your bag as well as your forehead and heart areas. Hang the gris gris above the doorway to banish fear and anxiety. Alternately, you can wear it around your neck from a leather cord, or in your pocket, on the right side if a man and on the left side if a woman.

Gris Gris for Good Luck

Here is an old gris gris charm reported by Pitkin that was reportedly for good luck. It shows how gris gris is very adaptable to whatever is available at the moment for the individual in need, and certainly does not require the purchase of any expensive ingredients. Still, all of the ingredients are not specific, so it is a good example of how one can creatively adapt what is at hand and even figure out what may have been used during the early 1900s as ingredients in good luck gris gris. According to Pitkin, this charm contained:

- 50 black pepper seeds
- Spice
- Glistening mineral-like polished lead but brittle as coal
- Flakes of dried herbs
- Crumbs of moldy bread
- A wisp of hair
- Half of a white bean
- Tarnished brass medal of St. Benedict
- Rose colored flannel

Obviously, these ingredients are subject to substitution. For example, what is meant by a "glistening mineral-like polished lead but brittle as coal"? For this ingredient, I would substitute a lodestone, because a lodestone will attract good luck due to its magnetic properties. What about the spice? This could be cinnamon or nutmeg, two spices that were popular in conjure during this time period (and still are). The flakes of dried herbs would be of a variety that contains money-drawing properties, but are also readily available—like mint, parsley, or collard greens. The white bean would likely be a navy bean or a great white northern bean, as opposed to a black-eyed pea (black-eyed peas are used in whole form). The other two varieties have been popular in Cajun and Creole cuisine for a long time. Finally, the wisp of hair should be from the person for whom the charm is made. All of the ingredients are wrapped in a red flannel bag and tied shut. The entire charm should be soaked in rum every Friday while making the sign of the cross. (The exception to this was Good Friday, when the recharging ritual was not considered necessary.) Hang the gris gris above the doorway draw good luck into your home. Alternately, you can wear it around your neck from a leather cord, or in your pocket, on the right side if a man and on the left side if a woman.

Gris Gris Powder to Break Up a Couple

A special gris gris powder reportedly used by Marie Laveau for breaking up couples.

- Gunpowder
- Mud from a dirt dauber nest
- Flax seed
- Cayenne pepper
- Bb shots
- File
- Bluestone
- Dragon's blood resin

The above ingredients are mixed together and thrown on the front steps of the more undesirable of the two people to keep that person away from the other.

Gris Gris to Remove an Enemy

Here's a powerful gris gris for taking down enemies: grind up some snake sheds, dirt dauber nests, powdered blue glass, and a little cayenne pepper (oh hell, make it a lot of cayenne pepper), and mix it up real good. Sprinkle it where your target will be walking. If you are not near them, sprinkle some on a photo of your target and wrap everything up in a neat little package, folding the paper away from you, and bind with black thread. Bury it in a cemetery or throw it away in the trash.

Gris Gris to Get a Husband

Take a silver dime and wrap it in a piece of stale bread. Throw the gris gris in the middle of a river. Then go immediately to a church, light a candle, and say a flying novena. A flying novena is a novena said for an emergency. Novenas are typically said over a period of nine days. A flying novena is said every hour for nine hours.

The Flying Novena
O Jesus, who have said: "Ask and you shall receive, seek and you shall find, knock and it shall be opened to you," through the interces-

sion of Mary, Your most Holy Mother, I knock, I seek, I ask that my prayer be granted. (State the request.)

Gris Gris Bag for Protection

- 3 x 4 red flannel bag
- Snake sheds
- Frog bones
- Cigarette ashes
- Horsehairs
- Evil eye bead

Combine everything in the red flannel bag and string an evil eye bead onto the string before tying it shut. Hold the bag in the palm of your hands with both hands closed together, bring the gris gris up to your mouth, and gently blow into the bag to activate it. It will ward off all evil. Hang the gris gris above the doorway to keep evil from entering your home. Alternately, you can wear it around your neck from a leather cord, or in your pocket, on the right side if a man and on the left side if a woman.

Gris Gris to Make a Couple Quarrel

This gris gris is made to be thrown in the path of the people who you want to quarrel. Get some hair from a black cat and a black dog and cut it up until it is very fine. Mix it with salt and pepper, and a little red pepper as well. Throw it down in front of your target's door, on the sidewalk, or next to their car door where they will be sure to walk through it. Soon they will be fighting like cats and dogs.

Protection Gris Gris

Combine the following ingredients in a 2 x 3 red flannel bag to create a powerful gris gris.

- Dried toadstool top
- Camphor
- Piece of High John the Conqueror root
- Powdered jellyfish
- A hand drawn protection talisman

Hold the bag in the palm of your hands with both hands closed together, bring the gris gris up to your mouth, and gently blow into the bag to activate it with your breath.

Soak the gris gris bag in whiskey every Friday to recharge it. Hang the gris gris above the doorway to keep evil from entering your home. Alternately, you can wear it around your neck from a leather cord, or in your pocket, on the right side if a man and on the left side if a woman.

Sweet Glove Gris Gris to Charm a Man

Here is another gris gris attributed to the infamous Voodoo Queen, Marie Laveau. If a woman is in love with a man who has not reciprocated her feelings, the woman is to get one of his gloves and fill it with honey and sugar to sweeten him up, and steel dust to gain power over him. She should then tie the glove closed with red string and sleep with the glove under her mattress every night until her loved one comes to her. A slightly modernized modification of this gris gris is to use honey granules as opposed to honey in its sticky state.

.

CHAPTER THIRTEEN

SACHET POWDERS

Sachet powders are one of the oldest forms of fragrance. Powder perfumes can be traced back many centuries to when the ancients used naturally occurring fragrant flowers, leaves, and woods to perfume their bodies and living quarters. Over time, the art developed—the various naturally fragrant botanicals were ground together and other plant and animal products called *fixatives* were added to the mixtures to enhance and lengthen the life of the fragrance.

Sachet powders are commonly used in hoodoo magick. The word *sachet* actually refers to a small bag or packet that contains a fragrant mixture. As hoodoo became commoditized, the focus expanded to the powder's intent as well as its fragrance. In truth, there is a thin line between many hoodoo powders and gris gris. Certainly there are many that should not be used as perfumes at all. However, all powders can be used in spells, charms, mojo bags and gris gris, dressings letters, job applications, business cards, blends with other powders, dressing candles, and foot track magick. These days, the fragrant powders are utilized as magickal perfumes. One can do many things with sachet powders, such as blowing, sprinkling, dressing, wearing, or drawing diagrams with them. They can be thrown on the ground and used to create magickal boundaries across doorways or around ritual works.

Sachet powders are made in several different ways. Usually the ingredients are ground down to a fine powder or dust and often cut with rice flour or corn starch. Freshly crushed botanicals that are more coarsely ground will retain their fragrance longer than finely ground powders. Herbs are ground by hand using a mortar and pestle, or with a coffee grinder. Then the ingredients are blended together with focus and intent. The higher the quality of the ingredients used, the more effective the final product.

If you plan to make up a batch of powders, you should have a selection of botanicals on hand that function to fix the fragrance of the powders. Some of these include:

- Balsam of Peru
- Orris root
- Gum benzoin
- Calamus root
- Kus Kus (vetivert root)
- Patchouli leaves
- Tonka beans
- Clary sage

This is just a partial list, but it is good to have these botanicals on hand. Just remember their magickal correspondences when adding them to the recipes.

Here are a few recipes to assist you in your conjuring endeavors. Unless otherwise indicated, all ingredients would be ground together and blended well. The addition of any oil should be done after the botanicals are crushed and blended. The suggestions for use are merely suggestions; do not be bound by them. Use your creativity and intuition, as with all magickal works.

Formulas

Adam and Eve Powder

This powder is used to bring together two people, or to heighten or strengthen an existing relationship. It can help draw a couple closer after a fight or conflict as well. To use, sprinkle on the body, bed sheets, and the four corners of the home and bedroom.

- Orris root
- Balm of Gilead buds
- Rose geranium
- Melissa

African Ju Ju Powder

African Ju Ju powder can be used in a number of ways. It can be used to strengthen the power of any work, or as a crossing agent. It can also be used to develop psychic powers and to make a person more intuitive. It's great as an addition to gris gris with corresponding intent.

- Galangal root
- Sandalwood
- Patchouli leaves

Algiers Powder

Used to attract love by dusting the body or adding to a gris gris formula.

- Patchouli
- Orris root
- Vanilla oil

Grind herbs and add to a base of rice flour or corn starch. Mix in a few drops of vanilla oil.

Algiers Fast Luck Powder

This powder is used when you need luck in a hurry. For luck in gambling, dust your hands before going out to play. Dust your body, money, and wallet for luck in general.

- Wintergreen oil
- Patchouli
- Cinnamon

Grind herbs and add to a base of rice flour or corn starch. Mix in a few drops of wintergreen oil.

As You Please Powder

This is a form of commanding and compelling powder. Use to make other people want to please you at all costs. Sprinkle some in the shoes of the person you wish to control, or throw some on the ground where they are sure to walk.

- Orange rinds
- Orange blossoms
- Mint leaves
- Musk oil
- Orris root

Aunt Sally's Dream Powder

Make some of this to have prophetic dreams. Sprinkle on your sheets and inside your pillowcase before going to bed. May also be tossed under and around your bed.

- Licorice
- Cinnamon
- Cardimon
- Coriander

Grind herbs and add to a base of rice flour or corn starch.

Bat's Blood Powder

Use in enemy works and as an effective addition to any left-handed gris gris.

- Cinnamon
- Dragon's blood
- Myrrh

Blessings Powder

This is a great powder to use for cleansing a space and attracting good energy and benevolent spirits. Sprinkle it all around a space, paying close attention to corners, windows, and doorways. Rub a little on your body in order to purify your spirit before holding any ritual.

- Lavender flowers
- Jasmine flowers
- Oil of ylang ylang
- Frankincense gum
- Magnetic sand

Grind herbs, add magnetic sand, and add to a base of sandalwood powder.

Boss Fix Powder

Boss Fix products are double action, meaning they can be used for two specific purposes: to sweeten up an employer; or to dominate that employer. To sweeten up your employer and create harmony in the workplace, use Boss Fix Powder. If you have a supervisor who is harassing you and making your life miserable, or if you are trying to get a promotion or raise, this powder will work wonders. Write your supervisor's name nine times on a piece of torn brown paper from a grocery bag. Turn the paper ninety degrees and cross it with your statement of intent. Sprinkle a little of the powder on the statement. Wear it in your right shoe to "walk on" your boss. You can also sprinkle your boss's office or paperwork where he/she will walk in it on touch it, or sprinkle a little on their chair so they will sit on it. Or, you can dust the doorknob of their door, if they frequently open and close it.

- Tobacco
- Sage
- Chili
- Sugar
- Master root
- Gravel root

Confusion Powder

Use confusion powder to make someone quit meddling in your affairs and to cause their minds to get foggy so they can't think straight.

- A mess of spiderwebs
- Old snake sheds
- Black pepper
- Vetivert

Mix in a base of ground patchouli leaves.

Controlling Powder

Use this powder to make someone do what you want. Blend equal parts:

- Corn starch
- Saltpeter
- Epsom salts

Drawing Powder

Use this powder to draw luck, love, or success to you.

- Corn meal
- Magnetic sand
- Confectioner's sugar

Add to a base of rice flour or corn starch.

Fiery Wall of Protection

Use for protecting yourself and your environment and as an adjunct to any protection work.

- Dragon's blood powder
- Sea salt
- Frankincense
- Myrrh
- Dried chiles
- Cayenne peppers
- Powdered ginger
- Powdered cinnamon
- Black peppercorns

Go Away Powder

This powder is very important: it's the antidote to Follow Me Boy products as well as a general go away powder. If you decide the guy you got to follow you around like a little puppy is just too pitiful for words, but you don't want to hurt his feelings, use this. You can also use it on customers that you want back, but you don't want them nipping at your heels all the time. The effect of this powder is to get someone to leave your home or property without engaging in a confrontation.

- Chili powder
- Cayenne pepper
- Powdered brown chalk
- ½ teaspoon black pepper powder
- ½ teaspoon powdered patchouli herb
- ½ teaspoon powdered ginger
- ½ teaspoon powdered John the Conqueror root

Goofer Dust

Goofer Dust is a very old African American hoodoo blend used to cause serious trouble or harm. It can even kill an enemy, so be very careful with it. There are a number of recipes, no doubt reflecting the intent of the conjuror. Goofer dust can also be used for its protective properties. **You should not use goofer dust**; I have included it here for its folkloric value.

- Graveyard dirt
- Black salt
- Ground sulfur
- Snake skin
- Magnetic sand
- Dried pigeon shit

To this basic blend, one would add particular items to enhance its effects, such as ground insects, powdered bones, or black pepper.

Graveyard Dirt

Graveyard dirt is also known as graveyard dust. There are a number of different kinds of graveyard dirts, depending on the type of grave they are gathered from. For example, graveyard dirt gathered from nine separate graveyards, with one from a child's grave, is considered powerful for good works. Dirt gathered from the graves of nine criminals is considered ideal for left-handed works.

Graveyard dirt should never be gathered flippantly or without proper reverence. According to Madrina Angelique, a respected Southern-style hoodoo rootworker, New Orleans Voodoo practitioner and Palo-initiated Madre Nganga of Munanso Centella Ndoki Nkuyo Malongo Corta Lima Cordosa, and Iyalorisha of Ile Ori Yemayá, there are a number of different types of protocols to follow when gathering cemetery dirt. The following is excerpted from *Hoodoo and Conjure Quartely Volume 1:*[88]

> My way of gathering cemetery dirt is to first make sure I am cleansed and in a proper frame of mind. A lot of times I will wrap my head in white to cut down on spiritual chatter and to keep out negative spirits. I pour rum at the entrance of the cemetery and ask permission to gather the dirt. There is always a guardian spirit at the entrance of every cemetery. After pouring the rum, I stand quietly and listen. If I feel no negativity, I enter the cemetery. There have been times when I felt an overwhelming sense of negativity, danger, sadness and just plain fear. When this happens, I back away from the cemetery and leave. If I'm allowed entrance, I spend some time just walking through the cemetery, talking quietly with the spirits. I will then gather my dirt, leaving 3, 7 or 9 blessed pennies as payment, sometimes fruits and bread. I always say a blessing for all the souls in the cemetery. When leaving, I again pour rum at the entrance and thank the guardian spirit. Most times I will go home a different way than I went and make 3 stops before heading home to confuse any spirit that is trying to follow.

Happy Times Powder

This hoodoo powder is used to change luck, reverse unfortunate circumstances, and eliminate poverty. Sprinkle around your home.

- Orange peel
- Vanilla oil
- Strawberry oil

---

88 Alvarado, D. & Marino, S. (2010) *Hoodoo & Conjure Quarterly, Vol 1.* Prescott Valley, AZ: Planet Voodoo.

Hot Foot Powder

This powder helps to drive away unwanted people in your life. Sprinkle around the doorway or a picture of the person you want to get rid of. Throw some down where they will be sure to walk on it. Dust their shoes with it or sprinkle some in their socks.

- Chili powder
- Cayenne pepper
- Black pepper
- Sulfur powder
- Ground cinnamon

Mix in a base of ground chicory root.

Jinx-Removing Powder

Jinx-Removing Powder is used to kill jinxes, break curses, and remove crossings or hexings.

- Mint
- Wintergreen
- Chamomile
- Angelica
- Crabshell powder

Grind herbs and add to a base of ground mullein and aloeswood.

Basic Love Powder

- ½ teaspoonful of sugar
- Teaspoonful of peppermint
- Teaspoonful of grated candied orange peel

Give a teaspoonful of this mixture in a glass of sweet red wine to your target. That person will love you forever after he or she drinks it.

Money Drawing Powder

- Cedar
- Patchouli
- Galangal
- Ginger
- Five finger grass

Grind herbs and add to a base of cinnamon powder.

CHAPTER FOURTEEN

TALISMANS

A talisman is a small amulet or other object, often bearing magical symbols, worn for protection against evil spirits or the supernatural. In Afro-Caribbean syncretic religions like Voodoo, Umbanda, Quimbanda, and Santería, drawings are used as amulets or talismans and placed in mojo bags. In New Orleans, they are often an ingredient in gris gris bags as well. Other symbols, such as magic squares, angelic signatures, seals of Solomon, seals from the Sixth and Seventh Books of Moses, magickal alphabets, and kabalistic signs have been employed to a variety of ends, both benign and malicious. All of these can be used as talismans in hoodoo.

In common tradition, if a horseshoe is hung on a door with the two ends pointing up, then good luck will occur. However, if the two ends point downwards, then bad luck will occur.

The difference between an amulet and a talisman is negligible in terms of their effects. In some magick circles it is said that amulets are charged when the moon is waning and talismans are charged when the moon is waxing.

In the following section, I will describe one way in which a talisman can be consecrated prior to use. I have also provided some examples of seals and sigils that can be drawn and used in your own magickal works.

How to Consecrate a Talisman

Your talismans and amulets should be consecrated to infuse them with the power of your intent. There are an infinite number of ways to do this—here's one.

Light some incense as an offering to the divine (or whoever you believe is your higher power). Light three white candles that have been placed in a triangle form on your altar. Place the amulet or talisman upon your altar in the center of the triangle between the candles.

Sprinkle the amulet/talisman with salt, and say:

I consecrate you with the element of earth, that you will provide an aura of protection to the person who holds you.

Pass the amulet/talisman through the incense.

I consecrate you with the element of air, that you will provide an aura of protection to the person who holds you.

Pass the amulet/talisman through the candle flame.

I consecrate you with the element of fire, that you will provide an aura of protection to the person who holds you.

Sprinkle the amulet/talisman with water.

I consecrate you with the element of water, that you will provide an aura of protection to the person who holds you.

Place the amulet/talisman back on your altar. Place both hands over the amulet/talisman. Visualize a white light from above pouring into the amulet/talisman.

I charge this amulet/talisman to serve as (name its purpose) for I [your name] am servant of the Divine. So be it!

Extinguish your candles (always pinch out the flame, never blow). Your amulet or talisman is now ready to use.

The Talismans

The following talismans can be used in your mojo bags, nations sacks, and gris gris bags. They come from a variety of traditions related to New Orleans Voodoo and hoodoo. Talismans should be drawn with dragon's blood ink on parchment paper for the best effect. Alternately, you may print out the page, cut out the desired talisman, and fold it either towards you to draw the talisman's properties to you, or away from you to repel negativity. For an added boost, anoint the four corners of the paper on which you draw the talisman with a conjure oil specific to the purpose. You can also sprinkle the talisman with a corresponding sachet powder.

A number of sacred and authoritative texts contain many more talismans. Abramelin's *Magickal Word Squares,* the Sixth and Seventh Books of Moses, and the *Black Pullet* are some of the texts from which many hoodoo talismans derive. See the back of this book for a list of grimoires and texts that are classic sources of talismans and seals in hoodoo.

Satori Square

The Satori Square is a word square containing a Latin palindrome featuring the words *sator arepo tenet opera rotas* written in a square so that they may be read top-to-bottom, bottom-to-top, left-to-right, and right-to-left. Use for removing jinxes and hexes, to protect from evil influences, and to protect against fatigue when traveling.

Pentagram

A pentagram is the shape of a five-pointed star drawn with five straight strokes. Use as an amulet to attract money and love and to protect against envy, misfortune, and other disgraces.

Seal of the Choir of the Ministering Angels

According to the Sixth Book of Moses, "the most useful ministering archangels of this seal are the following: Uriel, Arael, Zacharael, Gabriel, Raphael, Theoska, Zywolech, Hemohon, Yhael, Tuwahel, Donahan, Sywaro, Samohayl, Zowanus, Ruweno Ymoeloh, Hahowel, and Tywael."

The particularly great secret and special use of this seal is that if it is buried in the earth, where treasures exist, they will come to the surface by themselves, without any presence during a full moon.

Love

This design for an amulet comes from the *Black Pullet* grimoire. The *Black Pullet* is a grimoire that proposes to teach the "science of magical talismans and rings," including the art of necromancy and Kabbalah. Embroider it upon black satin, say "Nades, Suradis, Maniner," and a djinn is supposed to appear; tell the djinn "Sader, Prostas, Solaster," and the djinn will bring you your true love. Say "Mammes, Laher" when you tire of her.

Four Leaf Clover

Deriving from the ancient Celts, the clover, if it has four leaves, symbolizes good luck (not the Irish shamrock, which symbolizes the Christian Trinity).

Pomba Gira

Use the ritual symbol of Pomba Gira for wild sex and passion and to add spice to your relationship.

Papa Legba

Use this amulet or talisman to remove obstacles, open doors, and receive opportunities.

Marie Laveau

Use the Marie Laveau talisman for protection.

Power

This is the power to destroy talisman. Use when you need to break up or end a situation. This talisman can be used against a person, but this is **not recommended**.

La Sirène

Use the La Sirène talisman for seduction.

Ayida Wedo

Use the Ayida Wedo talisman for gaining control of your future.

Sexual Potency

Use the talisman of Erzulie Freda to increase sexual prowess and potency.

Winning Court Cases

Use this talisman for winning court cases.

Prosperity

This prosperity talisman is alchemical in origin and combines the properties of winter and the element of air with the properties of the signs of the zodiac Aquarius.

Seal of the Spirits of Good Luck (from the Seventh Book of Moses)

This seal gives good luck and fortune. Its spirits give the treasures of the sea. In hoodoo, this seal is used for good luck and success in games of chance. Place beneath a green candle anointed with Fast Luck Oil.

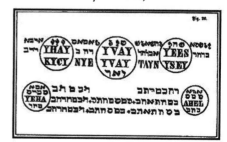

Celestial Powers

Use this talisman to conjure the celestial and infernal powers. Make a ring of the talisman, with the bottom words written inside the band of the ring. Wear the talisman on your finger and put it over your heart, then pronounce the following words: "Siras, Etar, Besanar." You will soon perceive the effects.

Seal of the Choir of Hosts of the Ministering Archangels (from the Sixth Book of Moses)

If a man carries this seal with him, it will bring him great fortune and blessing. Use this seal in mojo hands and gris gris bags for money drawing. Combine with lucky hand root, black-eyed peas, five finger grass, High John the Conqueror root, and a piece of pyrite and dress daily with Crown of Success Oil. Wrap in green flannel for gris gris and red flannel for mojo.

Seal of the Power-Angels (from the Sixth Book of Moses)

If a man wears this seal in bed, he will learn what he desires to know through dreams and visions.

Seal of the Spirit of Air (from the Seventh Book of Moses)

Use this seal to gain employment, necessities, and relief from want. Place beneath a yellow candle anointed with Lucky Nine Oil.

Seal of Black and White magic

Use this seal to compel spirits to appear and to serve your needs. Place beneath a white candle anointed with St. Jude Oil.

Seal of Jupiter (from the Seventh Book of Moses)

This seal assists in overcoming lawsuits and disputes; assists in winning games of chance and attracting luck and fortune; helps in business matters, legal cases, religious affairs, overseas travel, and buying and selling real estate or other property.

CHAPTER FIFTEEN

Tħε Spεℓℓs

Chants are not typically used in hoodoo as they are in Paganism, high magick, or Wicca. Rather, selections from the Bible, like the psalms, may be read for the spell's intent. For example, one could read Psalm 91 for uncrossing or jinx-removing purposes. The psalm is recited three times while you are focused on a candle. An uncrossing bath may be used in conjunction with this ritual—take the bath before you light the candles or after they have finished burning. Incantations are used in some spells that are influenced by European folk magic and the grimoires.

Another note about Voodoo hoodoo spells: most are quite simple in their application. No long, drawn-out ritual is usually necessary to perform effective magick (although there are a few longer ones). Once you have your hoodoo medicine chest stocked, it becomes a matter of using your intuition combined with certain techniques to quickly assemble some gris gris or a trick in order to get the job done.

In performing any type of spell, if there are no specific directions for disposing of the left over water, wax, ashes, roots, powders, and so forth, then take them to a crossroads and dispose of them there by throwing them into the center. You should then walk away and not look back. You can also leave them under a tree in the woods, or toss them into a running stream of water.

A Note about Animal Sacrifice

For the most part, animal sacrifice is not currently practiced in New Orleans Voodoo, except by those initiated in related traditions, and then only under specific guidelines at specific times. Sacrificial offerings are made in numerous other forms that do not require the killing of animals. Moreover, an independent practitioner should never have the need or desire to engage in ritual sacrifice of animals. To do so is an indication of some greater issue, and it is unwise and unsafe.

Animal sacrifice is still practiced in Haiti and Africa, as well as in parts of the United States by some practitioners of Santería and other variant religions of African origin. There are a couple of reasons for this. One reason for animal sacrifice is economic. Hunger and poverty prevail in Haiti and parts of Africa, and when an animal is sacrificed in a ritual, it is afterwards consumed by the community. Thus, the ritual also serves the purpose of feeding the people and building connectedness between members of the community through the power of the ritual. None of the spells or rituals in this book includes the practice of animal sacrifice or the use of sacrificial blood. If you are is interested in this type of practice, you will have to look elsewhere. I am not able to address this issue with any degree of real authority, nor is it appropriate to do so in this book or any other.

> If you are going with a man and you don't want him to come back, get some of his hair and put it in a bottle. Go to the river and throw it in, and the man will go whichever way the bottle goes.

Banishing Spells

Banishing spells are spells designed to get rid of an enemy or unwanted person. They can be used to banish illness, emotions, a lover's jealousy, or unwanted spirits. Banishing spells are best done during a waning moon.

To Banish Illness

For this spell you will need a handful of salt. Take the salt and toss it into the flames of a fire. The flames will turn blue. Gaze into the blue flames and focus intently on the illness leaving. As you visualize the illness going away, repeat the following words:

Sickness burns, good health returns.

Following this, take a Green Bath for Health. This spell can be used on yourself or on another person.

Ritual to Get Someone Out of the House

This is a ritual by Marie Laveau as reported by Zora Neale Hurston in her seminal work, *Mules and Men*. The narrative has been left intact to retain its folkloric value. I have edited the punctuation minimally to increase its readability.

Too many women in my house. My husband's mother is there and she hates me and always puttin' my husband up to fight me. Look like I can't get her out of my house no ways I try. So I done come to you."

We can fix that up in no time, dear one. Now go take a flat onion. If it was a man, I'd say a sharp pointed onion. Core the onion out, and write her name five times on paper and stuff it into the hole in the onion and close it back with the cutout piece of onion. Now you watch when she leaves the house and then you roll the onion behind her before anybody else crosses the doorsill. And you make a wish at the same time for her to leave your house. She won't be there two weeks more." The woman paid and left.

That night we held a ceremony in the altar room on the case. We took a red candle and burnt it just enough to consume the tip. Then it was cut into three parts and the short lengths of candle were put into a glass of holy water. Then we took the glass and went at midnight to the door of the woman's house and the Frizzly Rooster held the glass in his hands and said, "In the name of the Father, in the name of the Son, in the name of the Holy Ghost." He shook the glass three times violently up and down, and the last time he threw the glass to the ground and broke it, and said, "Dismiss this woman from this place." We scarcely paused as this was said and done and we kept going and went home by another way because that was part of the ceremony. [89]

To Get Rid of a Troublesome Neighbor

Light a black candle and dress with castor oil. Write the neighbor's name on a piece of paper along with the word "goodbye." Place the paper under the candle. Mix powdered mud dauber's nest with graveyard dirt and throw it at the neighbor's front door. Recite Psalms 74, 101, and 109 three times each and let the candle burn out. Dispose of the candle remains at a crossroads, along with three pennies.

---

89 Hurston, Z. N. (1935) *Mules and Men*. New York: Harper's Perennial.

To Get Rid of a Friend

If you have a friend who you don't want coming back to your house, try this simple trick. Get a photo of the person and dig a hole in the ground in your front yard. Pour some salt in the hole, and place the photo face-down on top of the salt, with the head away from your house. Cover the hole with dirt and stomp on it with your foot. Your friend will not come back.

Bend Over Spells

Bend over spells are designed to subjugate someone else to your will. With these types of spells, you can force your boss, coworker, family member, friend, or rival to treat you the way you would like to be treated and remove any type of confrontation. These spells can also be used for sexual domination. To make another person do what you want them to do, try one of these spells.

To Gain Power over Another

Get the largest white stick candle you can find. Pour some Bend Over Oil in your palm and begin twisting the candle with your hands. Then roll the candle in a powder made of salt and camphor. Light the candle and let it burn all the way down. On the third night, take the remaining powder mixture and throw it in the path where the one to be dominated will walk.

To Make People Love You[90]

Take nine lumps of starch, mime of sugar, and nine teaspoons of steel dust. Wet it all with Jockey Club Cologne. Take nine pieces of ribbon, blue, red, and yellow. I suggest using wide ribbon for the blue and red ribbons, and thin ribbon for the yellow. Take a teaspoonful of the mixture, put it on a ribbon, and tie it in into paket (a small bundle). As you do, call out the name of the person or persons you want to love you. Wrap the paket with yellow ribbon, and as you do so, call out the person's name. Do this nine times, making nine bags wrapped with yellow thread. Place the pakets under a rug, under a bed, behind a piece of furniture, under a step, or over a door. Distance makes no difference with this trick. Your target(s) will be unable to take their mind off of you.

---

90 Adapted from Zora Neale-Hurston's *Mules and Men*.

Binding Spells

Binding spells are designed to prevent someone from doing harm to themselves or others. They are used to control the behavior of others or to stop undesired behavior.

Charm to Bind an Enemy

Gather cobwebs from your house and put them all in a mess on a black cloth. Find a dead fly and set it on the mess of webs. Then write the following words on a piece of paper:

> *North, South, East, West*
> *Spider's web shall bind him best*
> *East, West, North, South*
> *Hold his limbs and stop his mouth.*
> *Seal his eyes and choke his breath*
> *Wrap him round with ropes of death.*

Fold the paper four times and wrap it, along with the mess of webs and the fly, in the black cloth, forming a small packet. Wrap it tightly with a long cord, leaving a length of cord so it can be hung in a dark corner of the home. Let it hang there until it is thickly covered in dust, and then bury it near the person's home.

Binding Spell

Take a Guardian Angel candle and dress with Peace Oil. Light the candle and some frankincense incense. Find a twig large enough to write on. Write on the twig all the negative things you wish to bind in your life. Take some thread and wind it around the twig, then bury it in the earth under a tree away from your home. Repeat Psalms 130 and 133 nine times each.

Blessing Spells

Across cultures, a blessing is perceived as the consecration of something with holiness, divine will, or one's hopes. In ancient times, a blessing referred to a Germanic pagan custom of making something sacred or holy by marking it with blood. In Christian terms, to be blessed means to be favored by God. In Catholicism, formal blessings are carried out by priests and bishops, by raising their right hand over the person and making the sign of the cross over the person or object to be blessed. While it is typically the spiritual leader who is recognized as having the power to bless someone or something, in hoodoo, anyone can bless someone or something if they know how.

In hoodoo, there is the belief that charms and such do not necessarily have to be blessed because they are created with natural items that are inherently powerful and sacred, and infused with *ashé*—the power of the universe. Nonetheless, items are ritually "charged" by anointing with oils and using special prayers to enhance their power. Doing so aligns them with your energy and intent. Some people prefer to bless their tools and works as a sort of insurance policy against any negative influences.

A Simple Ritual for Creating Sacred Space

This ritual calls for a Native American spiritual practice called "smudging" wherein objects, people, or spaces are lightly covered with the smoke of incense, or the smoke of smoldering herbs such as cedar or sage. For this ritual you will need a sage bundle or incense and some Florida Water. If using sage, light one end, blow out the flame, and lightly blow the bundle until you have a nice smoking ember. Offer the smoke to the helper spirits by fanning the smoke with your hand or a large feather. Respectfully ask the spirits to help you clear the area of all negativity.

Begin fumigating the area, beginning with the doorway. Smudge it, and all of the corners moving from the floor up, going clockwise. Smudge everyone present, starting from their front, going from their feet to their head. Have each person turn around and repeat the procedure. Next, sprinkle (or use a spray bottle to mist) Florida Water on the floor of the room or area you wish to have blessed. Mist each corner and move to the center of the room. You may now light some incense and thank the helper spirits for their special attention.

Express your love and say goodbye. Your space is now properly dressed for ritual work.

Rose of Jericho Home Blessing

The Rose of Jericho is known as the resurrection plant. It is believed to bring peace, power, and abundance to the home. To restore or revitalize peace and abundance in your home, light a blue candle and anoint with

Peaceful Home Oil on a Monday. Place a rose of Jericho in crystal bowl of spring water and say Psalm 62 over it daily. Watch the plant come to life. As it grows, so shall the peace and abundance in your home.

Bottle Spells and Jar Spells

Bottle spells and jar spells are some of the most traditional hoodoo works. They are essentially a type of container spell in which specific ingredients are placed inside a jar or bottle and then manipulated through magick. Any type of jar or bottle will work; it just depends on what is available and the size and amount of the ingredients to be placed inside.

One of the most popular jars is the honey jar. Honey jars are used when the rootworker wishes to sweeten up or attract a person in a particular direction. Alternately, vinegar jars are used when the goal is to sour a situation, person, or relationship.

Bon Voyage Spell

This is a cut and clear type of spell, to be done when you want to cut all ties from negative people or end a relationship absolutely and completely. This spell will need to be done nine times, nine days in a row. You will need the following items:

- Piece of paper torn from a brown grocery bag
- Bon Voyage incense
- Personal effect of the target person (i.e. hair, nails, piece of clothing, letter)
- Four Thieves Vinegar
- Mason jar
- Black fabric

- Red string
- 9 razor blades
- Sulfur
- Patchouli
- Ginger
- Storax
- Guinea pepper
- Black snake root

Write the name of the person you wish to be rid of nine times on a piece of brown paper torn from a grocery bag. Each time you write the person's name, turn the paper counterclockwise, then write it again, turn counterclockwise again, and so on. Do this process nine times. Then, fold the paper away from you three times and stick in the jar along with one razor blade and one personal effect. While you are doing this, burn a little Bon Voyage incense. Once the incense burns to ash, add the ashes to the bottle. Repeat this ritual each night for nine nights, each night adding an additional ingredient. On the final night, fill the jar with the Four Thieves Vinegar. Wrap the jar with black fabric and tie in place with a piece of red string, being sure to tie it closed with nine knots. Take the bottle to the cemetery and stand quietly. Listening closely to the spirits, ask if there is one who would help you cut the ties of the relationship. When you find the right grave, leave the jar there with a small bottle of rum, three carnations, and nine pennies. Leave the cemetery in a different direction from whence you came, and be sure to thank the spirits for helping you to finalize the relationship once and for all.

Bottle Spell to Curse an Enemy

Gather the dirt from a footprint of your enemy. Put it in a bottle along with some Hot Foot Powder and bury it under your target's front porch or in their front yard. The only way this spell can be broken is by digging up the bottle and throwing it in a fire. If this is done and the bottle bursts, the spell is considered broken.

Get Someone to Move

Get a small jar or bottle with a lid. On a piece of paper, draw a house with a big "X" through it. Then write the target person's name on it nine times, but not inside the house. Fill with Four Thieves Vinegar, cap, and cast into a river or ocean. Back this up by splashing War Water on all the target's outside door knobs and porches. Do this as you build energy, visualizing the person packed up and driving away.

Hoodoo Honey Jar

Write the full name of the person you desire nine times with Dove's Blood Ink on a piece of parchment paper that is cut into the shape of a heart. Turn the paper ninety degrees and cross their name by writing your name on top of theirs nine times, each time turning the paper ninety degrees. Anoint the three points of the heart with Fire of Love Oil or Come to Me Oil.

Fold the paper towards you three times and place into a jar of honey. Add a teaspoon of cinnamon to the jar, and then close it. Place the jar on a fireproof dish. Take a red candle. Write the name of your lover on one side of the candle, and your name on the other side. Anoint the candle with the Fire of Love Oil. If you are looking to increase the passion and sex between you and your lover, use Fire of Love Oil to anoint the candle. Affix the candle to the top of the honey jar and light it. Focus on your intention and allow the candle to burn down. You may use another candle by dressing it in a similar fashion as many times as is necessary until your lover comes to you or you see the desired changes. Once this occurs, bury the jar in your front yard to keep your lover near you.

Lavender Lust Bottle Spell for Same-Sex Couples

Write the names of you and your lover on a piece of paper which you have anointed on all four corners. If you have a photo of your lover, write on the back of the photograph instead of a piece of paper. Then, put the paper inside the bottle so the side with the writing is facing outwards.

Grind up the following dried herbs. Note that they need not be completely pulverized—just grind them long enough to give you time to focus your intention on being deeply in lust or happy in love.

- Pomegranate rind (dried)
- Ginger
- Clove
- Cinnamon
- Jasmine
- Lavender
- Violet
- Magnolia (if seeking a faithful partner)

Place the ingredients into the bottle. Add a condom to ensure prevention of STDs (and be sure to wear one when you have sex with your lover, too). Add nine drops of musk, nine drops of lavender essential oil, and nine drops of Desire Oil. Anoint a Hierophant tarot card and two identical skeleton keys with the musk oil. Tie the two keys together with a red silk cord and place in the jar along with the anointed Hierophant tarot card. Fill the jar with almond oil and screw on the lid. Light a red candle that has been anointed with Desire Oil, and allow the wax to drip on the rim of the jar. You will have to hold the jar in one hand and the candle in the other, or place the jar on a table that is covered with tin foil and roll the jar towards you as the wax drips and seals the lid onto the jar. Continue until the lid is completely covered with the wax and the jar is sealed. Keep the jar under your bed until your loved one comes to you, at which point you can bury the jar in your front yard to keep your lover close.

St. Expedite Bottle Spell

For help with any concern in a hurry, make this bottle spell for St. Expedite.

- Bottle or jar
- Red candle
- Images of St. Expedite, crows, crosses, Virgin of Guadalupe, the planet mercury
- Statue of St. Expedite or framed image
- Red paint
- Fast Luck Oil
- Metal cross
- Glass of water
- Sara Lee pound cake
- Fresh flowers
- Cinnamon
- A piece of pyrite
- Magnetic sand
- Feather from a crow
- Red wine
- Herbs: juniper, pine, basil, geranium, lilac
- Red stones

Set up your altar in a triangle formation with the statue or framed image of St. Expedite on the front right, the glass of water on the front left, and the St. Expedite bottle spell in the back center.

Wash the bottle with salt water and consecrate it to the purpose at hand. Paint the bottle or jar red and affix the image of St. Expedite to the bottle. Add the other images onto the bottle in a manner that pleases you. Write the word "hodie" on the bottle, or print it out and glue it to the bottle. Attach the cross to a chain or cord and tie around the mouth of the jar, allowing the cross to hang down in front of St. Expedite's image.

Prepare your candle by washing it with Florida Water. Florida Water is used to draw things to you. Set it aside to air dry. Anoint with Fast Luck Oil. Write your petition on a piece of parchment paper with Dove's Blood Ink. Alternately, write your petition with red ink and spray some floral perfume on the paper after you write the petition and anoint with Fast Luck Oil.

Place your petition inside the bottle. Add some fresh flower petals, cinnamon stick, piece of pyrite, five herbs, magnetic sand, red stone, and crow feather. Stick the red candle into the mouth of the bottle. Set the bottle on a fireproof dish. Light the candle and pray to St. Expedite:

Our dear martyr and protector, Saint Expedite,
You who know what is necessary and what is urgently needed.
I beg you to intercede before the Holy Trinity, that by your grace my request will be granted.
(State your petition exactly as it reads in the bottle.)

May I receive your blessings and favors.
In the name of our Lord Jesus Christ, Amen.

This is to be said daily until the candle burns all the way down. Take the candle remains and place into the bottle; then top it off with the red wine. Keep the bottle on your altar. Continue to pray to St. Expedite daily until he answers your prayer. Then be sure to pay him with a piece of pound cake and fresh flowers. Don't forget to tell someone how he has helped you.

To Get Rid Of an Enemy

Take three sticks of artemesia, blood weed, or sage. Write the name of your enemy on a piece of paper and tie it to the sticks. Place the sticks in a glass jar and fill the jar with vinegar (the sticks should not be longer than the jar). Cover the top of the jar and turn it upside down. Take a white candle and tie a black ribbon around it. Butt it and turn it upside down, placing it on the bottom of the glass. Carve the bottom of the candle to a point so the wick is exposed. Light the wrong end of the candle and say:

> *As Jesus turned vinegar into water, so shall (name of enemy) turn into nothing, so that they go far away and so that I will never have to see them again.*

Let the candle burn down and dispose of all of the items used in the spell in a graveyard along with nine pennies.

Break Up Spells

To Break Up a Couple (1)

Here's is the simplest of simple hoodoo tricks to break up a couple. All you have to do is make a mixture of half salt and half pepper and put it down where your targets are sure to walk. It is said that they will start fighting soon thereafter.

To Break Up a Couple (2)

Take nine needles; break each needle into three pieces. Write each person's name three times on paper. Write one name backwards and one forwards, and lay the broken needles on the paper. Take five black candles, four red, and three green.

Tie a string across the door from the needles, and suspend a large candle upside down. It will hang low on the door. Burn one each day for one hour.

> **If a woman's husband dies and you don't want her to marry again, cut all of her husband's shoes into little pieces, just as soon as he is dead, and she will never marry again.**

If you burn your first in the daytime, keep doing so in the day; if at night, continue at night. A tin plate with paper and needles should be placed under the candle to catch the wax.

When the ninth day is finished, go out into the street and get some white or black dog dung. A dog only drops his dung in the street when he is running and barking, and whoever you curse will run and bark likewise. Put it in a bag with the paper and carry it to running water. Soon after, one of the parties will leave the other.

To Break Up with Someone

There is nothing more annoying than having a man who you aren't interested in anymore hanging around. To remedy this situation, get some of his hair and put it in a bottle. Then, go to a river and throw it in. It is said that the man will go whichever way the bottle goes.

Better Business Spells

Spell for Attracting Business

This spell is designed to give the self-employed some much-needed economic relief. Pour a cup of fresh basil into your bath water and add three lodestones to the bath. Soak in the bath for twenty minutes. Drain the bath, keeping a cup of the infused water and the lodestones. Carry the lodestones with you or keep them where you do the majority of your work (your computer desk, artist studio, etc.). Put the water in a spray bottle and spray the lodestone-infused water over the entrances and thresholds of your business area, as well as in corners, behind doors, and anyplace where the energy could be stagnant. Alternately, you can place the basil, lodestones, and three cups of water in a non-metal container for three days instead of taking a bath. Then, proceed with the rest of the spell.

Cleansing Spells

Cleansings are a staple in New Orleans Voodoo and Southern hoodoo practice. Many works require a basic cleansing to be performed first, to remove any negative energy that may interfere with the work to be done. Cleansings are also done by themselves whenever a "clean slate" is needed.

Basic Egg Cleansing
By Madrina Angelique (2010)

A basic egg cleansing is something everyone can do to absorb negativity and remove impurities from their life. Eggs have been used for cleansing in many parts of the world. Eggs that come from black chickens are used when witchcraft is involved. Eggs from white chickens are used for general cleansings, and brown eggs are all-purpose.

Fill a clean clear glass with regular tap water or for a little more power, Blessed Peace Water. Add a little Protection Oil. Light a white candle. For a basic cleansing, use a cold plain white egg. A cold egg absorbs negative energy better than one at room temperature. Place the egg on the top of your head and recite a prayer or chant of your tradition. Roll the egg down the back of your head, the back of the neck, the center of the back, and around to the chest. Then continue downward across the open palms and over the soles of the feet. Always move the egg in a downward motion, never up. You can also begin at the top of the head and make spiraling motions around the body in a downward motion. Then break the egg into the glass of water, checking for abnormalties such as color, blood, shape, and texture.

Some basic interpretations:

1. If the water smells bad with blood present, this is a sign of evil work being done.

2. If there are blood spots in the water, this is a sign of bad luck and harm being caused by strong spell work—especially if the water is murky.

3. If the water turns murky with no smell or blood, this is a sign of susto (soul loss) as long as there is no blood present.

4. If the yolk of the egg has the shape of a face, this is a sign of an enemy. A thin face indicates a male enemy, a round face indicates a female enemy.

5. If the yolk is in the shape of an eye, this is a sign of the evil eye.

6. If there are small bubbles in the water, this is a sign that the negative energy was absorbed by guardian spirits.

7. If the water is clear, with no abnormal shapes, smells, or blood, this is a sign that nothing unnatural is happening.

To Detect and Remove Negative Energy

Before performing a home cleansing, you may want to know if there are any specific areas in the home where there is a concentration of negative energy. To detect any areas in need of special attention, while at the same time absorbing the negative energy, try this simple spell. To do this spell, gather the following:

- Fresh lemons
- Fresh garlic cloves

Gather as many lemons as you can. Cut the lemons in half, and insert a clove of garlic into each half. Place the lemons face down in the corners, doorways, and windowsills of your house at nightfall and leave until dawn. In the morning, gather up the lemons, and as you do, examine each one for changes. If any of the lemon halves have been damaged or changed colors or show some sort of visible difference, then that is an area of the home in need of attention. If the lemon halves look the same as they did when you placed them the night before, then those areas are free of negative energy.

For the areas that show signs of uncleanliness, repeat the procedure daily until the lemons appear clean.

Ellegua Cleansing Ritual

This ritual is done every day for three days. You will need:

- 3 eggs
- Palm oil
- Rum
- Cigar
- Paper bag

Take the eggs, rub them with palm oil, and spray them with rum and cigar smoke. Place all of the items in a paper bag, then rub the bag over your body from head to toe. Ask Ellegua to cleanse you of your negativity, and visualize the negative energy leaving you. Take the eggs and crush them on three separate street corners away from your home. While you are crushing the eggs, ask Ellegua to cleanse you of all negativity and to remove all obstacles from your way, the same way the eggs are being crushed. Start this ritual on Monday, which is Ellegua's day; it ends on Wednesday.

Commanding Spells

Commanding spells are among the unholy trinity of spells of this nature; the other two are domination and controlling spells. Commanding spells are performed to gain dominance and influence over people and situations, and to easily direct people to do your will. They are performed by people in positions of power, or people desiring to be in positions of power. Commanding spells allow a person to have influence over people and gain admiration and respect in the process.

To enhance spells of this nature, you can add Commanding, Master, Master Key, Nature Power, John the Conqueror, Domination, and Crucible of Courage oils and powders to the work. A helpful saint to appeal to is St. Martha (Espiritismo). Helpful herbs include calamus, licorice root, and dragon's blood.

Basic Commanding Candle Spell

Carve the initials of the one you wish to influence in a day candle or commanding candle. Anoint with Commanding Oil and burn. If you are seeking influence in general, do not carve any initials in the candle. Instead, write a petition stating what you want (power, influence, leadership) and place under the candle. Perform during a full moon for best results.

Damballah Wedo Do As I Say Spell

The snake is revered in New Orleans Voodoo, with most Voodoo temples and houses possessing their own boa constrictor or python for ceremonial purposes. Marie Laveau publicly danced with her snake known as Li Grande Zombi in what is now Congo Square in New Orleans. The snake is called upon for many purposes, including transformation, transcendence, ancestral knowledge, righteous retribution, and wisdom. Damballah Wedo is likened to St. Patrick, the Catholic patron saint of Ireland.

This spell is designed to help you sway a person in a particular direction.

- One piece of ribbon each in red, yellow, and black
- Photo of person you want to do your bidding attached to a red Voodoo doll
- High John the Conqueror root
- Damballah Wedo Oil
- Ritual symbol for Damballah Wedo

Take three pieces of ribbon—one red, one yellow, and one black. Tie them together at one end and then knot them nine times. Each time you tie a knot, repeat the name of the person you are trying to influence.

Create a doll from red flannel and attach a photo of the person you are trying to influence. If you do not have a photo, then write their name nine times on a piece of brown paper with Dragon's Blood Ink and attach it to the doll. Insert a piece of High John the Conqueror root and the ribbon tied with nine knots.

Draw the ritual symbol for Damballah and place it on a small table you have dedicated to this work. Alternately, you may photocopy the design and use the copy; though, your spell will be more powerful if you draw the symbol yourself. Set your doll on top of the symbol and concentrate on the person you are targeting. Chant the following nine times:

Damballah, may I, (your name)
come out victorious in dealing with (the person's name).

Anoint the doll with Damballah Wedo Oil. Keep in a box lined with Spanish moss, with the box sitting on top of the ritual symbol. Repeat the ritual as often as necessary until the desired results are achieved.[91]

Command and Compel Spell

The purpose of this spell is to command someone to love you. Gather the following items:

- Brown paper
- Red pencil

Take the piece of brown paper and cut it into a square. Using a red pencil, write the name of your loved one nine times. Turn the paper ninety degrees

---

91 From Alvarado, D. (2010). *The Voodoo Doll Spellbook: A Compendium of Ancient and Contemporary Spells and Rituals*, Prescott Valley, AZ: CreateSpace, p. 167.

to the right and write your name over hers nine times. Fold the paper three times. While doing this, focus intensely on your desires. Repeat the following as you hold the paper to your heart:

I command you, I compel you
Love me, as I love you
I command you, I compel you,
(Name) return to me now!

Now, burn the paper and scatter the ashes to the wind. The rest is up to the universe.

There is an incubation period that occurs after a spell is cast. Be patient for the results. In twenty-seven days, if you have not heard from your beloved, repeat the above actions. You can do so once every twenty-seven days to strengthen and recharge the work.

Consecration

The act of consecration involves opening up to and tapping into the universal divine force from which all possibilities, solutions, and miracles emanate. To consecrate an object for ritual use is to connect to this universal divine force and to declare sacred or appropriate for sacred use the object at hand. Consecrating an object removes any negativity that may be attached to the object and purifies it. It removes the vibrational energies of anyone who has handled the object other than you. This is the foundation of any effective magick or ceremonial work.

How to Consecrate an Object

Consecrating an object is simple. You will need:

- Item to be consecrated
- White candle
- Some sage, cedar, or sandalwood incense
- Something to burn the herbs or incense in

Step One

Light a white candle. White is the color for purity. Light the herbs or incense.

Step Two

Pass the object through the smoke. This is referred to as "smudging." Repeat the following:

> *I hereby consecrate this _____ with the powers of earth, water, fire, air, and spirit. That it shall be used only for good, according to my will and divine law. May it serve me well in this world, between worlds, and in all worlds. So be it.*

Repeat Step Two six more times, a total of seven times. Your object will now be ready for ritual use.

You may personalize what you say; the above is only meant as a guideline. There is no one right way to consecrate an object, place, or person. Once consecrated, you should not allow others to handle the item. Place it on an altar, or wrap it up safely in a white bag and put in a safe place where it will not be disturbed.

Court Case Spells (Court Scrapes)

Court case spells are used in all kinds of ways: for getting and staying out of jail, helping someone else in jail, putting someone else in jail, having someone released from jail, and keeping someone in jail. There are spells to enhance testimony, spells to silence the witness, spells to make the judge and jury sympathetic, and spells to confuse attorneys. In short, there are court spells to suit any and every occasion.

Here are some herbs commonly employed in court case spells:

- Black poppy seeds—to cause confusion amongst your adversaries
- Calendula (marigold) flowers—to promote legal victory and self-respect
- Deer's tongue—for eloquent speech by you and your attorney
- Slippery elm—against gossip, lies, and those trying to slander you in court
- Galangal (little john)—this is considered the "court case" root and should be carried or chewed whenever you go to court
- High John the Conqueror—for personal power and mastery
- Solomon's seal—for judge's wisdom (especially when you are wrongly accused)

You should be familiar with Psalms 7 and 35, and if using candles, make sure they are brown for victory. Purple can be used for power over the opposing parties. Seven day saint candles to use include Just Judge and El Niño de Atocha. Court case oils, powders, incense, and baths can be used to enhance any work.

Helpful spirits to appeal to are Joe Feraille or Ogun, Ochosi, Marie Laveau, and Manman Brigit (especially for cases of murder and rape where you are the victim). Helpful saints include El Niño de Atoche and St. Martha.

Black Candle Tobacco Spell For Court Cases

On a Wednesday, during a waxing moon, mix together some powder from High John the Conqueror root, powder from the Low John root, clove, rosemary, sage, and a good aromatic pipe tobacco. At least seven days prior to going to court, combine the mixture with some blessed salt. Salt can be blessed by praying Psalm 23 over it. Anoint a black candle with Court Case Oil and burn it for eight minutes as you concentrate on winning your case before the judge. Use charcoal for the incense mixture, and allow the candle to burn for only eight minutes. Repeat this each day until your court date. Wear the oil as a perfume when in the courtroom and before the judge. According to an old New Orleans tradition, this spell aids in getting justice before the bar.

Day in Court Spell

To win court cases and influence the judge and jury, make this oil.

- Oil of cinnamon
- Oil of calendula
- Oil of frankincense
- Oil of carnation
- Piece of devil's shoestring
- Galangal root

Blend the above oils in carrier oil and add a piece of devil's shoestring and a piece of galangal root to the mixture. Add to the bath for three days before your court date. Anoint your arms, chest, and throat on court day. Place a few drops on your hands, and rub together briskly before signing important legal documents.

Dressed for Court

Write the judge's name three times, the prisoner's name three times, and the district attorney's name three times, and fold the paper small. Tell the prisoner to wear it in his shoe.

Then, get some oil of rose geranium, lavender oil, and verbena oil. Put three drops of each oil in ½ ounce club soda. Shake it and give it to the prisoner. He must use seven to nine drops on his person in court by rubbing it on his hands and body, from his face down his whole front. His clothes must also be dressed with seven to nine drops. Get to court before it starts and dress the court room, jury box, and judge's stand in the same fashion. The courts will rule in the prisoner's favor.

Hoodoo Spell for Justice

Go to a cemetery, and with your right hand gather dirt from the graves of nine children. Put the dirt in a white bowl and put it on your altar, facing east, between three white candles. Light the candles.

Add three teaspoons each of sugar and sulphur to the graveyard dirt. Recite Psalm 35. Ask the spirits to come with all their power to help you. Afterwards, buy a new pair of underclothes and a tan pair of socks, turn them inside out, and dress them with the graveyard dust. Place on your altar until your court date. Read Psalm 35 every day until your court date. On the day of court, turn the underclothes right side out and wear them. Keep the left sock inside out and wear it that way. The court will do as you wish.

Ochosi Spell for Justice

This spell petitions the help of Ochosi, the orisha of prisoners and the falsely accused.

- Three fresh fruits
- Three bird feathers
- Three rooster feathers
- Hair from a cat
- Hair from a dog
- High John the Conqueror powder

Write on parchment paper with pencil the names of the people involved, as well as their office or position. Wrap the feathers and powders in the papers with the names written on them and bind with crimson and green ribbons. This work can be buried until the case is solved, but it is necessary to give Ochosi the three fruits, replacing them when they rot, taking them to the jungle or the mountain, requesting your desire.

Silence Opposing Witnesses

To silence opposing witnesses, take a beef tongue, nine pins, and nine needles. Split the beef tongue. Write the names of your opponents on paper, cut the names out, and stuff them into the split tongue. Add some red pepper and beef gall. Pin the slit up with crossed needles and pins. Hang the tongue up in a chimney, tip up, and smoke the tongue for thirty-six hours. Then, take it down and put it in ice. Stick three black candles in the ice and light them. Read Psalm 22 (and 35 too, if for murder). Then ask the spirits for power more than equal to man.

To Win a Court Trial

Take the names of all the good witnesses, the judge, and the client's lawyer, and write them on a piece of parchment paper. Put the name papers in a dish and pour sweet oil over them. Burn a white candle beside the dish every morning for one hour, from nine to ten. On the day of the trial, put the dish upon your altar and don't take it down until the trial is over.[92]

To Silence a Court Rival

For this spell you will need a piece of parchment paper and two bricks. Take the names of your opponent, his witnesses, and his lawyer, and write them a on a piece of paper. Place the name paper between two whole bricks. Put the top brick crossways. On the day of the trial, set a bucket or dishpan with ice in it on top of the bricks. That's to freeze them out so they can't talk. [93]

To Win a Court Case (1)

Write the names of your opponent's lawyer, witnesses, and judge on a piece of parchment paper. Buy a beef tongue and split it from the base towards the tip, separating the top from the bottom. Put the name paper into the split tongue, along with eighteen pods of hot pepper, and pin it through and through with pins and needles. Put the tongue in a tin pail with plenty of vinegar and keep it on ice until the day of court. That day,

---

92   This spell is a root doctor formula taken from Zora Neale Hurston's *Mules and Men*.
93   Ibid.

pour kerosene into the bucket and burn it. Your opponent will destroy him or herself in court.[94]

To Win a Court Case (2)

Put the names of the judge and all those on your side on a piece of paper. Take the names of the twelve apostles after Judas hanged himself and write each apostle's name on a sage leaf. Stand six white candles in a tray of holy water and burn them. Wear six of the sage leaves in each shoe on the day of court, and the jury will decide in your favor.

To Win a Court Case (3)

Write all of your opponents' names on a slip of paper. Put the paper in a can, take soot and ashes from your chimney, and add salt to it. Stick pins crosswise in six white candles and burn them at a good hour. Set the can in a bucket of ice. Recite Psalm 120 before court and in court.

To Win a Court Case (4)

For this spell you will need:

- ½ pint of whiskey
- 9 pieces of John the Conqueror root acquired before September 21
- White rose perfume

Put the nine pieces of John the Conqueror root in the whiskey and let soak for thirty-eight hours. Shake it up really well and drain off root into another bottle. Get one ounce of white rose perfume and pour into the mixture. Wear this before going to court.

Crossroads Spells

"If you want to learn how to make songs yourself, you take your guitar and your go to where the road crosses that way, where a crossroads is. Be sure to get there just a little 'fore twelve that night so you know you'll be there. You have your guitar and be playing a piece there by yourself . . . A big black man will walk up

---

94 Ibid.

there and take your guitar and he'll tune it. And then he'll play a piece and hand it back to you. That's the way I learned to play anything I want."

—*Tommy Johnson*

In the folk magic of many cultures, the crossroads is a location where two realms touch and thus represent a place "between worlds" or "neither here nor there." As such, the crossroads is a site where supernatural spirits can be contacted and paranormal events can take place. Crossroads magic is prominent in conjure, rootwork, and hoodoo. It is said that special favors and talents, such as playing a musical instrument, throwing dice, or dancing, may be attained by going to a crossroads a certain number of times, either at midnight or just before dawn, where one will meet a "black man," presumably Legba though often mistaken for the Devil, who will bestow the desired skills.

Probably no other aspect of popular culture has spoken about, or I should say sung about, the crossroads more than blues musicians. The crossroads of blues legend was the intersection of Highways 49 and 61 in Mississippi, where many bluesmen allegedly "sold their souls" to the Devil (Legba) in exchange for fame and extraordinary playing ability. The preeminent archetype for the "bluesman who sold his soul to the devil" is Robert Johnson, even though some say it is actually the lesser-known artist, Tommy Johnson, who is first credited with the whole crossroads legend.

In the New Orleans Voodoo and related traditions, Papa Legba, Ellegua, and Exú are the spirits of crossroads. All of these manifestations of the crossroads "god" serve a similar role in that they act as intermediaries between the divine spirits and humans. They stand at the spiritual crossroads and give or deny permission to speak with the spirits of Guinee, and are believed to speak all human languages.

The crossroads play a prominent role in Voodoo and hoodoo. Not only are they a place where one can petition Legba and interact with the various loas; but they are where ritual remains are left; where leftover water from spiritual baths is disposed of; where cursed objects can be nullified; where any number of spells can be performed.

Crossroads Spell

Get three shiny pennies. Hold them in your right hand and tell them your problem. Put them in your left hand and envision the solution to your problem. Now cup both hands together, placing the pennies on the seam line between them, and ask Legba to help you decide.

Walk three blocks from your house in either direction. Stop at a crossroads; walk in a square, stopping at each corner. Then, walk diagonally through the crossroads. When you reach the center, toss the pennies over your left shoulder.

Go home and do not worry about your problem anymore. Legba will influence people and situations in such a way that the best option will become clear to you.[95]

Quick Decision Candle Spell

For this spell you will need the following items:

- 1 red glass seven day novena candle
- 3 pennies
- 3 pieces of candy
- 3 cigars with 3 wooden matches
- Small bottle of rum
- Petition written on paper

Clean the candle with saltwater and let dry. Write the issue about which you need to make a decision on the petition paper with Dragon's Blood Ink. Take all items to a crossroads. Lay down the petition paper, covering it with the pennies and candy. Place the candle in the center of the petition paper or document. Arrange the cigars at the 12 o'clock, 4 o'clock, and 8 o'clock positions, with the candle being in the center of this cross configuration. Place the unlit wooden matches at the 2 o'clock, 6 o'clock, and 10 o'clock positions.

Next, open the bottle of rum and take small swig, swishing it around in your mouth. Spray it out over the paper, candle, and everything. Place the remaining rum in the bottle down next to candle. Light the candle and walk away.

Do not turn to look back at what you have left. Return home a different route than the one you traveled to get to the crossroads. If there is no change in your situation within three days, repeat the offering until a decision is made or the desired change has occurred.

---

95 Teish, L. (1991). *Jambalaya, the Natural Woman's Book of Personal Charms and Practical Rituals.*, San Francisco: Harper One.

Crossing Spells

Crossing spells are a form of foot track magic—one of the oldest types of magick. When you decide to perform a crossing spell, you must be absolutely sure of what you want to achieve, and that the action is justifiable. When performing any kind of adversarial magick, be prepared to be confronted with antagonizing forces from which you should use all of your resources, magickal and non-magickal, to protect yourself. You should also use those resources available to you in society, such as the law, to help you achieve your means.

To Cross an Enemy (1)

Carve the name of one you want to cross in a black cross candle. Turn the candle upside down and carve away at the wax until the wick is exposed from the bottom. Burn upside down. Dispose of the wax remains in a cemetery.

To Cross an Enemy (2)

Carve the name of your oppressor into a black image candle and anoint it upside down with Revenge Oil. Say Psalm 55 over the candle nine times while it burns. Throw the wax remains in a cemetery.

To Cross an Enemy (3)

Use a stick to draw a cross mark with wavy lines in the ground in the path of your target. Sprinkle a crossing powder made of salt, sulphur, black pepper, cayenne pepper, and graveyard dirt onto the cross mark. Activate the cross mark by spitting on it and cursing out your enemy.

Cure-Alls

In Voodoo spells, the "cure-all" was very popular amongst followers. Though there are different recipes, a "cure all" was a spell that could solve all problems.

Cure-All

Mix some jimson weed with sulphur and honey, place in a glass, rub against a black cat, and then sip slowly.

Cure for General Illness

Take a beef tongue and boil in water and honey to make a broth. Feed the afflicted nine drops three times a day for nine days.

Psalm to Become Free from Danger and Suffering

Mix rose oil, water, and salt in a vessel. Pray the most holy name Jeho, Psalm 20, over it seven times. Add a heartfelt prayer of your own. Anoint your face and hands with the oil, water, and salt mixture and sprinkle it on your clothing. You will remain free from danger and suffering that day.[96]

A Powerful Tonic

Pour a full quart of wine in a pot and place over a fire. Add three pinches of uncooked rice, one tablespoon of cinnamon, five small pieces of pomegranate hull, and five tablespoons of sugar. Stir all of the ingredients together and bring to a boil. Cover tightly and remove from the fire, allowing it to cool slightly. Take one tablespoon with each meal for added energy and to build immunity to illnesses.[97]

Curses, Jinxes, and Hexes

Hex, bind, curse, jinx, trick, cross, goofer . . . all of these terms are ways of describing something very similar in the Voodoo hoodoo vernacular. A curse is the result of a spell or prayer asking that a god, natural force, or spirit bring misfortune to someone. To perform such a "trick" is to work the left hand of Voodoo. Curses, jinxes, and hexes are considered black magic spells because they are concerned with hurting, harming, goofering, jinxing, or hot footing enemies.

If a woman can get a little of your blood on a piece of cloth and tie it up in a bag and wear it on her leg, she will run you crazy in nine days.

On the other hand, certain types of spells can be used to repel negative energy, to keep a perpetrator from hurting someone, or for driving away bad neighbors.

---

96 Adapted from Selig, G. A. (1982). *Secrets of the Psalms,* Arlington, TX: Dorene Publishing Co.
97 From Pelton, R. W. (1974). *Voodoo Signs and Omens.* South Brunswick and New York: A. S. Barnes and Company.

Create Confusion

Carve the name of one you want to confuse in a black skull candle. Anoint the candle with Confusion Oil and sprinkle with black salt. Burn the candle. Dispose of the wax remains in the woods.

Cross 'o Stones

To create chaos in the life of an enemy, lay a series of stones in the shape of a cross in their path, with a button belonging to the target placed in the center as a sympathetic link to that person.

Damnation Spell

The purpose of this spell is to undo your enemies and take the power to harm you away from them.

Take two drachmas of the damnation powders and two drachmas of the water powders. Make a package of them and send it to the home of the one who has spoken badly of you or treated you poorly. This will cause damnation and trouble for the enemy.

The Curse of Marie Laveau

Set an altar for a curse with black candles that have been dressed in vinegar. Write the name of the person to be cursed on the candle with a needle. Then place fifteen cents in the lap of death upon the altar to pay the spirit to obey your orders. Then place your hands flat upon the table and say this curse-prayer:

To the Man God: Oh great One, I have been sorely tried by my enemies and have been blasphemed and lied against. My good thoughts and my honest actions have been turned to bad actions and dishonest ideas. My home has been disrespected; my children have been cursed and ill-treated. My dear ones have been back-bitten and their virtue questioned. Oh Man God, I beg that this that I ask for my enemies shall come to pass: That the South wind shall scorch their bodies and make them wither and shall not be tempered to them. That the North wind shall freeze their blood and numb their muscles and that it shall not be tempered to them. That the West wind shall blow away their life's breath and will not leave their hair grow and that their finger nails shall fall off and their bones shall crumble.

*That the East wind shall make their minds grow dark, their sight shall fail
and their seed dry up so that they shall not multiply.*

*I ask that their fathers and mothers from their furthest generation will
not intercede for them before the great throne, and the wombs of their
women shall not bear fruit except for strangers, and that they shall become
extinct. I pray that the children who come shall be weak
of mind and paralyzed of limb and that they themselves
shall curse them in their turn for ever turning the breath
of life into their bodies. I pray that disease and death
shall be forever with them and that their worldly goods
shall not prosper, and that their crops shall not multiply
and that their cows, their sheep, and their hogs and all
their living beasts shall die of starvation and thirst. I pray
that their house shall be unroofed and that the rain, the
thunder and lightning shall find the innermost recesses of their home and
that the foundation shall crumble and the floods tear it asunder. I pray that
the sun shall not shed its rays on them in benevolence, but instead it shall
beat down on them and burn them and destroy them. I pray that the moon
shall not give them peace, but instead shall deride them and decry them
and cause their minds to shrivel. I pray that their friends shall betray them
and cause them loss of power, of gold and of silver, and that their enemies
shall smite them until they beg for mercy which shall not be given them. I
pray that their tongues shall forget how to speak in sweet words and that it
shall be paralyzed and that all about them will be desolation, pestilence and
death. Oh Man God, I ask you for all these things because they have dragged
me in the dust and destroyed my good name; broken my heart and caused
me to curse the day that I was born. So be it.*[98]

**If a hoodoo person wants
to show you something,
let them put their own
hand on it, for if you touch
it they can poison you.**

Hex That Perp

This ritual is to be performed against someone who has perpetrated evil
against you or a loved one. This one is particularly good for sexual preda-
tors and pedophiles. For this spell, you will need:

- Parchment paper
- Four Thieves Vinegar
- Dragon's Blood Ink

---

98 From Hurston, Z. N. (1932) *Mules and Men.*

- Patchouli oil
- Black candle

Wet the piece of parchment paper in Four Thieves Vinegar. Let it dry. Write the name of the person you wish to hex using Dragon's Blood Ink (red ink will do in a pinch). Hold the paper in the flame of a black candle which has been dressed with patchouli oil. Sprinkle the ashes by your enemy's place of residence. If you do not know where they live, blow the ashes in the wind while asking the wind to take the ashes to the perpetrator's home. Your enemy's life will soon become a living hell.

> **An evil person can take the length of your fingers and hoodoo you in two days, to make you do whatever they want.**

To Keep a Man Drunk

A person can cause you to become very thirsty by putting a whiskey bottle under your porch for three weeks, and then throwing the bottle into a fire. This will make you very thirsty for whiskey.

Marie Laveau's Confounding an Enemy Spell (1)

Dip a piece of parchment paper into Four Thieves Vinegar. On this sheet write the names of your enemies. Send the paper to the house of your enemies, tightly sealed with the wax of a porcupine plant.

Marie Laveau's Confounding an Enemy Spell (2)

Sprinkle War Water in front of the house of your enemy as you pass by.

Marie Laveau's Punishment Ritual

This ritual is designed to punish a person who is already indicted, or to punish a person who has severely harmed a loved one.

When you want a person who is already indicted punished, write his name on a slip of paper and put it in a sugar bowl or some other deep bowl or dish. Now put in some red pepper and some black pepper. Put in one eightpermy nail, a splash of ammonia, and two door keys. Drop one key down in the bowl and leave the other one against the side. Now you got your bowl set. Go to your bowl every day at twelve o'clock and turn the key that is standing against the side of the bowl—that is to keep the man locked in jail. Every time you turn the key, add a little vinegar. Now, I know this will do the job. All it needs is for you to do it in faith.

Salt and Saltpeter Bath for Puttin' de Enemies Under Yore Feet

To thrive and prosper to the chagrin of your enemies, take a tablespoon of saltpeter and a tablespoon of salt and add to a pot that contains five quarts of water. Place on a stove set to medium-high heat. Just as it is about to boil, stir the mixture and remove from heat. Repeat this three times, allowing it to just start to boil, stirring the mixture, and removing it from the heat. After the third time, remove it from the heat for good. Add it to a bath that you have drawn, and bathe in it. When you are finished bathing, save the water and throw it to the east. Say, "Lord moves thine evil influence."[99]

To Swell a Man

This ritual is done to stop a person from bragging and belittling you or another. For this ritual you will need:

- A new brick
- 9 black candles
- Piece of paper
- Twine

Steal a new brick. Dress nine black candles by writing the offender's name on each. Write the offender's name nine times on a piece of paper, and place it face down on the brick. Tie securely with twine. Light the black candles to burn, one each day for nine days. Then, dig a well to the water table and slip the brick slowly to the bottom. "Just like the brick soaks up the water, so that man will swell."

---

99   Hyatt. Waycross, Ga., (1118, small-time root woman), 1796:1.

Defensive Magick

Simple Defense Spell for Hoodoo Warfare

88ナ~ スひ 974226

If you are the victim of a spiritual attack, here is a simple spell to do to reverse the attack and send it back to the attacker, while providing you protection from further attack in the process. Take a brown candle. Butt the candle, and inscribe it with the name of St. Michael using the Theban alphabet. Anoint the candle with Fiery Wall of Protection Oil, and roll in Fiery Wall of Protection Powder. Set the candle on a mound of sugar. Light the candle and say the prayer to St. Michael before going to sleep. In the morning when the candle has burned down, put all of the remains of the wax and sugar in a paper bag and dispose of in your enemy's trash or at a crossroads.

Spiritual Defense Potted Plant Spell (see Potted Plant Spells)

- 4 red pots
- Protection talisman
- 4 railroad spikes
- Bottle of whiskey
- 4 strips of red flannel
- 4 St. Benedict medals
- Fiery Wall of Protection incense and oil

Wrap the protection talismans around the railroad spikes and tie in place with the red flannel. Anoint with oil and pass through incense. Plant spikes along with medals in each pot. Place a pot in each of the four corners of your home.

Doll Magick

Banishment and Equalizer Spell

This spell asks God to be the mediator between you and your enemy by protecting you and punishing the person who hurt you.

This spell can be used as a means to settle the score with an enemy by causing them to be ostracized, resulting in mental anguish. Since you are asking God to intervene for you, you are not in danger of any ill effects.

Write the name of your target on the parchment paper and anoint with Black Arts Oil. Tuck the paper into a black Voodoo doll. Recite Psalm 55 nine times over the doll, and stick one pin through the parchment paper and into the doll. Wrap the doll in a black cloth and hide in a dark place, careful to choose a spot where no one can find it and handle it.

If someone always comes to the house at dinner time, place a bottle of castor oil by their plate, which will make them so sick they will never impose on you again.

Each day for eight more days (for a total of nine days), take out the doll and recite Psalm 55 over it nine times. Stick a pin through the parchment paper and into the doll. Wrap the doll in a black cloth and hide away in a dark place, away from prying eyes.

On the ninth day, take the doll and the black cloth and bury it near a cemetery. Alternately, you can burn the doll and throw the ashes in a cemetery. Or, you may keep the doll and remove the parchment paper and nine pins from the doll and either bury them in or near a cemetery or burn and throw the ashes in or near a cemetery. If you keep the doll for future use, you may only use it to represent the same person, and you must keep it wrapped up and away from view, except when you wish to speak to your enemy through it.

Spell to Bind Someone Dangerous

This spell is best performed on Saturday (Saturn's Day—to bind a criminal, one who intends to do harm, to bring someone to justice). For this spell you need:

- A doll baby made to represent the target
- A black candle
- Salt water

- Personal effect of the target, if available
- Frankincense incense
- Red ribbon

Light a black candle and burn frankincense incense. Sprinkle the doll baby with salt water, saying:

I have made you to be _____ (name the person being bound)
It is he/she that you are.

Hold the doll baby and begin tying it up firmly with the red ribbon, binding all parts that could possibly do harm. Then bury the doll baby far from your home, under a heavy rock beneath a tree.

Doll to Drive Away Your Lover's Mistress

Make a doll baby out of red cloth to represent your man. Then make a penis out of the cloth to tie it onto the doll. To do this, cut a 2 x 1-inch piece of cloth and sew up three sides, then turn inside out. Stuff the penis with some of your lover's pubic hair, a piece of their underwear, nine drops of your menstrual blood, and Spanish moss. Sew the penis onto the doll, allowing some of the Spanish moss to show. Lay the doll on a bed of magnolia leaves inside a box. When you are sure your cheatin' man is going to see his mistress, tie a black cord around the doll's penis and pin the cord to the penis, using three black-headed pins. Now, take a black candle and anoint with Commanding Oil. Set it to the left of the doll and light it. Scratch the name of the other woman onto the candle (if you know it). Next, take a white candle and scratch your name onto this candle and anoint with magnolia oil. Set the white candle to the right of the doll and light it. Finally, take a red candle that you have anointed with Fire of Love Oil, set it at the head of the doll, and light it. Set a bowl of water at the foot of the doll and recite Psalm 85 to promote reconciliation between you and your lover.

Keep a Big Man Down Spell

This spell is designed to knock someone down a notch or two after they have gotten too big for their britches. For this ritual you will need:

- Blue candle
- Black pen
- Piece of paper

- Bitter aloes
- Cayenne pepper
- Black doll baby
- Black thread
- Black lace

Put the blue candle on your altar and light it. Write your target's name on a slip of paper with black ink. Take a small black doll baby and rip open its back. Put the paper with the name along with some bitter aloes and cayenne pepper inside. Sew the rip up again with the black thread. Tie the hands of the doll behind its back and make a black veil from the lace; then tie it over the face, and knot it from behind. Place the doll in a kneeling position in a dark corner where it won't be disturbed. Your target will be frustrated as long as the doll is not disturbed.

Fertility Spells

There are a number of saints that can be petitioned for fertility and childbirth.

To have a child:

- St. Anna, Mother of the Theotokos
- St. Elizabeth, Mother of the Forerunner
- St. Sabbas the Sanctified of Palestine
- St. Irene Chrysovolantou

For safe childbirth:

- St. Eleftherios

For the care and protection of infants:

- St. Stylianos

To Increase Fertility

Make this Ya Ya powder and sprinkle it on yourself regularly to increase fertility, prevent miscarriage, and increase male potency. For this powder you will need:

- Vetivert
- Cinnamon

- Sage
- Rose

Take a handful of each of the herbs and grind to a powder. Add to a base of cornstarch and mix well.

To Make a Woman Barren

Take an egg of a guinea fowl and write your target's name on the egg. Then, roll it in cayenne pepper and goofer dust. Boil it in a pot of clear rain water until it is hard. This will cause the woman to be barren.

Foot Track Magick

Foot track magick involves working sorcery using the dirt from someone's footprint placed in a bottle—or else placing a sprinkling powder such as goofer dust or graveyard dirt inside someone's shoes or in a place they're likely to walk through, in order to administer a curse. Walking over the buried bottle spell or contact between the powder and the victim's foot results in toxic magical consequences such as a streak of bad luck or unexplained illness.

To collect a foot track, locate a footprint in the dirt and gather the dirt that makes up the print. This is the dirt that goes into the bottle for the bottle spell.

Bring Back a Straying Lover

To bring back a straying lover, gather some dirt from the path that his or her left foot has walked on. Place the foot track in one of your lover's socks or stockings along with some devil's shoestring, and bury the charm in your front yard. Your loved one will come back to you within a short time.

Git Rid of a Hateful Husband

Take the right foot track of your hateful husband and put it in a dark bottle. Add a dirt dauber's nest and some cayenne pepper to the foot track and parch it in an old tin frying pan. Put all of this into a dirty sock and tie it up. Turn the bundle away from you as you tie it. Carry it to the river at noon. When you get within forty feet of the river, run fast to the edge of the water, whirl suddenly, hurl the sock over your left shoulder into the water, and never look back. Say, "Go, and go quick in the name of the Lord."

Running Feet

This spell is a root doctor formula taken from Zora Neale Hurston's *Mules and Men*.

This spell is to make someone run around like a chicken with their head cut off. Take the dirt out of the person's foot tracks and mix with red pepper. Throw some of this mixture into a running stream of water. This will cause the person to run from place to place until finally they run themselves to death.

Gambling Luck Spells

Hoodoo spells are often quite simple. For example, if you want to win the lottery, you might carry a mojo hand containing ingredients that bring luck in games of chance. These hands are considered as effective as more elaborate spells. The following spells and charms are good for improving luck with games of chance.

Place dried seaweed under the busiest portion of the house to draw luck and prosperity to you.

Gambling Luck

Write the Apostle's Creed backwards. Fold it around a whole nutmeg, tie with a green ribbon, and anoint with Fast Luck Oil. Carry it with you when you gamble.

For Gambling Advice

Take a lodestone and some brimstone (sulphur) to a crossroads at midnight. Light the brimstone with a match. A spirit will appear and give you gambling advice.

Lucky Gambling Mojo

To be lucky in gambling, make a mojo bag that contains a John the Conqueror root, a dime with your initials scratched on it, and a lodestone dressed with magnetic sand. Carry it in your pocket when gambling.

Lodestone and Brimstone Charm

To get advice in gambling from the spirits, take a lodestone and some brimstone (sulphur) to a crossroads at midnight. Light the brimstone with a match, and a spirit will appear and counsel you in winning at games of chance.

To Win at Every Game One Engages In

This spell comes from John George Hohman's (1820) *Pow-wows or the Long Lost Friend*. The pow wows book is a collection of magical formulas and veterinary recipes of Germanic origin; it has had a big influence on hoodoo.

Tie the heart of a bat with a red silken string to the right arm, and you will win every game at cards you play.

Good Luck Spells

The best times to do work that draws luck in money and love are Thursdays and Sundays under the waxing moon or full moon. Colors associated with this type of work include gold (money), green (to draw), pink (luck in love), and red (sexual luck).

A spider found crawling on a person is good luck.

For Good Luck

Wear an alligator's tooth around your neck and avoid going near the ocean or a river with it as it will lose its power.

Magic Broom Good Luck and Prosperity Spell

The purpose of this spell is to bring good luck and abundance into your life.

- Charcoal block
- Money Drawing incense
- Hemp cord
- Miniature broom
- Cowry shell
- Coin
- Piece of abalone shell
- Hemp cord

Place a piece of charcoal on a fireproof dish and light it. Take a pinch of the Money Drawing incense and put it in the charcoal. As the incense burns, tie the hemp cord onto the broom and attach the charms: cowry shell for general good luck, coin for wealth, abalone for protection in business and personal affairs. Tie seven knots in the cord, and with each knot, focus on what you specifically desire in the areas of luck and prosperity.

Hang the talisman in your home or office, or wherever you want to concentrate your efforts.

Healing Spells

To Heal Physical Pain

Sit in a quiet place and clear your mind of everything you can. Take a glass of holy water and hold it in the hand that is closest to the hurt (if the pain is in the center of the body, hold it in your writing hand). Begin rubbing the glass of holy water over your body and concentrate on the area in need of healing. Focus all your healing energy into this area. If this doesn't work the first time, then repeat. You should feel better soon.

Voodoo Doll Healing Spell

For this spell you need a white Voodoo doll—white is the color for healing and purifying. Write the name of the person in need of healing on a piece of paper, and attach it to the doll along with a personal effect that belongs to the person. Anoint two white candles with holy oil and set them on either side of the doll. Anoint the doll with the holy oil as well. Light the candles and pray for good health and healing.

Guardian Angel Spell for Protection from Evil Spirits

For protection from evil spirits and to cast evil out of your home, take seven sprigs from a willow tree and seven leaves from a date palm and bring to a gentle boil in a pan of water. Allow to cool, and transfer to a glass bowl on your altar. Say Psalm 29 over the bowl of water nine times in the evening, while burning a seven day Guardian Angel candle for protection. Then recite the following prayer, which is usually found on the back of the candle:

Spirit protector, who gives constant protection to me; my loved ones and my friends who help me, give guidance to those who assist me with answers to my life's problems and give comfort to my soul. Reveal to me what I must do tomorrow, and give strength and courage to my afflicted spirit. Make my problems disappear and restore my faith. (Concentrate on your desires) Amen.

Repeat the above daily for seven days or until the candle is completely burned down. Then take the bowl of water and pour what remains of it on your front doorstep. Evil spirits will no longer be able to cross over the threshold of your home.

Love Spells

Many practitioners advise against doing love spells that are directed towards any specific person. You are encouraged to perform spells to attract love in general, and allow the universe to bring the right person to you, rather than attempting to manipulate a person's will. There is a general consensus that the best times to do love drawing spells are on Thursdays and Sundays when the moon is waxing or full.

Adam and Eve Love Mojo

This simple mojo uses the power attributed to the Adam and Eve root. This spell is for two people who are already in love and who wish to strengthen their love and commitment to each other.

Make two mojo bags out of red flannel, one for each partner. Inside the bags, place the Adam root (cone shape) for the man and the Eve root (round shape) for the woman. Add some Dittany of Crete (to increase love and passion), damiana herb (to draw your lover closer and to improve sexual relations), and some coriander seeds (to promote fidelity). Pray Psalm 139 together to increase and preserve your love, and anoint your bags with Adam and Eve Oil. The woman should keep the mojo in her bra, and the man should carry in his right pocket. Every Friday, take out your mojo bags and pray Psalm 139 over them, recharging with Adam and Eve oil. This ritual will keep you and your lover close for as long as you continue to do it.

Adam and Eve Love Spell

For this very simple spell you will need some Adam and Eve incense. Using Dove's Blood Ink, write the names of the two lovers on parchment paper and draw a heart around the names. Anoint the edges of the name paper with Adam and Eve Oil. Place the paper beneath an incense burner and light some Adam and Eve incense. Focus your intention while the incense burns. Repeat as necessary.

Algiers Love Charm

An old root doctor taught me this trick on one of my many visits to Algiers. Algiers is one of the oldest neighborhoods in New Orleans, situated across the Mississippi from the French Quarter. His name was Samuel Brown, and he was considered a strange man by many, keeping mostly to himself. One afternoon, I walked up the sidewalk to Sam Brown's front porch. A young black man walked by me in a relative hurry, carrying a brown paper sack. He nodded and smiled, and I greeted him as well. When I got to Sam's front door, he laughed, and said, "Here she come! 'Lil Voodoo Mama comin' to learn me some tricks!" (I was much younger then, in my twenties; hence the "lil.") Obviously he was being facetious, as I was one doing the lernin', though he did often ask me about the Indian medicine I "brought" with me. He used to say that Indian medicine was powerful stuff.

Anyway, I asked him what was in the paper bag the young man was carrying. He said he gave the man some May Water that he needed to perform a love charm he was prescribed. May Water is rain water collected from the first rain in May. I couldn't resist, and asked him about the love charm he prescribed. He said something to the effect of "Now you know I can't tell you nuthin' 'bout nuthin' right now. I let you know when the time is right." I figured he wouldn't tell me at that time because he had just prescribed the work, and since I was not part of that work, it would be inappropriate for him to tell me anything about it. I did eventually get it out of him, at a later date. I always remembered it, because it was an unusually floral trick, not the typical kind he was known to prescribe. This is what I remember about his love charm.

Get a large pot and fill it three quarters full with May Water. To this, add nine honeysuckle flowers, nine petals from magnolia blossoms, a bit of graveyard dirt, a wishbone from a chicken that you have wished your intention on, and three tablespoons of maple syrup. Boil all of this down to half its original amount, then add nine more honeysuckle flowers, nine more petals from magnolia blossoms, and three more tablespoons of maple syrup. Boil it down again, and then allow it to cool. Transfer half of it to a large jar or bottle. Set the bottle or jar on the Bible for nine days. The Bible supposedly strengthens the charm. Each day for the next nine days, take a bath with a little of the May Water in the bath water. After the nine days, take the jar and bury it in the yard of the one to be charmed. Alternately, it can be placed under the person's front porch.

Attraction Love Spell

The purpose of this spell is to attract the person you love. This spell is most effective when performed during a full moon or when the moon is waxing. Take a pink candle and engrave a heart into it with a toothpick or new nail. Place the candle on a windowsill with the heart in the moonlight. Place a bottle of Come to Me Oil in front of the candle . Write a petition in Dove's Blood Ink that states what and who you want, anoint with the Come to Me Oil and place the paper under the candle. Once the candle burns out naturally, carry the perfume with you and apply every time you go out to meet people.

A love powder is a half teaspoonful of sugar, a teaspoonful of peppermint, and a teaspoonful of grated candied orange peel; give a teaspoonful of this mixture in a glass of wine and the person will love you forever.

Bring Back Yo' Ex

Try this spell to bring back your ex. For this spell, you will need:

- Your lover's dirty left sock (or another personal item if you can't get a sock)
- Piece of paper
- Fresh basil
- Red candle
- Glass of water

Write your lover's name three times on a piece of paper. Dig a hole in the ground. Put the paper with the name in the hole first, then the sock or other personal item. Light a red candle on top of it all and burn it. Put a spray of sweet basil in a glass of water beside the candle. Light the candle at noon and burn until one o'clock. Pinch the candle flame out. Light it again at six o'clock and burn until seven o'clock. After the candle is lit, turn a barrel over the hole. When you get it in place, knock on it three times to call the spirit and say: "Tumba Walla, Bumba Walla, bring (name your lover) home to me."

Recipe to Make a Man Love You

The following is a recipe from the *Great Book of Saint Cyprian*, a book that became widely used in popular religion, especially Umbanda and Candomble. Saint Cyprian is the legendary patron saint of witches, conjurers, root doctors, and spiritual workers, both good and evil. The book is said to derive from a manuscript made by the saint himself. Although the book is attributed to St. Cyprian, the first edition was published in 1849, centuries after his death.

It is considered a sin by many to possess or even touch the *Great Book of Saint Cyprian*. In fact, it is a common belief in Portugal that reading the book from back to front will attract the Devil. The fear surrounding the consequences of touching, reading, and possessing the book are so pronounced that owners of book shops are said to keep it chained inside a box.

This recipe calls for the woman to give the chosen man a cup of chocolate, to which she must add two pinches of powdered cinnamon, five spikes of clove, ten grams of vanilla, and a pinch of ground nutmeg. After it is ready, take out the cloves and add two drops of Spanish fly *(cantharides)*. To eat it is better, and the ingredients can be added to a sweet cake that is then served to the man. The chocolate can be substituted by coffee, but in this case the coffee must be prepared with anise, adding a drop of Spanish fly later.[100]

To Keep a Partner Faithful

If you are concerned about fidelity in your relationship, you can keep your partner faithful by doing this little trick. Write the name of your partner on a piece of brown paper with Dove's Blood Ink and anoint the four corners of the note with Stay With Me Oil. Place it in the chimney of your home. Pray upon the note with Psalm 23.

Rule da' Man Spell

This spell was adapted from Zora-Neale Hurston's *Mules and Men*. It is used to gain control over the man you love. You will need:

- A sock worn by your man
- One silver dime

---

100 From *Antigo Livro de São Cipriano*, 1993, Editora Espiritualista, Ltda, Rio de Janeiro, Translated by Ray Vogensen.

- Some of his hair
- Piece of paper
- Steel dust
- Lodestone (male)

Lay the sock out on a table, bottom up. Write your man's name three times on the piece of paper and put it on the sock. Place the dime on the name and the hair on the dime. Put a piece of male lodestone on top of the hair and sprinkle it with steel dust. As you do this, say, "Feed the he, feed the she." That is what you call feeding the lodestone. Then fold the sock heel on the toe and roll it all up together tight. Pin the bundle by crossing two needles. Then wet it with whiskey and set it up over a door. And don't allow him to go off no more, or you will lose all control.

To Make a Man Come Home

Take nine deep red or pink candles. Write your man's name three times on each candle. Wash the candles with Van Van. Write the name on paper three times and place under the candles. Call the name of the party three times at the hours of seven, nine, or eleven. [101]

To Keep Your Man from Running Around

If your husband is running around, take some of his hair and a piece of his necktie and put them in a bottle. Then throw that in the river; when that necktie rots, your husband will change his ways.

To Keep a Man

To keep your husband to yourself, take your first urine on a Monday morning and put it in a jar. Place the jar under the bed for nine days, and it will hold him close to you.

To Make a Man Crazy for You

Cut some hair from your pubic area and some from your man's head, and tie it all together to wear in your left shoe. This'll make him crazy about you.

---

101 Hurston, Z. N. (1990). *Mules and Men*, First Edition. Harper Perennial.

To Keep a Man from Talking to a Woman

If you don't want your man to talk to another woman, take a nail and drive it at the end of his heel prints. He will run from her the next time he sees her.

Spell to Get a Man

For a woman to get a man away from another woman, gather these ingredients:

- Salt
- Bowl
- Red pepper
- Lemon
- Parchment paper
- Graveyard dirt

Write the name of your target on the piece of parchment paper nine times. Cut a hole in the end of the lemon and pour some of the graveyard dirt into the hole. Roll up the name paper and stick it in the hole. Pour the salt into the bowl, and wrap the bowl and the lemon up in a red cloth. Dig a hole in a sunny part of your target's yard and bury the lemon, standing it up. Sprinkle some salt and red pepper over the place where you buried the lemon, and say:

"Fuss and fuss 'til you part and go away,
Then (insert person's name) come to me and stay."

Spell to Bring Back a Love

To bring a lover back, you need:

- Piece of paper
- 2 silver dimes
- 6 red candles
- Glass of water

Write the name of the absent party six times on paper. Put the paper in a water glass with two silver dimes in it. Write his or her name three times eachon six candles and burn one on a windowsill in the daytime for six days.

To Make Love Stronger

To bring back a wayward love, gather these items:

- 6 red candles
- 60 straight pins
- Parchment paper
- Cinnamon incense

You will do the following ritual six nights in a row. Prepare each candle in the following manner: Stick thirty pins into one side of a red candle, and thirty more pins into the other side of the same candle. Write the name of your beloved three times on a small square of parchment paper and place it underneath the red candle. Light the candle and let it burn down. Then take six pieces of parchment paper and write the name of your beloved one time on each slip of paper. Save the pins from the candle. The following morning, take four of the pins and stick them into one of the name papers, one on each side of your beloved's name. Smudge the name paper in the smoke of cinnamon incense. Then take the paper and the pins and bury them under your doorstep. Burn one candle this way each day for six days. Save all of the papers with your beloved's name written three times, and the wax from each candle, until the end of the six days. After you have done this ritual for six days, take all of the papers, wax, and pins and bury them in the same hole.

Magick Lamps

Old-time rootworkers use magick lamps in hoodoo because of their power and effectiveness—they produce results. Lamps are also used in New Orleans Voodoo and Haitian Voodoo to gain favors from the spirits. The reason they produce quick results is because they are hotter than candles and can be mounted by the spirits. Once you recite a saint's novena or utter the secret words of a spirit over the lit lamp, you draw that spirit down into the work.

Magick lamps can be made out of any number of containers. The first issue of concern is that the container be fireproof—that it can withstand the heat that is produced by burning oil. The second concern is the nature of the work—is it for protection? Love? Money? You can use a variety of different containers for burning oil, and some have properties that lend themselves to the particular work you are trying to do. Here are a few examples:

- For a work of protection, use a hollowed-out pineapple with the barbs intact
- To petition Eleggua, use a coconut shell
- To petition Yemayá, use a crystal bowl or a thick seashell
- For general purposes, you can use a coffee can or tin can
- Use a hurricane lamp for all general works (common in New Orleans for obvious reasons, but also because they are built for heat—you can fill up the base with oils and herbs and whatever else you want to use in the spell, put on the glass top, and everything is nice and safely contained)

For other containers, you will need a wick, which you can purchase at any craft supply store. The wick is then suspended in the oil through a piece of aluminum foil or a cross of bones. The type of oil mixture you use is consistent with the particular spirit and purpose. If calling upon a spirit, the lamp should be placed on an altar that is consecrated for that spirit and refilled daily until the desired result is obtained. Please refer to my book, *A Guide for Serving the Seven African Powers*, for instructions on how to make altars.

The following are some recipes for magick lamps to get you started.

Magick Lamp for Black Hawk

If you have battles to fight and feel you need the spirit of the Indian warrior behind you, create this magick lamp for father Black Hawk. Petition him to fight your battles for you.

- Olive oil base
- Sage
- Cedar
- Arrowhead
- Large abalone shell or other fireproof container

Fill the abalone shell or other container with the olive oil up to about a half inch from the top of the container. Add some sage, cedar, and an arrowhead in the oil; then add your wick. Place the lamp on an altar you have created for Father Black Hawk. The Spiritualist churches of New Orleans will have things like bananas, sugarcane stalks, sweet potatoes, apples, oranges, peppermints, and four groups of three red candles that are configured in a triangle pattern. A plaster or resin figure or bust of Black Hawk will sit prominently in the center, with two groups of four candles at either side. You can place images of the St. Michael, Dr. Martin

Luther King, and other Native American-themed items on the altar as well. Place the lamp in front of his altar. Light the lamp.

To petition Black Hawk, offer him some Indian tobacco and say the prayer to Black Hawk in chapter 4. Tell Father Black Hawk that you have prepared these offerings for him in return for his help. You can now talk to him about what you need. When you are done praying, you may share in eating the food with him by preparing a special plate for him with some of everything on it, and a plate for yourself. You should not waste the food, so don't make more than you can eat, plus one extra plate. Be sure to thank him when you are finished. The food may be discarded under a tree when you are done.

Magick Lamp for Erzulie Dantor

Erzulie Dantor can be petitioned by women who are victims of domestic violence who seek her protection. She is also petitioned for business matters and to improve money flow, bring in customers, and the like.

- Olive oil base
- Palmascriti (just a dash)
- Honey
- Ginger
- Cinnamon
- Chili peppers
- Dash of crème de cacao

Create an altar for Erzulie Dantor. Drape your altar with navy blue and gold cloth, and place some silver jewelry, knives, and perfumes on the altar. Place offerings of cooked pork, crème de cacao, and sweet potatoes in special bowls reserved just for Erzulie Dantor. Place a blue or yellow in candle in each plate; use both colors if you have more than one food offering. Light the candles.

Create your lamp while sitting in front of her altar. Combine the above ingredients and secure the wick in place. Light the lamp. Now, invoke Legba with the following words:

Legba, Papa Legba, open the gate for the loa!
Open the gate for Erzulie Dantor, Papa Legba!
Open the gate allow Dantor safe passage!
I have arrived, I am waiting for her.

Now you may communicate with Erzulie Dantor. Say the following:

> *Erzulie Dantor, you are strong and powerful! Do you see these offerings I have for you?*

Pick up each offering up and hold it above you, presenting it to the four sacred directions.

> *I offer some of your favorite things to eat and drink and these beautiful objects for you.*

> *Erzulie Dantor, I am in need of your protection and intervention. Help me, defend me, fight for me and my family!*

Now you must be specific about what you need her to do for you. Talk to her and tell her about your problems. Write down your request on a piece of parchment paper with blue ink. If you have written about problems you are having, fold the paper away from you several times. If you have written about something you want, fold the paper towards you several times. Place the paper on the altar and stab it seven times with a knife. Each time you stab it, say something to the effect of:

> *I win!*
> *I am empowered!*
> *I prevail!*

When you are done, sit quietly in front of your altar. Thank Erzulie Dantor for her help. You can use this time for divination if you would like. Allow the candles in the food offerings to burn down.

Dispose of the ritual remains at a crossroads. Now all you have to do is wait for her to answer your petition. Pay attention to your dreams, and be most respectful of your mother and the women and children in your life. Keep the lamp filled with oil and burning constantly in a safe place until your prayers are answered. When this happens, bottle the oil and use it in future works that are related to the original intention of your work.

Magick Lamp for Exú for Protection

Here is a lamp spell from my book, *Exú, the Divine Trickster* that leaves you with a nice oil you can use for other works.

To make powerful Exú oil for protection, fill the bottom of an oil lamp with olive oil and add some salvia, basil, ginger, an arrowhead, and top off with castor oil. Place the lamp on your altar before a statue or doll of Exú, light it, and leave it burning while you evoke Exú. Knock three times on the altar in front of the lamp and say:

Exú! Exú! Exú! It is me, (state your name).
I need your protection Exú,
from (state why you need protection).
Exú, owner of the crossroads, with your trident, cape, and hat,
Take care and provide protection at the break of dawn.
Take all the evil that came here, grab it by the tail,
and throw it into the depths of nothingness.
I make this prayer so that my enemies topple over
and I am left surrounded in your fiery wall of protection,
purified by flame, transformed by the night.

When you are finished, snuff out the lamp. Repeat this for seven days. After you have said these prayers, strain the oil from the herbs and put it in a glass bottle. You now have a powerful Exú oil for protection that you can use to anoint the doorways of your home, car, workplace, or anywhere you feel the need for protection.

To Make a Wick that is Never Consumed

Take an ounce of asbestos and boil it in a quart of strong lye for two hours; then pour off the lye and clarify what remains by pouring rainwater on it three or four times, after which you can form a wick from it which will never be consumed by the fire.[102]

Magick Lamp to Petition the Seven African Powers

This is a recipe for a magick lamp to petition the Seven African Powers from my book, *A Guide to Serving the Seven African Powers*. To create this magic lamp, you will need the following ingredients:

---

102 Hohman, 1820.

- Coffee can
- Palm oil
- Olive oil
- Magnetic sand
- Seven African Powers Oil
- Honey
- Parchment paper
- Piece of hematite
- Seven cashews or pine nuts
- Purple basil
- Pinch of sea salt
- Orange water
- 7 peppercorns
- Cocoa butter
- 7 bay leaves
- Rosemary
- 7 rosebuds
- Wicking material
- Mixed bouquet of flowers
- Coconut cake

Write your petition on the piece of parchment paper and set it in the bottom of the bowl. On top of the petition paper, place the ingredients listed above. Drizzle some honey over these base ingredients, and then cover with equal parts palm oil and olive oil. Place a wick in the mixture. Go to the seashore and petition Yemayá and all the orishas to come to your aid as you light the lamp. Next to the lamp, place a glass of water with cocoa butter, a mixed bouquet of flowers, and a coconut cake.

Money Spells

La Santísima Muerte (Holy Death) Spell for Money

La Santísima Muerte (Holy Death) is a Mexican saint who is petitioned for matters of daily living such as love, luck, money, protection, health, recovery of stolen items, and kidnapped family members. She is not officially recognized by the Catholic Church and so she is considered a folk saint. The Holy Death Spirit appears as male and female; however, for this spell we are appealing to the *skinny lady* as she is affectionately called by her servitors. The candle is prepared and a novena is said every day for nine days, followed by a day of rest. The nine-day novena is repeated up to three times until your petition is answered. The novena consists of a prayer or invocation called a *soneto* (sonnet) followed by a short, powerful prayer called a *jaculatoria* (this does not translate as *ejaculation* in this context, as is commonly misperceived).

Burn a white Santísima Muerte Holy Death Candle for protection, good fortune, or money. If you can get a gold Santa Muerte statue for the ritual, all the better.

Place the candle on a plate. Drizzle some honey next to the candle in the shape of a cross and sprinkle with gold glitter. Place a glass of water next to the plate. Place three coins from different countries or of different currency in a triangle formation around the candle on the plate. Then pray the following prayer to the Holy Death:

Holy Death, I plead to you urgently. As you constitute Immortal God with your great power over all mortals—until you send us to the great celestial stars to enjoy a glorious day without night for all eternity! In the name of the Father, Son, and Holy Spirit, I ask this . . . (State your petition.) Amen.

Recite three Our Fathers prayers and repeat this ritual every day for nine days.

St. Expedite Spell for Financial Relief

St. Expedite is the patron saint of those who need fast solutions to problems, who strive to put an end to procrastination and delays, and who seek financial success. Here is a St. Expedite spell for money emergencies. Take a white and a green candle, and carve your name on them lengthwise with a pin. Anoint the candles with St. Expedite Oil or Fast Luck Oil. Light the candles and pray to St. Expedite until he grants your request. The prayer should go as follows:

I call forth the power and the presence of St. Expedite in my time of financial trouble. I offer my body, heart, mind and soul upon your altar of light. I have faith and trust and complete confidence that you will be my strength in this time of need. Quickly come to my assistance. Bring to me _____ (Clearly express what you want, and ask him to find a way to get it to you.)

My financial need is urgent. Be my Light and Guide in this situation so that I may live with peace, love, prosperity, and abundance and in the Praise of God. Amen.

Now promise to give St. Expedite some Sara Lee pound cake if your desire is granted. Tell him you will spread news of his work by taking an ad out in your local newspaper so that his fame will grow.

To Attract Money

Take a whole buckeye and wrap a dollar bill around it. Anoint with Fast Luck Oil. Carry it in your pocket to attract money.

Money Drawing Ritual

This is one of the coolest rituals for drawing money I can think of. It is also a great way to contribute to the balance of give and take energies.

- Dollar bills
- Permanent marker

Take one or more one dollar bills and write a blessing on them with a permanent marker: "May you be blessed with health, wealth, and love." These are your blessed bucks. Grab a glue stick and head out into the world to hide your blessed bucks. Never let anyone see you hiding them, and never drop one so that it looks like an accident. This is an intentional spell that works when it looks intentional. It sets into motion the principle of "reap and sow," so that what you give you shall receive a hundred-fold.

If you desire money, each week offer Saint Anthony a loaf of bread.

Great places to hide these dollar bills are:

- In Help Wanted sections of the newspaper
- On a gallon of milk
- On a pack of diapers

The only rule is that you should never stay to see who finds them!

To Make a Debtor Pay

If someone owes you money and won't pay up, try this trick.

- Three needles
- Honey
- Rose honey
- A candle
- Ellegua bust or effigy

Write the name of the debtor on a piece of paper. Pierce the paper with the needles. Place it in a glass containing equal parts of the two honeys.

Place the glass before your Ellegua. Light the candle and place it next to the glass. Petition Ellegua for your money. If you receive it, you must make a sacrifice to him. Offer him three pieces of candy, three small toys, and a healthy glass of coconut rum as payment.

New Year's Ritual

Bringing in the New Year has always been an ideal time for renewal and hope for change for the better. It marks a period of time when it is easy for the human mind to measure and compare how one fared in the past to how one wishes to fare in the future. Many cultures celebrate the beginning of the New Year, but in the South, the celebration for enslaved people marked a special time of community organization for planned escapes and uprisings. Contrary to popular opinion, enslaved Africans and Indians alike did not easily submit to their masters. Whenever they could, they strategized for a way out, exchanging ideas and supporting each other in their endeavors.

Africans and Native Americans hold special reverence for ancestors. Thus, it is not surprising that some of the rituals for New Year celebrations in New Orleans and in the South can be traced back to when these practices were tradition for families, friends, and members of the plantation slave communities.

Meal for the Ancestors

One practice that has been adopted by the larger culture for bringing in the New Year is the preparation of certain foods to be eaten on New Year's Day. It is believed that eating these foods will bring good luck to the family for the coming year. Many people have forgotten why the tradition persists, and merely go through the motions. But for the rootworker, every type of food holds special significance because it is a meal made for the ancestors. In my family, my mother cooked collard greens and cabbage, black-eyed peas, hoe cakes, and sweet potatoes.

To ensure success and prosperity for the New Year, money greens are prepared. Money greens are typically collard or mustard greens and cabbage. Place a dime in the pot when cooking the greens down. Whoever finds the dime in their portion is said to have special blessings for the upcoming year. Cabbages are also used in New Orleans on St. Patrick's Day, when they are thrown off of the floats during the St. Patrick's Day parade. Whoever catches a head of cabbage is said to have caught good luck and prosperity—but the cabbage must be cooked and eaten, or the blessings will not manifest. Cabbage can be cooked and smothered or made into cole slaw.

Black-eyed peas are eaten for good luck and purification. They are still used by some traditional families as a cleansing agent to be rubbed all over the body before entering the home. The beans are then disposed of at a crossroads. In New Orleans, black-eyed peas go into gris gris as a good luck curio.

Sweet potatoes scrubbed and washed well and baked represent wealth and health. All that is added is a little (or a lot) real butter and a little salt and pepper.

A portion of each of these dishes is placed on a special plate reserved for your ancestors. I will set a place at the table and invite them to come and eat the meal with us. We thank them for their help and the suffering they went through for us when they walked on this earth and ask for guidance for the coming year. After everyone finishes eating, the plate is set under a tree outside. After four days, the plate is retrieved and whatever has not been eaten is disposed of at a crossroads.

For instructions on how to prepare the recipes for the Meal for the Ancestors, see my book, *13 Proven Hoodoo Recipes for le Bon Appétit.*

Potted Plant Spells

Potted plant hoodoo spells are spells of convenience and discretion. If privacy, or lack thereof, is an issue for you, and you do not have a place to perform candle rituals or honey jar spells, a potted plant spell can be an excellent alternative—and no one will be the wiser.

Potted plant spells are container spells. Like bottle spells, special ingredients that are consistent with the work to be performed can be placed inside a hollowed-out piece of fruit or vegetable which is then placed at the bottom of the pot. This is then covered with soil and a plant. The ingredients, which are biodegradable, will decay in the pot and as they do so, the spell is energized.

There are a variety of types of spells that can be done in potted plants. Sweetening spells are among the most popular. Fertility spells, protection spells, success spells, stop-gossiping spells, road opener spells, and hot foot spells are also possible.

Use a good potting soil as the base soil for your potted plant spells. Special dirts can be added to the base dirt to enhance the spell. The pots are anointed with a special magickal oil to reinforce the intent. Petition papers should be written in magickal ink on brown paper or virgin parchment paper.

Keep Away Thieves

For this spell, mix up some potting soil consisting of your base soil to which a bit of dirt from a police station, jail, or army base has been added. Plant a fern in the pot. Ferns act as guardians of the home, keeping burglars away, preventing jinxes, and warding off evil. As you are planting the fern, talk to it about why you are planting it, and tell it you will take good care of it so it can take good care of you and your family. Then, write a statement of intent with Dragon's Blood Ink on parchment paper. Stick the petition paper into the soil by pushing it into the earth with a railroad spike that you have wrapped in red flannel. Place the pot at the front door, on the outside if possible; if not, place it as close to the front door as possible. Anoint the pot with Fiery Wall of Protection Oil every Tuesday, the day of Mars. You will be protected as long as the nail is in place. This ritual should be repeated every year, when you refresh the soil, repot the plant if it needs a bigger pot, and rewrite your petition.

Peaceful Home Potted Plant Spell

To create a peaceful and harmonious atmosphere in your home, or to maintain an already existing peaceful environment, try this potted plant spell using a Peace Lily.

Mix up some potting soil consisting of your base soil to which a bit of dirt from a church or the bank of a body of calm water (i.e. a pond or lake) has been added. If you are using water from the banks of a peaceful pond or calm lake, be sure the body of water is clean and not polluted. Hollow out a pomegranate so that all you have is the rind. Inside the rind, place some basil, rue, and hyssop. Add your written petition, and if you are so inclined, write down Psalm 23 or tear out a page from the Bible and add it to hollowed rind as well. Use Dove's Blood Ink to write your petition. Fill the pot one-third of the way with your special soil mix and then place your filled pomegranate in the pot. Cover with some more soil. Plant a Peace Lily. Peace Lilies do not need excessive light or water to survive, so they are perfect for virtually any situation. They attract good energy and help to maintain peace and harmony in the home. As you are planting the Peace Lily, talk to it about why you are planting it, and tell it you will take good care of it so it can take good care of you and your family. You can add a few earthworms to the pot, which will help to nurture and fertilize your plant and thus, your spell. Water the plant with holy water and anoint the pot with Peaceful Home Oil every Sunday. Keep this plant in your living room or whatever room functions as the heart of your home. Be sure to periodically wipe the leaves down with holy water to keep dust and dirt from collecting on them. This ritual should be repeated every year, when you refresh the soil, repot the plant if it needs a bigger pot, and rewrite your petition.

Keep Away the Law Potted Plant Spell

For this spell, mix up some potting soil consisting of your base soil to which a bit of dirt from a police station, jail, or court house has been added. Plant some oregano in the pot. Write a petition on a piece of parchment paper or from a torn piece of envelope from the courts, the IRS, etc. Place an Indian head penny or nickel in the middle of the petition, fold the petition over the coin, and wrap the little bundle with red string. Plant the bundle into the soil. Anoint the pot with Law Keep Away Oil weekly. Keep the plant in your backyard or by your front door. If you want to enhance this spell, glue a row of four Indian head pennies or nickels to the outer rim of the pot to mobilize the watchful eyes of Black Hawk, who will act as a guard for your home. This spell is best performed during a waxing moon.

Seal of Fortune Hoodoo Spell

For this spell, mix up some potting soil consisting of your base soil to which a bit of dirt from a bank has been added. Place a 2- to 4-inch layer of mulch at the bottom of the pot and add about an inch of your special soil. Throw in a handful of earthworms. Plant a male and a female sweet basil plant so they grow together in the pot. Write a petition on the back of a seal of fortune from the Sixth Book of Moses and wrap the seal around a whole nutmeg. Secure the petition with green string and plant in the pot. Water your basil with collected rainwater whenever possible. Basil benefits from regular pruning, which will stimulate growth. Simply pinch off growing tips with your thumb and forefinger when each plant is about six inches tall; always pinch off blossoms as they appear, as they affect leaf growth and the oil content of the leaves. As the basil grows, so will your fortune.

Protection Spells

It is generally agreed that the best days to do spiritual protection works are Tuesdays and Thursdays under a waxing moon or full moon. Colors associated with this type of work include white and yellow for purity and blessings, and red for standing up for yourself.

Create a Spiritual Barrier

To make a spiritual barrier between you and evil influences, make spiritual protection magic oil that contains the following:

- Angelica essential oil
- Rosemary essential oil
- Bay leaves
- Piece of mandrake root

Add to a base of almond oil. Anoint entryways, windowsills, and doorknobs in your home and workplace to keep out negative influences.

Red Brick Dust

One of the most common means of protecting one's home from evil and negativity is the use of red brick dust. To keep negativity from entering your home, take an old red brick and pound it into dust. Take the dust and pour it across your doorway.

Salt and Black Pepper Floor Wash for Protection

To give natural protection against anything evil, mix salt and black pepper in a bucket of water and scrub your home from the inside out every morning before sunrise.

St. Expedite Spell to Get Things Fast

Here is a popular spell that you can use to petition St. Expedite for just about anything you need fast. Perform this spell on a Wednesday. Light a red candle in a glass jar—I like to use a cinnamon candle. Place a holy card of St. Expedite on your altar and set a glass of water next to his image. Write your petition on a piece of paper and place it under the candle. Then, say the following prayer:

St. Expedite, you lay in rest.
I come to you and ask that this wish be granted.
_____ *(Express exactly what you want, and ask him to find*
a way to get it to you.)
Expedite now what I ask of you.
Expedite now what I want of you, this very second.
Don't waste another day.
Grant me what I ask for.
I know your power, I know you because of your work.
I know you can help me.
Do this for me and I will spread your name with love and honor
so that it will be invoked again and again.
Expedite this wish with speed, love, honor, and goodness.
Glory to you, St. Expedite!

Recite the prayer once a day until your prayer is answered. Allow the candle to burn down. When your request is granted, pour the water into the empty glass candle holder, and place fresh-cut flowers into the candle glass. When your request is granted, thank St. Expedite by offering him a piece of Sara Lee pound cake and be sure to tell someone how he has helped you.

To keep evil spirits out of your home, throw down a handful of grits before your front door. The evil entities will become obsessed with counting the number of grits on the ground and forget why they came.

Spells for Revenge

For Bad Work

Get a coconut that has three eyes. Take the name of the person you want to get rid of and write it on the paper like a gravestone. Bore a hole in one of the coconut eyes and drain the liquid. Put the name paper into the nut. Add some vinegar, and write the person's name all around the coconut with black ink. Stand the nut up in a mound of sand and set one black candle on top of it. Burn the candle for fifteen days, and mark the coconut each day at twelve o'clock. in the morning or the evening. By the fifteenth day your enemy will be gone. Never let the candle go out. You must add a new candle and set it on top of the old stub that has burnt down to a wafer and continue in this way until the fifteenth day. When the last candle has burned, place everything in a paper bag and dispose of it at a crossroads or at a garbage dump.

Traditional New Orleans Coffin Spell

This spell is a variation of a traditional New Orleans Voodoo doll coffin spell. Perform this spell during a waning moon to remove an enemy from your life. This spell is also good for transformative magick, where the doll symbolizes the transformation of something negative into something positive, or the death of something old into something new. For this spell you will need the following items:

- 1 black taper candle
- Reversible Oil
- Fiery Wall of Protection sachet powder
- Graveyard dirt
- Fireproof dinner plate
- Cross
- Angelica root
- Clean white cloth
- Black Voodoo doll
- St. Michael the Archangel holy card

Lay the cross in front of the plate and anoint with the Fiery Wall of Protection Oil. Dress the Angelica root with the Fiery Wall of Protection Oil as well. Lay a circle of protection around the cross and Angelica root with the Fiery Wall of Protection sachet powder. As you are dressing the cross and the Angelica root, repeat the following:

Saint Michael the Archangel, protect me and defend me in battle.

When you are done preparing the cross and Angelica root, lay the St. Michael the Archangel holy card in the center of the circle and sprinkle with a little Fiery Wall of Protection powder. Place the white candle in the circle. Then, take the seven purple offertory candles and inscribe the names of seven people, angels, saints, or spirits who represent your personal army of protection on the candles; one name per candle. Anoint the candles with the Fiery Wall of Protection Oil and roll in the sachet powder. Set the candles on the circle of protection around the cross, Angelica root, and St. Michael the Archangel holy card. Sprinkle a bit more of the Fiery Wall of Protection sachet powder on the St. Michael the Archangel holy card, cross, and Angelica root.

Place the graveyard dirt in a fireproof dinner plate. Attach a photo of your target to the Voodoo doll with a black pin and/or write your target's name nine times on a piece of parchment paper. On top of and crossing the person's name, write nine power words that describe your feelings for this person, such as *wicked, evil, hate, sick*, etc. Attach the name paper to the doll with a black pin. Lay the doll on the graveyard dirt in the plate. Place the doll in the plate to the left of the circle. Do not put the doll and plate inside your circle of protection.

Begin lighting the purple candles going clockwise. Light the white candle next. Then repeat the following prayer:

> *St. Michael the Archangel, defend me in battle.*
> *Be my protection against the wickedness and snares of the devil.*
> *May God rebuke him, I humbly pray;*
> *and do Thou, O Prince of the Heavenly Host*
> *by the Divine Power of God*
> *cast into hell, Satan and all the evil spirits,*
> *who roam throughout the world seeking the ruin of souls. Amen.*

Now, speak a heartfelt prayer of your own, asking your spiritual army led by St. Michael the Archangel for protection and ask for divine assistance with the expulsion of your enemy. Light the black Voodoo doll on fire. As it burns, say:

> *Your evil is returned!*
> *Your evil is undone!*
> *Your evil is done!*
> *You are done!*

Let the doll burn out in the fire-proof dish. When it is extinguished, place the plate with the graveyard dirt and the remains of the doll in a paper bag.

Take the cross, Angelica root, and St. Michael the Archangel holy card and wrap in the clean white cloth. Anoint with Fiery Wall of Protection Oil and sprinkle with Fiery Wall of Protection powder. Tie it closed with seven knots to represent your Divine Army of Seven. Hang it behind your front door for protection. You can also carry it with you as a protection talisman.

Take the paper bag with the remains of the black Voodoo doll, the plate, and the graveyard dirt and go to one of the 42 Cities of the Dead (a New Orleans cemetery). Find a tomb with a cross and throw the wrapped dish with the doll and graveyard dirt as hard as you can against the wall of the tomb, breaking the plate. Turn around and leave the cemetery and never return to that spot.

If you do not live in New Orleans, you can go to any cemetery and find any grave with a cross to use to finalize this spell.[103]

Spells to Obtain Employment

A Charm to Get a Better Job

The purpose of this spell is to secure better employment with better pay, and to attract wealth and prosperity.

- Green fabric
- Salt, magnetic sand, pyrite
- Hemp rope
- Money Drawing incense
- Charcoal block

Take piece of green flannel cloth and lay it flat with one of the corners facing you. Place in the middle of the fabric the salt, magnetic sand, and pyrite. Fold up the corners until you have a bundle, and tie it closed with the hemp string. Place the charcoal block on a fireproof dish. Place a pinch of the Money Drawing incense on the charcoal block and light the charcoal. Pass the better job charm through the smoke, and say the following nine times:

> Essence of light, earth, and fire, send me the job that says 'please hire.' Send me better money, a better job, that I will be happy, wealthy, prosperous, and proud!

Before each interview, hold this bundle and visualize yourself walking into the interview room, radiating confidence. Imagine yourself being in a position to pick and choose jobs at will. Carry this better job charm with you to your job interviews. Accept that any rejection is a sign from the universe that the job was not right for you.

---

103 From Alvarado, D. (2010). *The Voodoo Doll Spellbook: A Compendium of Ancient and Contemporary Spells and Rituals, Vol. 1.* CreateSpace.

To Get a Job with Ogun

Ogun is the patron loa to the unemployed. If you need a job, I can't think of a better loa to ask for assistance. I have never seen anyone who served him correctly fail to get a job. In fact, they usually get more than one offer, so they can pick the best one!

- Three railroad spikes
- Green and black ribbons
- Parchment paper
- Get a Job powder and Ogun Oil
- Bottle of rum

Anoint the railroad ties as you would a candle with the oil. Then sprinkle them with the powder. Write your petition on the parchment paper, and make sure you are very specific about the kind of job you want, the hours you need, the pay you want, and so on. Then sign your name. Wrap the paper around one of the ties and then wrap the green ribbon around the paper. Take another railroad tie, wrap it with the black ribbon, and turn it in the direction opposite of the first. Take the third railroad tie and wrap it with the green ribbon. Lay it next to the first two, in the same direction as the first tie. Then, using both the green and the black ribbons, tie all three railroad ties together in a bundle. Take the bundle along with a small bottle of rum to a railroad crossing and tell Ogun you are leaving it there for him. Tell him you need a job and that you are paying him with the bottle of rum. Leave the bundle and the rum at the railroad crossing, thanking Ogun as you leave.

Snake Bite Cures

Here are few snake bite cures provided for their folkloric value:

When mosquito hawks are seen flying about, take it as a warning sign. A dangerous snake is nearby. Be on guard against gossiping friends.

Split open a black hen and bind it warm tie it to the bitten place while the animal is still warm after killing it to the bitten place. If the flesh of the fowl darkens, the poison has been drained from the bite; if not, the victim has absorbed the poison.

Apply soda and lye soap to the bite.

Suck the poison from the bite. This must be done by a person with red gums who has chewed a piece of tobacco before starting.

Kill the snake and tie it around the victim's foot. Dig a hole and bury the bitten foot.

Various Lagniappe Spells

Spell to Stop a Nosey Neighbor

The purpose of this spell is to stop a neighbor from meddling in your business and to keep them away from you. It can also be used to get them to move away. This spell must be repeated for nine consecutive days. For this spell you will need:

- 1 black candle dressed with Black Arts Oil
- Crossing powder
- Slip of parchment paper

Dress the black candle with Black Arts Oil. Write the name of your neighbor and the word "farewell" on the slip of parchment paper and place it underneath the candle. Light the candle and recite Psalms 74, 101, and 109. When you are done, take the crossing powder and throw it in the path of your neighbor where they will step on it and track it inside their house.

Repeat this ritual for nine days, reusing the same candle. At the end of the nine days, burn the slip of paper and take the ashes and leftover wax and throw it away in a garbage can outside of your home.

Success

Take a picture of St. Peter and put it at the front door. Place a picture of St. Michael at the back door. Put some paradise seeds in little bags and put one behind each saint. It is known as "feeding the saint."[104]

---

104 Hurston, 1935.

Spell to Rent a House

Do this spell to ensure that a house will be rented. Tie up some rice and sycamore bark in a small piece of goods. Tie six fig leaves and a piece of John the Conquer root in another piece. Cheesecloth is good. Boil both bundles in a quart of water at the same time. Strain it out. Now sprinkle the rice and sycamore bark mixed together in front of the house. Put the fig leaves and John the Conquer root in a corner of the house and scrub the house with the water they were boiled in. Mix it with a pail of scrub water.[105]

Uncrossing Spells

Here's what to do if you think someone has put a hex or curse on you: Before going to bed, cleanse a white household candle with Florida Water and/or holy water. Anoint the candle with psychic or dream oil, light the candle, place a glass of water next to the candle, and pray to your spirits for clarity and understanding of whatever is causing you distress. Do this for three nights in a row, beginning on a Monday night. If you receive no clear answer by the end of the week, contact a rootworker or tarot reader to see if he or she can determine why these issues have arisen in your life.

> If someone is putting an evil spell on you, sit for an hour and close your eyes while imagining that everything around you is orange in color. It is said this will break the spell.

Salt and Saltpeter Bath for Undoing Tricks

When taking spiritual baths to remove jinxes or negativity in general, you should always wash with downward strokes. This uncrossing bath is for when you are a victim of foot track magic, i.e. something has been buried in your path or under your porch. You will need:

- ½ teaspoon of saltpeter
- 8 quarts of hot water

Wash with downward strokes from your face all the way down, nine times. Take the left over water and throw it towards sunrise early in the morning before the sun comes up.

---

105 Hurston, 1935.

Wish Spells

Seven Bean Mojo Wish Spell

The purpose of this spell is for making wishes. For this spell you will need seven Job's tears or seven mojo beans. Place one Job's tear or mojo bean in your pocket every day for seven days. On the seventh day, go to a river or stream and make your wish "in the name of the Father, Son, and the Holy Ghost." Throw the seven beans or seeds over your left shoulder into the running water, and walk away. Do not look back or your wish will not come true.

Mojo Wishing Bean Spell

Mojo beans are also called African wishing beans. Mojo beans are believed to have the power to make wishes come true. Make seven wishes (one per bean) and for each wish place one mojo bean in a cloth bag. Carry for seven days to make a wish come true.

Final Note from the Author

I hope you have enjoyed reading the revised edition of *The Voodoo Hoodoo Spellbook*. It took an incredible amount of work to compile all of the information in a format that is useful for the beginning as well as the seasoned conjuror. I have spent hundreds of hours selecting the content from the original version to keep, and weeding out those works that were not purely New Orleans Voodoo or hoodoo in origin. As a result, there is a lot of new material in the book, and some reworkings of previous spells. The first edition was just the beginning. This edition is so much more.

This book represents a lifetime of learning and living New Orleans Voodoo hoodoo. I have never before written down so much of my personal knowledge and experience for public consumption. I admit, I was hesitant to share much of it; but ultimately I felt it was important to preserve the cultural knowledge that was passed on to me through multiple channels. Many of the old ways have been lost or forgotten. Many of the old ways have been diluted through the commercialization of hoodoo. I know that much of what I learned as a child in 1960 was impacted by this phenomenon. Like so many things, however, the New Orleans tradition adapted to the changes. As an adult, I have come to understand those things that were "created" by marketeers and those that are pure hoodoo and conjure. In the end, hoodoo is about what works.

One of my goals for this book was to emphasize the many influences that are found in the New Orleans tradition. Voodoo and hoodoo as it is expressed in New Orleans does not look the same as it does in other areas of the country in some very significant ways. A major hallmark is the fusion of Voodoo and hoodoo—or lack of separation of the two. Voodoo is not just a religion, and hoodoo is not just a magickal system in New Orleans. It never was. And gris gris is not just a mojo bag. For many of us, Voodoo, hoodoo, and gris gris are each a part of a whole Creole tradition. Just like the merging of my ancestors—indigenous, Spanish, and French—makes me a whole Creole woman, the merging of multiple cultures makes New Orleans Voodoo hoodoo a whole Creole tradition.

Another goal for the rewriting of this book was to better explore the history of New Orleans. I have never read and researched so much about my hometown in my life! I did my best to provide accurate information and present the facts. I also did my best to provide the sources of my information. You are encouraged to explore some of the sources for yourself and see what else can be gleaned from them. In the end, there is no end to the study of Voodoo, hoodoo, and conjure in New Orleans.

Whether or not you agree with what you read in these pages is not important. What I write is my experience and my understanding. I am but one person. But, I am one person for whom the tradition lives on in my blood and in the blood of my children and my children's children. I am not writing as an outsider looking in. I write as an insider looking out, and there is a big difference in the two perspectives.

May the blessings of our beloved Voodoo Spirits be with you always!

—Denise Alvarado
June 7, 2011

References and Bibliography

Alvarado, D. *A Guide to Serving the Seven African Powers*. West Liberty, IA: The Mystic Voodoo, 2009.

———. *Exú, the Divine Trickster*. Createspace, 2010.

———. *The Gypsy Wisdom Spellbook*. West Liberty, IA: The Mystic Voodoo, 2009.

———. *The Voodoo Doll Spellbook: A Compendium of Ancient and Contemporary Spells and Rituals*. Prescott Valley, AZ: Planet Voodoo, 2010.

———. *Voodoo Dolls in Magick and Ritual*. Createspace, 2009.

Brown, A. and Hill, E. *African American Heritage and Ethnography: A Self-Paced Training Resource*, Ethnography Program, National Park Service, Washington, DC, 2006. Retrieved February 10, 2011 from: *www.cr.nps.gov/ethnography/aah/AAheritage/index.htm*

Crowley, A. *Magick: Liber ABA, Book Four, Parts I–IV*. York Beach, ME: Weiser, 1997.

Davis, W. "On the Pharmacology of Black Magic," *Caribbean Review, XII*, Summer, 1983.

———. *The Serpent and the Rainbow*. New York: Simon and Schuster, 1985.

Davis, Wade. *Passage of Darkness: The Ethnobiology of the Haitian Zombie*. Chapel Hill, NC: University of North Carolina Press, 1988.

De La Torre, M. A. "Dancing with Ochún: Imagining How a Black Goddess Became White," *Aesthetics within Black Religion: Religious Thought and Life in Africa and the African Diaspora*, Anthony Pinn, ed., Cambridge University Press, 2010, pp. 113–134.

Debien, Gabriel, and Le Gardeur, René. "Les colons de Saint-Domingue refugies a la Louisiane (1792-1804)," *Revue de Louisiane* 9, 1980: 101–140.

Deren, M. *Divine Horsemen: The Living Gods of Haiti*. New York: Vanguard Press, 1953.

Diederich, B. "On the Nature of Zombie Existence," *Caribbean Review, XII*, Summer, 1983.

Dieterlen, G. *Essai sur la religion Bambara*, Paris, 1951.

Fanger, Claire, ed. *Conjuring Spirits: Texts and Traditions of Medieval Ritual Magic*. University Park, PA: The Pennsylvania State University Press, 1998.

Gamache, Henry. *The Master Book of Candle Burning*. 1942.

—————. *The Magic of Herbs*. New York: Power Thoughts Publishing Co., 1942.

Hall, G. M. *Africans in Colonial Louisiana: The Development of Afro-Creole Culture in the Eighteenth Century*. Baton Rouge and London: Louisiana State University Press, 1993.

Hanger, K. S. *A Medley of Cultures: Louisiana History at the Cabildo*. Louisiana State Museum, 1997.

Haunted New Orleans Tours. *www.hauntednewQrleanstours.com*

Hearn, Lafcadio. "New Orleans Superstitions," *Harper's Weekly*, December 25, 1886.

Hohman, J. G. *Pow-Wows or The Long Lost Friend*, 1846.

Hurston, Zora-Neale. *Mules and Men*. Philadelphia: Lippincott Publishers, 1935.

Hyatt, H. M. *Folk-Lore from Adams County Illinois*. Alma Egan Hyatt Foundation, 1935.

—————. *Hoodoo—Conjuration—Witchcraft—Rootwork*. Five Vols. Memoirs of the Alma Egan Hyatt Foundation, 1970–1978.

Jacobs, C. F. & Kaslow, A. J. *The Spiritual Churches of New Orleans: Origins, Beliefs, and Rituals of an African-American Religion*. Knoxville, TN: University of Tennessee Press, 2001.

King, P. J., and Stager, L. E. *Life in Biblical Israel*. Westminster: John Knox Press, 2001.

Lawless, J. *The Illustrated Encyclopedia of Essential Oils: The Complete Guide to the Use of Oils in Aromatherapy and Herbalism*. Rockport, MA: Element, 1995.

Malbrough, R. *Hoodoo Mysteries: Folk Magic, Mysticism, and Rituals*. St. Paul, MN: Llewellyn Publications, 2003.

—————. *The Magical Power of the Saints: Evocation and Candle Rituals*. St. Paul, MN: Llewellyn Publications, 2001.

Martinié, L. "New Orleans Voodoo Sacred Rhythms of the Third Coast." *Journal of New Magick 3*, 2005.

—————. *A Priest's Head, A Drummer's Hands: New Orleans Voodoo: Order of Service*. Oakhurst, NJ: Black Moon Publishing, 2010.

Mathers, M. S. L. *The Book of the Sacred Magic of Abramelin the Mage*, 1897. Reprinted by Dover Publications, 1975.

Matory, J. L. *Sex and the Empire That Is No More*. New York: Berghahn Books, 1985.

McAllister, E. *Rara! Vodou, Power, and Performance in Haiti*. Berkeley, CA: University of California Press, 2001.

New Orleans Voodoo Crossroads. *www.neworleansVoodoocrossroads.com*

O'Neill, C. E. *Church and State in French Colonial Louisiana: Policy and Politics to 1732*. New Haven, CT: Yale University Press, 1966.

Pitkin, H. *An Angel by Brevet*. Philadelphia, PA,1904.

Rebennack, M., and Rummel, J. *Under a Hoodoo Moon*. New York: St Martin's Griffin, 1994.

Selig, G. *Secrets of the Psalms: A Fragment of the Practical Kabala*. Arlington, TX: Dorene Publishing Co., 1982.

Surrey, N. M., and Waselkov, G. *The Commerce of Louisiana During the French Regime, 1699–1763*. University of Alabama Press, 1968.

Teish, L. *Jambalaya, the Natural Woman's Book of Personal Charms and Practical Rituals*. San Francisco: Harper One, 1991.

Valdman, A. *French and Creole in Louisiana*. Plenum Pub Corp, 1997.

Walter, M. N., and Fridman, E. *Shamanism: An Encyclopedia of World Beliefs, Practices, and Culture, Volume 1*, ABC-CLIO, 2004.

Yronwode, C. *Hoodoo Herb and Root Magic: A Materia Magica of African-American Conjure*. Lucky Mojo Curio Company, 2002.

Sources for Talismans, Seals, Magick Numbers, and Symbols

The Ancient's Book of Magic, Lewis de Claremont

Aunt Sally's Policy Players Dream Book, Aunt Sally

Book of Talismans, Amulets and Zodiacal Gems, William Thomas and Kate Pavitt

The Black Pullet, or *The Hen with the Golden Eggs* (anonymous)

The Egyptian Witch Dream Book and Fortune Teller, (anonymous)

Grimorium Verum, or the *True Grimoire*, Solomon

Herman's Book of Black Art, Herman

The Holy Bible

Legends of Incense Herb & Oil Magic, Lewis de Claremont

The Oracle of Human Destiny or *Book of Fate*, Madame le Normand

Pow-Wows or Long-Lost Friend, John George Hohman

The Secrets of Numbers Revealed, Godfrey Spencer

Secrets of the Psalms, Godfrey Selig

The Seven Keys to Power, Lewis de Claremont

The Sixth and Seventh Books of Moses

The Ten Lost Books of the Prophets, Lewis de Claremont

Resources and Suppliers

The following websites carry many of the supplies, ingredients, and background information related to the spells and formulas contained in this book.

Planet Voodoo
   www.planetvoodoo.com   email: planetvoodoo@planetvoodoo.com
This website is owned and operated by the author, Denise Alvarado. Its focus is on New Orleans Voodoo, hoodoo, and gris gris magick. It features Alvarado's handcrafted Voodoo dolls, Day of the Dead dolls, and altar dolls, as well as books, jewelry, and ritual supplies. You can find the entire line of Voodoo Mama's hoodoo Oils, Potions, and Gris Gris, which is based on authentic New Orleans formulary here.

13 Moons
   www.13moons.com   email: info@13moons.com
Witchcraft supplies, wiccan supplies, gothic & occult supplies since 1997.

Medicines and Curios
   www.medicinesandcurios.com
Mecidinesandcurios.com is part of Miller's Rexall, a third generation family-owned business operating in the Atlanta, Georgia area. They are the largest and most comprehensive "Old Fashion hoodoo drugstore" in the South.

Dr. Snake's Voodoo Spells and Conjure Shack
   www.doktorsnake.com   email: drsnake@doktorsnake.com
Doktor Snake is a legendary cult author, hoodoo bluesman, and Voodoo spell-caster. His books include *Doktor Snake's Voodoo Spellbook* and *Mary Jane's Hash Brownies*. He provides high-quality spellcasting services and old-time hoodoo card readings to clients around the world.

Root Mama Conjure
   www.madrinaangelique.com/
The website of Madrina Angelique. Root Mama Conjure offers the finest authentic occult handcrafted items for all of your spiritual needs.

Index

Abramelin, 110, 117-119, 302
abre camino, 107, 151, 176, 198
absinthe, 121-125
    see also *Green Fairy*
Adam and Eve, 11, 92, 104, 108
    candle spell, 108
    in the garden of Eden, 209
    incense, 271-272
    love mojo, 271
    love spell, 271
    lover's candle, 108
    oil, 108, 126, 271-272
    powder, 218
    root, 92, 126, 149, 271
advice, 45, 269
    for gambling, 268
affair, 36, 108
afflictions, 82
    to heal from, 86
Africa, 2, 4–5, 7–8, 10–11, 16, 26, 28, 33–36,
    42, 44, 51, 149, 202, 205, 234, 301
 central, 10, 205
African Diaspora, 4
African holocaust, 5
African Muslims, 11, 203–204
African Voodoo, 4, 8–9
Agwé, 26, 35–36, 44, 47, 75
Algiers, 2, 69, 157, 164, 203, 210, 219,
    Fast Luck, 219
    Love Charm, 272
    flakes of, 144–145, 157
alligator, 98
    teeth, 98
    feet, 98
ammonia, 87–88, 101, 132
amulets, 47, 49–52, 103, 114
Ancestor, 25, 2, 6, 17, 47, 50
    worship, 9
ancestors, 1, 3, 14, 23–25, 47, 54, 56, 72,
    75–76, 97, 105, 144–145, 207,
    285–286, 299
aphrodisiac, 47, 63, 65–66

ashé, 44, 238
astrology, 58, 204
astronomy, 204
Atocha, Nino de 30, 58, 76, 250
attorney, 146, 250
azalea, 131
    oil, 131

Babalú-Ayé, 37–38, 63, 76, 172
Bakongo, 205
Baleine, La, 27, 47
Balm of Gilead, 128, 131–132, 135–136, 218
Bambara, 5, 203–204
banishing spells, 234
Baron Samedi, 27, 38, 62, 76
basil, 92, 113, 148, 156, 164, 193, 196, 242, 244,
    273, 281–282, 287–288
Bayou St. John, 36, 47, 49–50, 188
Bible, 9, 72, 77, 84, 97, 117, 131, 154, 190, 207,
    233, 272, 287,
black-eyed peas, 99, 213, 230, 285–286
Blanc Dani, 40–41, 57
blessing, 82, 91, 93–97, 99, 110, 117, 127, 148,
    152, 148, 187, 223, 230, 238, 284
    spells, 237
bluestone, 97, 214
    see also laundry blueing
boa constrictor, 12, 47, 247
Brigit, Manman, 27–28, 38, 48, 61, 76, 251
    see also Brigitte
Brigitte, 76
    Gran, 46
    Grande, 27
    Maman, 48–49
burial, 38, 59, 106

Cajun, 202, 213
candle magick, 3, 9, 101
Catholic, 2–4 , 8, 9, 10, 25, 29–30
    saint worship, 9
    saints, 2, 8
Chango, 27, 28, 31–33, 61

charm, 9, 11, 50, 91, 98–99, 201, 204–205, 210,
212–214, 216
Code Noir, 4, 10
see also Black Code, Louisiana's Black Code,
Louisiana's Code Noir
Congo, 5, 10, 16, 21, 27–28
conjure, 2, 8, 12, 14, 23, 50, 77, 85, 89, 90, 94,
95, 97, 107, 111, 113, 116, 118, 121–122,
124, 126, 131
cosmogram, 21, 206–207
Creole, 3, 4, 16, 47, 111, 116, 179, 202, 213, 299
culture, 7
language, 7
phase, 7, 8
crossing, 18, 46, 68, 96, 146, 170, 197, 218, 257,
275, 292, 294
powder, 295
crossroads, 16, 18, 21, 22, 27, 29, 38–39, 42, 44,
46, 48, 52, 106, 108–109, 154, 206–207, 210,
233, 235, 255, 286, 291
spell, 254–256, 263, 268–269, 280–281
Crucible of Courage, 247
crystal, 23, 34, 164, 189, 239, 278
see also quartz crystal
curios, 15, 89
curse, 18, 92, 100, 103, 196, 244, 258–260, 267, 296
an enemy, 240
of Marie Laveau, 259
prayer, 259
reversal oil, 108, 138
reversal spell, 109
see also jinx, hex, crossing
customers, 19, 51, 64, 97, 174–175, 182, 222,
279
cypress, 93

Dahomean, 4, 5, 26
Dahomey, 27, 35, 48
Damballah Wedo, 26, 32, 36, 40, 51, 57, 65,
247–248
dauber, mud, 39, 98, 132, 164, 214
Davis, Wade, 13–14, 18, 203
doll, 2–3, 11–12, 94
domination, 20, 31, 95, 140, 170, 236, 247
Dr. John, 9, 17, 41, 42, 208

Egyptian, 22–23, 99, 167
Elegba, 29, 34
Ellegua, 29, 30 42, 58, 60, 65

employment, 88, 99, 137, 212, 231, 293
enemies, 31, 57, 60–61, 65, 76, 79, 82, 85, 87,
88, 92–94, 97
Exú, 11, 29, 44, 255, 281

Fast Luck, 2, 69, 107, 143, 157–158, 164, 174,
210–212, 219
floor scrub, 174
oil, 69, 107, 143, 157–158, 164, 210–211,
229, 242, 268, 283–284
powder, 219
fava beans, 71
feast days, 48, 56, 72–73
Four Thieves Vinegar, 187
folk magic, 8–9, 14, 47, 233, 255
French, 2–4, 6, 22, 111
perfumery, 22, 111
frankincense, 91, 126–127, 129–130, 132, 135,
137, 140, 142

ghede, 28, 76
ghost, 47, 92, 235, 297
water, 183
graveyard, 21–23, 39, 99, 132, 164, 202, 206–
207, 211, 222, 223, 235, 243, 252, 256, 267,
272, 276, 291–293,
gree gree, 201
see also gris gris
gris gris, 3–4, 6–9, 11, 22, 27, 37, 47–48, 50–52,
66, 79, 102–112, 114–115, 117–118, 145,
151, 154
see also gree gree
Guinea, 10,
peppers, 56, 93–94, 148,
Guinee, 29, 38, 138, 255
Guédé, 28, 38, 46, 52, 63
see also ghede, guede

Haiti, 7, 13, 16, 25, 27, 28–29, 37, 46–47, 204,
234
see also Saint Domingue
Haitian, 2, 11, 12–14
healing, 1, 9, 10, 14, 20, 22, 33
herbs, 19, 21, 41, 45, 48, 90, 92, 96
hoodoo, 2–4, 8–9, 12, 15–16, 21, 27, 29–31, 36,
40, 44, 46, 50–53, 55, 57–58, 61, 64, 66–67,
71, 74, 76–77, 84, 86–87, 90–92, 94, 100,
102–103, 110, 113–116, 118, 121, 123–124,
129, 131–132, 136, 140, 145, 151–152, 154

hoodoo,
   marketeers, 8
Hurston, Zora Neale, 4, 13, 89, 235

image magic, 14
Indian, 7
   see also Native American
Indian Spirit, 2
indigenous, 3, 5, 6, 50, 58, 85, 203, 299
initiated, 2
initiation, 1

jazz, 8
Jewish mysticism, 9
jury, 133, 137, 250–252, 254
justice, 26, 30, 39, 49, 52, 57–58, 70, 74, 87,
   251–252, 264

Kabbalah, 228
King of France, 4, 5

Laba, 29
LaCroix, Baron, 62, 67
lagniappe, 124–125, 295
lamp, 61, 133, 167, 277–282
laundry bluing balls , 194
Legba, 26–30, 42, 44, 46, 48, 52–53, 58, 60, 63,
   65, 73, 74, 105, 198, 228, 255–256, 279
   Oil, 151, 198
   see also Papa Legba, Elegba
Laveau, Marie, 14, 47, 49–51, 73–74, 103, 134,
   145, 175, 182, 214, 216, 228, 235, 247, 251,
   259
Li Grande Zombi, 10
live things in you, 12
Louisiana, 3–8, 10, 14, 16, 57, 59, 62–62, 65,
   100, 140, 154, 161, 173, 174, 193
   Van Van Oil, 152
love spells, 271
lover, 19, 43, 67, 93, 94, 104, 106, 108, 126, 130,
   141, 174, 199, 240–241, 265, 267, 271, 273,
   276

Madrina Angelique, 223, 245,
Mami Wata, 33, 35, 49
Manman, 27–28, 38, 48, 61, 75–76, 251
marabout, 203–204, 207
Mardi Gras, 8, 15–17, 34, 70, 73

Mardi Gras Indians, 15–17, 39, 70
marketeers, 2, 8, 39, 50, 185, 299
   see also hoodoo marketeers
marketplace, 32–34, 37
masking, 8, 15–16
Martiné, Louis, 2, 11, 41
materia medica, 2, 8
Mentor, Felicia Felix, 13
mojo, 2
Mombu Mombu, 51
Montanée, John 42
Moses, 41, 54
mysteries, 3

Nago, 5, 27–28
Narcisse, Clairvius, 14
Native American, 2, 6, 14
   herbalism, 2, 8
   Indians, 6
   spirituality, 2, 8
   tribes, 5
New Orleans, 1–4
   Creole, 3
   Voodoo, 2–4, 10
New Orleans Voodoo Spiritual Temple, 2, 11
novenas, 71, 77, 81, 103, 214
Nzambi, 10–11

Obatalá, 32, 40, 57, 59, 75, 99, 105
obstacles, 29, 44, 53, 57, 62, 73–74, 80, 100, 103,
   134, 151, 172, 198, 228, 247
Ochosi, 52, 74, 251–252
offerings, 24, 30, 33, 36–37, 41, 47, 51, 73, 75,
   177, 233, 279, 280
Ogun, 27–28, 30, 36, 44, 47, 52, 57, 62–63, 73,
   75, 105, 155, 184, 251, 294
   oil, 155
oils, 111
opportunities, 29, 44, 73–74, 100, 103, 151–152,
   173, 198, 228
orisha, 26, 29, 31–35, 44, 52, 57, 155, 172, 252
Oshun, 30–31, 34–35, 44, 59, 61, 73, 75, 95
   oil 155
Oyá, 30–33, 66, 73

paket, 236
pantheon, 7, 25
Papa Legba, 29, 42, 53, 105, 228, 255, 279
   see also Legba, Ellegua

parchment paper, 108, 131, 205–206, 208, 226, 240, 242, 252–253, 260–261, 264, 271, 276–277, 280, 282, 287–288, 292, 294–295
Petro, 26–28, 31, 51
Ponto Riscados, 205
power, 4, 12
psalms, 9
psalms, 9–10, 18, 22, 77, 84–86, 89, 101, 107, 207, 233, 235, 250, 295,
purification, 72, 91, 97, 157, 193, 197, 199, 286
python, 12, 47, 247

quarrel, 137, 215
quartz crystal, 96
    see also crystal

Rada, 26–28, 40, 43, 54
rain water, 12
rainbow, 14
realtors, 159
reconciliation, 265
revenge, 12
rootwork, 89–90, 102, 107, 255
rootworker, 2–3, 21, 116, 161, 223, 239, 285, 296

Saint Domingue, 7
    see also Haiti
saints, 2, 4, 8–10, 22, 25, 29, 33, 41, 49, 50–52, 55–57, 61, 67, 72, 77–78, 81, 93–94, 97, 100–104, 107, 133, 192, 251, 266, 291
seals, 9, 169, 202–205, 225, 227, 241
séances, 3, 9, 97, 101, 103, 106, 189
Senegambia, 4–5, 10
Senegambians, 5, 11
serpent, 10–12, 14
    cult, 10
    worship, 11
sigils, 9
slave, 4, 7, 10, 14
    owners, 4
    trade, 4, 5
snake, 11–12
sorcery, 13
spells, 2, 20–21, 44, 76, 84, 91, 93, 97, 98–99, 100, 102–104, 106–107, 111–112, 127, 143–144, 162, 167–168, 190, 196, 207, 211, 217, 233–234, 236, 247–248, 250, 255, 257–258, 263, 268, 271, 286, 293

banishing, 234
bend–over, 236
binding, 102, 237
blessing, 237
bottle, 239, 286
break–up, 243
business, 244
cleansing, 245
commanding, 247
court case, 20–21, 250
crossing, 257
crossroads, 254
domination, 20
fertility, 266
for revenge, 290
gambling, 102, 268
good luck, 269
healing, 270
jar, 239
love, 21, 271
money, 21, 282
potted plant, 286
protection, 21, 289
to obtain employment, 293
uncrossing, 296
wish, 297, 299
Spirit Guides, 9
spirits, 3–4, 7, 9, 11, 14, 16, 23, 25, 26, 28–29, 34–36, 41–42, 44, 46, 48–49, 56, 62–63, 67, 81, 87, 91, 94, 97, 102, 104, 106, 116, 127–128, 132–133, 148, 162, 173, 177, 179, 205, 220, 223, 225, 229, 231, 234, 238, 240, 246, 251, 252–253, 269, 277, 290–291, 292, 296
ancestral, 205
evil, 172–173, 270–271
guardian, 246
helper, 238
summon, 189–190
Voodoo, 4, 205
spiritual, 1–2, 9–12, 14, 18, 21–23, 25, 29, 41, 42, 48, 50, 52–54, 56, 58, 62, 69, 72, 91–92, 96–97, 99, 111, 116, 188, 122, 131, 133, 144, 158–159, 163, 171–172, 177, 179, 183, 187, 191–194, 199, 202, 203, 206, 209, 223, 238, 255, 263, 274, 289, 292, 296, 302, 305
tools, 9
Spiritualist, 2, 8, 39, 41, 55, 57–58, 70, 72, 101, 107, 157, 189, 278
Church(es), 2, 8, 9, 39, 70

swamps, 6, 140
syrup, 37, 97, 124–125, 135, 272

talisman, 9, 21, 77, 97, 215, 225–226, 228–230, 263, 270, 292
Tallant, Robert, 36, 50
tar, 164, 189
tarot, 241, 296
Taurus, 105
teepee, 39
Teish, Louisa, 14, 256
Temple snake, 11–12
    see also Li Grande Zombi
tobacco, 6, 38, 40, 133–134, 202, 221, 251, 279, 295
tradition, 2–5, 7–9, 12, 14–15, 17, 24–29, 33, 40, 44–45, 55–56, 64, 68, 70–72, 76, 84–85, 101, 111–112, 117–119, 122–123, 129, 143, 145, 149, 154, 161, 175, 179, 181, 189, 196, 201–205, 209, 225–226, 233, 239, 245, 251, 255, 285–286, 291, 299–301
tribe(s), 5–6, 15–17, 28
    see also Native American
trickster, 2, 29, 34, 42, 45, 280

uncrossing, 18, 50, 88, 93–95, 97, 118, 140, 144, 146, 148, 152, 161, 170, 193, 233, 296
    bath, 196
    oil, 163,
unfaithful, 154

vagina, 104, 110,
vengeance, 26, 31
Vévés, 36, 205
Vieux Carré, 111, 134
vinegar, 100, 141, 187, 243, 253, 259, 262, 290
violets, 176
Virgin Mary, 59, 78
Vodou, 2, 13, 16, 26–27, 29, 31, 33, 37, 44–45, 49, 58, 60, 73, 205, 302
Voodoo Crossroads Temple, 53
Voodoo, 2–13, 16, 18, 23, 25–30, 34, 38–39, 41–51, 53–55, 57, 62–63, 65–67, 72–73, 77, 85, 89, 90, 95, 98–102, 104, 11–112, 132, 134, 144, 148, 152, 162–163, 167, 171–172, 201–202, 205, 211, 216, 223, 225–226, 233, 245, 247–248, 255, 257–258, 264, 270, 272, 277, 291–293, 299, 300, 302, 305
    ceremony, 12

hoodoo, 9
pantheon, 7
Queens, 8, 12
rituals, 8
saint, 2
Voodoo doll, 2, 3, 14–15, 99–100, 132, 162, 201, 211, 248, 264, 270, 291–293, 301, 305
voodooists, 8, 11, 25, 35, 36, 43, 52–53, 56, 207

wangas, 202
War Water, 189, 240, 261
warrior, 31, 33, 38–39, 79, 278
Water of Notre Dame, 190
wealth, 1, 34, 41, 43, 47, 76, 94, 102, 103, 105, 194, 270, 284, 286, 293
Whydah, 10–11, 202
win, 31, 268–269, 280
    court cases, 39, 87, 93, 251, 253–254
wish spells, 297
witchcraft, 14, 34, 61–62, 207, 245, 302, 305
wormword, 114, 118, 121–124, 137, 158
worship, 36, 46, 55, 91, 97,

Xango, 31
    see also Chango Shango
XXX, 145
    Algiers Oil, 164

Ya Ya Powder, 266
yard, 20–21, 67, 110, 130, 199, 236, 240–241, 267, 273, 276
Yellow bath, 199
Yemayá, 30, 33, 75–76, 91, 223, 278, 282
    Oil, 164
ylang ylang, 115, 125, 134–135, 142, 186, 220
yolk, 245–246
Yon Sue, 35–36
    see also Aggasou,
Yoruba, 2, 5, 16, 25, 28–32, 34, 44, 205
Yoruban, 25–26, 29, 33–34, 44

zodiac, 116
zombie, 11, 13, 14, 301
    astral, 13
    bottle, 14
    spirits, 25
zoological curios, 98,
Zorba Oil, 165

About the Author

Denise Alvarado was born and raised in the Voodoo and hoodoo rich culture of New Orleans. She was first introduced to the world of spirits at the age of 5 by family members on the bayou. As an adult, she has studied mysticism and practiced Creole Voodoo and indigenous healing traditions for over four decades. She is a cultural anthropologist, psychologist, writer, artist, rootworker, and spiritual consultant. She currently lives in Arizona. You can visit her online at: *www.planetvoodoo.com* and *www.mysticvoodoo.com.*

To Our Readers

Weiser Books, an imprint of Red Wheel/Weiser, publishes books across the entire spectrum of occult, esoteric, speculative, and New Age subjects. Our mission is to publish quality books that will make a difference in people's lives without advocating any one particular path or field of study. We value the integrity, originality, and depth of knowledge of our authors.

Our readers are our most important resource, and we appreciate your input, suggestions, and ideas about what you would like to see published.

Visit our website *www.redwheelweiser.com* where you can subscribe to our newsletters and learn about our upcoming books, exclusive offers, and free downloads.

You can also contact us at info@redwheelweiser.com or at

Red Wheel/Weiser, LLC
665 Third Street, Suite 400
San Francisco, CA 94107